Against the Odds

AGAINST THE ODDS

Matt Te Pou and Māori Rugby

Matt Te Pou
with Matt McIlraith

HUIA

First published in 2006 by Huia Publishers,
39 Pipitea Street, P O Box 17-335
Wellington, Aotearoa New Zealand
www.huia.co.nz

ISBN 1-86969-251-9

Copyright © Matt Te Pou and Matt McIlraith 2006

All rights reserved. No part of this publication may be reproduced, stored in a retrieval system, or transmitted in any form or by any means, electronic, mechanical, including photocopying, recording or otherwise, without prior permission of the publisher.

National Library of New Zealand Cataloguing-in-Publication Data

Te Pou, Matt.
Against the odds : Matt Te Pou and Māori rugby / Matt
Te Pou with Matt McIlraith.
ISBN 1-869692-51-9
1. Rugby Union football—New Zealand—History. 2. Maori (New
Zealand people)—Sports. 3. Rugby football coaches—New
Zealand. [Tākaro. reo.] I. McIlraith, Matt. II. Title.
796.33308999442093—dc 22
Printed by Everbest Printing Co. China

Front cover:
The New Zealand Maori team performing their haka Timatanga
© PHOTOSPORT

*To the memory of Makuini Te Pou,
a lady of outstanding values whose influence
has spanned generations.*

Contents

Foreword

Timatanga

Introduction – An era of survival and prosperity   1

CHAPTER 1
Lion taming: 2005 – 'Kings of the empire'   5

CHAPTER 2
Beginnings – 'A life less ordinary'   23

CHAPTER 3
Into the 'Nam – 'Where boys became men'   31

CHAPTER 4
Bay of Plenty or bust! – 'Rebuilding a province's pride'   39

CHAPTER 5
Matt the Maori: 1994 – 'Welcome to my world'   47

CHAPTER 6
Night of the snow queens: 1995 – 'Hitting the ground running!'   57

CHAPTER 7
Into the Pacific: 1996 – 'Of frogs, kings and collapsed scrums'   63

CHAPTER 8
An Apia afternoon: 1997 – 'When an island went to war'   81

CHAPTER 9
The England massacre: 1998 – 'Remember the Treaty!'   95

CHAPTER 10
Murrayfield Maori: 1998 – 'The tour with a difference!'   109

CHAPTER 11
The 1988 New Zealand Maori World Tour – 'Planes, trains and slaves'   125

CHAPTER 12
On the back burner: 1999–2000 – 'New stars for a new century!'   133

CHAPTER 13
Taking on the world: 2001 – 'The ultimate Test'   147

CHAPTER 14
Boks, barbed wire and rugby – 'The 1981 Springboks recalled'   161

CHAPTER 15
The wild west: 2002 – 'Wallabies versus New Zealand Maori, episode II'   171

CHAPTER 16
Canadian capers: 2003–2004 – 'A Churchillian conquest!'   187

CHAPTER 17
Hearing the Lions roar: 1993 – 'Maori and Lions recalled'   207

CHAPTER 18
Focusing on the future – 'Maori rugby into the 21st century'   211

Statistics   223

Acknowledgements   243

Matt Te Pou and Matt McIlraith   244

Hon Parekura Horomia
Minister of Māori Affairs

When I was growing up on the East Coast in the 1950s and '60s it was every young boy's dream to play rugby for New Zealand and to be an All Black or a Maori All Black. That was my dream too; my namesake, Parekura Turei, had been a Maori All Black.

But there were a few steps to take along the way to that point, like playing for your province – in my case East Coast – which I did on more than a 100 occasions.

In contemplating this foreword, I've reflected both on my own time as a player, and also on the part Maori have played in the development and popularity of rugby union in Aotearoa. We took to the game like ducks to water. The British brought it here, and Maori began playing it in games with or against the Armed Constabulary. Our rugby history tells us that the first recorded Maori player was a bloke called Wirihana, who took part in a 20-a-side match playing for Whanganui Country against their Town counterparts in 1872. The first match was scoreless, and the replay was abandoned when the Town captain led his team from the field in protest against the 'rough and tumble' tactics of their rivals.

The first team to leave these shores was the 1888–89 New Zealand Natives side, organised by a private promoter to travel to Britain. The team pre-dated the formation of the New Zealand Rugby Union. Amazingly, the 21-strong team, captained by Joe Warbrick, was together for more than a year. They played 107 matches in this country, Australia and the United Kingdom. They won 78, drew 6 and lost 23. They also played the odd game of soccer and Aussie rules.

This book is about the more recent and highly successful New Zealand Maori team coached by Matt Te Pou. Maori teams over the decades have beaten every team in the world, and on Matt Te Pou's watch they enjoyed a remarkable run where the side went seven seasons before it was finally defeated and won 36 of their 40 matches. Their victories included a match against the touring British & Irish Lions. Their losses included two very close games against Australia, who were the world champions at the time, and a loss to the England team that went on to win the Rugby World Cup later that same year.

Matt's army background and his wairua Maori played a big part in his coaching style. It provided him with the skills to rebuild the Maori team from a low point, when players who were selected often failed to turn up to play, to a point where players – All Blacks included – said that the team they most enjoyed playing for was the Maori side. Under Matt's direction, playing for the New Zealand Maori side helped to develop the players' taha Maori as well as their rugby.

The importance of the New Zealand Maori side to the people, and its place within the national landscape of the game should never be underrated. In many ways, the story of how the side developed under Matt's leadership takes me back to my own time as a player. The team had all the elements of the game that I fondly remember from my days with East Coast – the mateship and fun and games off the field as well as the sheer hard work on it.

But it has one thing that I didn't experience – the great success Matt and his men had in the decade or so he was in charge, which is why it is important that this special story was recorded for posterity. This team very rarely lost; sadly, my time with East Coast was just the opposite. In the hundred or so games I played, we never won once.

I expect this book will be read for years to come as people reflect on a golden era of Maori rugby.

Kia ora

Hon Parekura Horomia
Minister of Māori Affairs
August 2006

Timatanga – the New Zealand Maori rugby team haka

I te timatanga	In the beginning
Ko te kore!	There was nothing
Ko te po nui	The big darkness
Ko te po roa	The long darkness
Wehenga Matua	The seperation of Rangi and Papa
Herenga Tangata	Formed man/people
He toa Rangatahi	Formation of young warriors
He toa Rangatahi	Formation of young chiefs
Whakaki ki te Maunga	If you aim for the mountains
Tae ki te Whenua	You will hit the plains
Hoki ki te Rangi	If you aim for the sky
Tae ki te Pukerunga	You will hit the mountain peaks
Piki ake piki ake	climb up, thrive
Ki te ara Poutama	to the pathway of knowledge
Ki nga Taumatatanga e	to achieve excellence
Wairua Hinengaro Tinana	spiritually, mentally, physically

Timatanga was written for the New Zealand Maori team by its kaumatua (elder) Whetu Tipiwai. It has been performed by the New Zealand Maori rugby side since 2001.

Introduction

An era of survival and prosperity

There's nothing especially remarkable about the Ashburton Showgrounds.

What, with its dilapidated grandstand and a main field that is exposed to bone-chilling north-west winds that rip across it on a flight path direct from the snow-covered Southern Alps, this is hardly a place that you would expect to have been the starting point for a major revolution in New Zealand Maori rugby.

Yet it was.

Even though Matt Te Pou wasn't the head coach for the 58–13 win over third division Mid-Canterbury on June 1 1994, the game does represent his entry point into the New Zealand Maori setting.

It is an environment that the former New Zealand Army Warrant Officer was to solidify significantly during a decade of success unparalleled for the New Zealand Maori team, going back even as far as its (and the All Blacks') forerunner, the 1888–89 New Zealand Natives touring side.

Having started off performing in front of a gathering in the central South Island that numbered in the hundreds, rather than thousands, Matt bowed out 11 years later with the New Zealand Maori side – for 80 minutes anyway – the centre of the rugby world.

Fittingly, given that he did more than any other single person to preserve and enhance the New Zealand Maori side amid the turbulence and uncertainty that was created as the professional game developed, Matt was sent out a winner.

In meeting and mastering the British & Irish Lions 19–13 in front of 32,000 passionate fans at a packed out Waikato Stadium in Hamilton, the New Zealand Maori side fulfilled Matt's vision of proving itself a major threat on the international stage.

That the contrast between the start and finish of the era could not have been greater is testament to Matt's impact on the team.

But the on-field picture only tells half of the story.

As much as the account of the last decade of the New Zealand Maori team is one of on-field success, it is also the story of how a people's pride manifested itself in some of this country's finest rugby players.

Maori society is all too often portrayed in a negative light. As an ethnic group, Maori feature prominently in the statistical categories of unemployment rates, lowest overall incomes, poorest health and housing conditions, and the highest percentage crime rate of all ethnic groups within New Zealand.

During Matt's time as coach of the New Zealand Maori team, the consistent level of success that was achieved filled fellow Maori, and indeed all New Zealanders, with a wonderful sense of pride.

In doing so, the players also provided tangible proof that a combination of history and social responsibility can still be blended to create success in the increasingly soulless environment that professional rugby has become.

As All Black and New Zealand Maori captain Taine Randell related to me during the interview process for this book, wearing the Maori jersey pulled on the emotional heart strings like nothing else for the majority of the players who appeared for the team.

The attachment the players feel for the side is something that has become increasingly rare in the cut-throat world of the modern game, where players seamlessly change teams, and even countries, in pursuit of the almighty dollar.

A number of the subjects I interviewed for this book have either spent time overseas or were resident at off-shore bases when we spoke.

Yet, all of them, to a man, spoke with great pride and enthusiasm about their time playing for New Zealand Maori, a team they described as like no other they'd ever appeared for. Many expressed genuine regret that those days were now behind them.

While the All Blacks will always be the pinnacle for New Zealand rugby players, I'm not alone in believing that there are specific aspects of the New Zealand Maori team environment that would enhance All Black life, were they to be incorporated into that setting.

Certainly, the relaxed tone that Matt set, and the humility and openness with which he operated, became a recurring theme in the feedback I received from the players with whom I spoke.

As, too, did their love of the infectious humour that punctuated the daily routine, the on-field freedom they were afforded to showcase their skills and, most importantly, their education via the cultural aspects of life in the New Zealand Maori side.

For many players throughout the decade, this was their first experience with that element of their heritage. Many freely admitted at having felt embarrassed that they had not known more about their culture.

Significantly, a number of international players, whose privacy I have happily respected where requested, outlined candidly to me why being involved with the New Zealand Maori side was a far more enjoyable experience overall than were their careers with the All Blacks.

It is an appreciation with which I can sympathise, having spent time inside both team environments.

While I will always be appreciative of the opportunity that I was afforded as All Black communications officer for two years during the stewardship of coaches John Mitchell and Robbie Deans, captain Reuben Thorne and manager Tony Thorpe, the New Zealand Maori team, too, will also hold a special place in my memory.

I was fortunate enough to be part of the New Zealand Maori team management for the 2001 programme, which included one of the most exciting games of rugby that I have ever witnessed: the showdown against Australia at the Sydney Football Stadium.

That match might have closed the chapter on a seven-year, 24-game (including non-first- class games) run where the side was unbeaten, but the quality of the New Zealand Maori team's performance that night – where it trailed the reigning world champions by just two points with seven minutes to go – was such that the players returned home with their heads unbowed.

It is true that the New Zealand Maori side doesn't generally carry the overwhelming, and at times unrealistic, level of expectation that burdens the All Blacks.

But, in the formative years of Matt's reign as coach, the players arguably carried an even greater load – the mere survival of the team as a worthwhile and high-profile entity in a professional landscape that was rapidly changing.

Had the results not been too good to deny, the New Zealand Maori side could easily have passed into the history books, condemned, as the New Zealand Universities representative side has been, to a position as a mere footnote in the modern game.

That the New Zealand Maori team instead survived and prospered in that most challenging of circumstances is a credit both to the commitment and ownership exhibited by the players, but also to the personality of the leadership and direction the team enjoyed during this time.

As Matt admits, having shouted at young men on parade during his work day as a drill sergeant in the military, why would he want to then yell at rugby players during the leisure hours he spent coaching the game he loves?

The military dynamic, which combines the pursuit of excellence and achievement with the internal disciplines that are required for communal living and dedicated preparation, cannot be divorced from the story of the New Zealand Maori team under Matt's charge.

Not only did the lessons he learned, both on the parade grounds of New Zealand and Australia and in the jungles of Vietnam, help to turn a young Tuhoe Maori lad from the Eastern Bay of Plenty into a successful leader, they also helped to shape a generation of elite rugby players as on-field winners, off-field role models and fiercely proud Maori.

That is why it was so important that the story of Matt and his team is told. It has been my pleasure to assist Matt to be able to tell it.

Matt McILraith
July 2006

1

Lion taming: 2005

'Kings of the empire'

Matt Te Pou was up and on the road at 6.00 am the morning following the New Zealand Maori team's historic 19–13 defeat of the 2005 British & Irish Lions.

It wasn't so much a case of scurrying away from the scene of the crime, as quietly closing a huge chapter of his life. The two-and-a-quarter hour drive back to Whakatane that peaceful Sunday morning did at least offer the former New Zealand Army Warrant Officer the chance to reflect on both his 11 years at the helm of the Maori team and the mission that had been accomplished the night before.

How do you say goodbye after all that time? It was also the nature of the schedule we usually had that the Maori team practically lived its life on the run. Over the decade that I was involved, it was always the same.

We often had very little preparation time together before our first game, and then we broke up again pretty much straight after our last engagement as the players had planes to catch to link up with the other teams they were playing for.

It was the same on the morning of Sunday, June 12.

As Matt slipped past the breakfast room, he noticed Leon MacDonald and a number of the other Christchurch-based players in the squad, tucking into their morning meal, prior to heading off for their 7.00 am flight home.

As was usually also the case, the team's noted 'night owls', either hadn't yet arrived back at the hotel, or were still in bed asleep as they recovered from the previous evening's 'exertions'.

There's no good way to say goodbye.

I suppose my feeling was one of sadness that it was finally all over, but mainly I was proud. Proud of what the team had achieved, proud of the way they had played, proud that we had given Carlos Spencer a fitting send-off in the Maori jersey but, most importantly, proud of how much our win had meant to the whole country. Our first game against Australia, in 2001, was the first occasion where I'd really felt that the whole country was right behind us, as if we were the All Blacks, and the Lions game had seen the same thing occur again.

The support we had in the lead up to, and during, the Lions' match was fantastic; but it wasn't until a few days afterwards that I, and the players, really came to appreciate how big a deal the whole thing had been.

Everywhere I went, people were thanking me and saying what a wonderful achievement it had been, and the feedback I was getting from all of the players was the same. Jono Gibbes told me that a number of the guys had rated that performance as the highlight of their careers, and he was talking about a couple of players who'd been All Blacks, among that group!

While I'd never doubted that my decision to step down at this time was the correct one, the performance against the Lions, and the reaction to it, confirmed that I'd done the right thing.

The vision, right from the first moment I became coach of the New Zealand Maori side in 1995, had been to establish the team as a threat on the international stage by winning at least 50 percent of our matches against the strongest nations –Australia, England, South Africa, and, of course, a traditional invitation team like the Lions.

Beating the Lions, when added to the earlier wins over the international opposition we had achieved, made me feel satisfied. We had fulfilled the vision that our management and senior players had created for the side.

The Lions had long loomed on the radar, from as far back as 2001 when it had been first mooted to Matt that his team might possibly feature on the itinerary for their next tour, shortly after the New Zealand Maori side's exciting loss to Australia.

The idea resurfaced in 2002, and was finally confirmed in 2004 when the itinerary for the Home Unions' side's tour of the following year was announced.

Ironically, had New Zealand Maori succeeded in their mission to beat Australia the second time around at Perth, in 2002, Matt wouldn't have been there to mastermind the Lions' demise.

> *I had thought about stepping down in 2002. At that stage, I was beginning to feel it was time to give another coach an opportunity – to give them the car keys so to speak – but I was also mindful of the likelihood that we had the Lions coming up. Going out in 2002 would have given my successor a good three-year lead up to that game, which was plenty of time to fashion the team along the lines he was thinking, and bed in his ideas and strategies.*

The only problem was that the Wallabies ruined the plan.

As they had the year before at the Sydney Football Stadium, the Australians again proved just a bit too strong for New Zealand Maori, although their 27–23 success was a close-run thing.

A close loss – as gallant as it might have been, however, was not good enough in Matt's eyes.

> *Close losses weren't in our vision. When we lost that game, it told me that we were still not quite where we needed to be – where I wanted the team to be. It meant that I still had some work to do before I could step down.*

In consultation with his former assistant coach, Jim Love, Matt opted to stay on.

Love, himself a former New Zealand Maori player, as it meant any potential succession for the giant former Marlborough second row was still some time off.

Love opted to take on the role as head coach of Tonga, taking the Pacific Islands side to the 2003 Rugby World Cup in Australia.

> *Jim needed and wanted experience as a head coach, which was completely understandable. He needed to be hands-on if he was to advance his own development as a coach. I understood that and thought it was a good thing for Maori rugby, for which I strongly believe Jim still has an important future role to play. It's about succession planning, and there was none at that stage within the New Zealand Rugby Union, as far as the Maori team was concerned. So it was a case of us helping our own although, unfortunately, that proved pretty costly for Jim.*

While Love took Tonga through to the World Cup, on his return to the New Zealand coaching scene in 2004, there were no vacancies around the New Zealand Maori, with Northland's Donny Stevenson having taken over as the team's assistant coach.

Stevenson subsequently succeeded Matt as head coach in 2006, with former All Black and New Zealand Maori representative loose forward Jamie Joseph coming in as his assistant. That appointment left Love with no option but to seek further coaching experience overseas, which he has done by taking up a position with Italian club Viadana.

Ironically, though he was subsequently overlooked for the assistant's position, Love played a key role in the preparation for the Lions match; coming on board at late notice after one of the team's forward coaches, former All Black hooker Hika Reid, had been forced to stand down due to illness.

> *With the Super 12 down to its final stages, we couldn't call in all of the players early, but we got together the Chiefs and Blues guys for a planning day in Auckland because they were already out of the tournament by the time the semi-finals took place. Hika was at the meeting, which was just over a week before we assembled, but he then rang me the next day to say he was no good. He'd felt so crook on the drive back home after our meeting that he'd pulled onto the side of the road and had a sleep. The next day he went to the doctor and was diagnosed with leukaemia!*

Fortunately for New Zealand Maori, Love was only too happy to down tools at his Maori Rugby Academy in Rotorua and step in to help the team.

> *It was a huge help having Jim around because he knew the environment and how we operated, and knew when to speak and when to sit back and let the players take control. I took a lot of confidence from having Jim around, especially when he commented to me at one stage up in Fiji that the environment hadn't changed a bit from when he'd last been involved in 2002. That feedback was important because it said to me that we were doing things how I wanted them to be done.*

While Love's return to the team environment only came after New Zealand Rugby Union officials had tried to force Matt to take on the services of a former Pakeha All Black player, who was coaching in Scotland but was back home during their off-season for a break, fortunately all of the other administrative matters around the side had gone smoothly.

The big one was around selection, where Matt describes the dialogue between the All Black selection panel and his selectors as having been 'excellent', which hadn't always previously been the case.

> *Graham Henry [All Black coach] had said to us in 2004 that we would have available the best possible team we could have. We interpreted that as meaning we would be able to select from all of our Maori players who would be in the All Blacks, and he stayed true to his word. Not only did Graham ensure that everyone was available, he also left the overall selection, and where we played each player, totally up to us. He didn't meddle at all in how we ran our team, and he deserves a lot of credit for that.*

Undoubtedly it suited Henry, as he put together his own plan for toppling the British invaders, to have a full strength and fired up Maori side thrown at the Lions in just their third match of the tour.

Not only was it guaranteed to be a physical assault, the potential for major psychological points to be scored was huge, especially if New Zealand Maori was able to lower the tourist's colours.

The self doubt that such an outcome would create within the Lions' ranks would make it much easier for the All Blacks in the Test series that followed, and so it proved.

Matt, however, also had the wishes and needs of other teams to consider as he sifted through the options for his 26-man squad for the Lions game, and the lead-up international against Fiji at Suva.

> *Both Bay of Plenty, who played the tour opener against the Lions, and Taranaki had matches against the tourists in the week before we played them, and their coaches naturally wanted the services of Wayne Ormond [Bay of Plenty] and Paul Tito [Taranaki], who were under consideration for selection in our group but were also the captains of their respective provincial sides.*

> *So we were in a position where we had to be consistent with the guidelines that had been set by the All Black selectors. They'd released players to us, so we were happy to do the same with the provinces.*

> *It meant that Wayne [Ormond] didn't travel to Fiji with us, playing instead for Bay of Plenty against the Lions, but I was okay with that. I knew that he would be playing a hard full game only the week before we played the Lions so knew that he would be ready if we needed him,*

although we were really only looking at him for the reserve's bench anyway. Wayne was more the type of player who we would use if he was needed, as opposed to being an impact player who was always going to come from the bench at some stage of the game.

The situation with Tito was a little trickier.

Not only was Taranaki's game with the Lions four days closer to the New Zealand Maori team's date with the tourists, than was Bay of Plenty's, as New Zealand Maori captain in 2003, Tito had every right to expect that he might be selected.

After accompanying the side to Fiji, where he played in the Test, Tito returned to New Zealand immediately following the match with the players who had been released from the Maori squad, linking up with his Taranaki provincial team-mates for their big night out against the Lions.

The situation with Paul hung on the availability of Chiefs' lock Sean Hohneck. Sean was the biggest lock in the country at the time, and we wanted him to play, but he wasn't fit and couldn't travel to Fiji because of an infected elbow. As a result, while we were happy to release Paul to play for Taranaki, he was still on stand-by in case Sean didn't come through our early training runs that week.

After Hohneck emerged unscathed from the New Zealand Maori team's opening training runs of the week, Tito became surplus to requirements, which Matt says was probably for the best because he believed the player had been injured in the midweek game against the Lions, and thus was not 100 percent fit.

It was tough on Paul, but the key thing was that he got to play the Lions. He did that, and did it well, leading his province on what, I am sure, would have been a very proud night for him.

If the situation surrounding the second row had caused some doubt because of injury, Matt's second major player selection issue caused him far less bother than he had originally anticipated.

Mercurial first-five-eighth Carlos Spencer, who was soon to depart the New Zealand game for a stint at English club Northampton, was a player Matt wanted to include, but his selection was complicated by a prior engagement to play in Jonah Lomu's comeback game in London the previous weekend.

That meant Spencer would miss the side's lead-up game in Fiji, while also not returning to New Zealand until five days before the side tackled the Lions.

As if this didn't complicate things enough, there was also the issue around Spencer's departure and whether the New Zealand Rugby Union would allow him to be selected, given that he was soon to be lost to the game in this country.

Matt had experienced such a scenario before, when the popular former skipper Errol Brain had been barred from a swansong tour of Scotland with the New Zealand Maori team in 1998, because he had already signed to play the following season with the Japanese club side Toyota.

As well as his huge regard for the talents of the former All Black as a player, Matt also had a strong personal motivation for wanting to involve Spencer, having been involved with him as far back as 1993, when the then youngster first attended the Prince of Wales Cup North–South Maori fixture.

As far as I, and our selection panel, was concerned, we were clear from the start that there would be a seat left on our bus for Los if he was available and wanted to play. There was a personal commitment there, for sure. I felt we owed him the chance to be involved and to go out with this game after all he had given to Maori rugby through the years. But there were also practical reasons. Carlos Spencer can turn a game, and his presence alone had lifted the guys around him in the past. To beat the Lions, we knew that we needed to have all of our big guns available and firing. Fortunately, on this occasion, both the Rugby Union and the All Black coaching panel agreed.

Not that Spencer was offered too many guarantees.

While Matt always had it in mind to inject Spencer into the game at some point, when his side was in need of the boost the presence of his star pivot provided, the player himself was not promised that.

He was told that, while he would be in the match-day squad of 22, he wouldn't be starting the game because he hadn't been involved in all of the lead-up trainings.

The move to include Spencer was a winner from the start.

Not only did he go on to play a key role in the game, his arrival at Tuesday morning's Hamilton training session prior to the match – fresh from an early morning arrival at Auckland airport straight from London – lifted the whole team, while graphically illustrating to them all the depth of commitment that was expected. After all, Spencer was only a reserve, yet he was seen to be pulling out all the stops so that the team would succeed.

> *It just so happened that Rangi [Leon MacDonald] had turned his ankle, so he didn't train, and Los ran at fullback for both of our trainings that day. There he was, just off the plane, yet he was throwing skipped balls and those no look passes of his. Showing off all of those magic skills that we already knew he had. It just added a real bounce to both those sessions, and put everyone on their toes. He then attended an official function we had that night in Hamilton before driving back to Auckland to see his partner and young son. Then he reported for duty again first thing the next morning, when he officially came into camp.*

Spencer's arrival saw the departure from the squad of the London Irish-bound Wellington utility back Riki Flutey, who had appeared as a substitute during the previous win in Fiji, and then remained with the squad as cover until Spencer's participation was confirmed.

Flutey was one of eight players who played for New Zealand Maori against Fiji at Suva but was not required for the Lions, with five of those players being backs: Flutey, fullback Shannon Paku, wings Neil Brew and Hayden Pedersen and halfback Craig McGrath.

> *One of the main reasons for the huge turnover was to allow the players who'd been involved in the Super 12 semi-finals and final, especially the Crusaders guys who'd won that tournament, another day or two at home with their families to unwind.*

> *One of the problems with the tight schedule we have in New Zealand nowadays, with the changeover from the Super 14 to the international 'window', is that the late May–early June period becomes pretty cramped.*

> *The Crusaders had obviously had a team session and spent a bit of time together after winning the tournament, and it was important we allowed those guys to unwind properly so that they would then be right mentally to refocus on the job they had to do with us.*

> *To ensure that was able to happen, we let those players have a couple of extra days at home, and they didn't officially join the rest of the team*

until just before we departed for Fiji. Obviously, because they hadn't been with us for the preparations, they couldn't then play that Test, so that meant that some of the younger guys had to carry the load – and they did a fantastic job.

Such was the feeling within the team, the departing players, prior to leaving Fiji after the match, honoured those who would do battle with the Lions.

While Flutey remained for a few days longer, returning to New Zealand with the rest of the squad on the Sunday prior to the Lions match, he too honoured his team-mates with a song he had specially prepared, and emotionally sung to the side prior to leaving the camp on the Tuesday before the international.

Those gestures were really special, and reinforced to the guys the job they had ahead of them. Not only were they playing for themselves, they were playing for the others who would have loved to have taken their places. It showed the spirit that existed between the whole group. While some of the players might have been leaving, and were surely disappointed not to be involved, their attitude showed that they were still with us in spirit, and that was inspirational for the players who had the job to do in the game.

Prior to their departure, the youngsters in the New Zealand Maori side had certainly made their mark fending off Fiji 29–27 in a game that Matt has no hesitation in labelling as the toughest of the three matches the side faced in Suva during his era.

They really came at us, but we knew they would. It perhaps surprised some of our guys, but Fiji really attacked us in the forwards. Their coach [former Auckland NPC-winning coach], Wayne Pivac, had them well drilled, and it was a very physical contest. While we got away with it in the end, it was a huge test of character, and in that way was probably a perfect build up for what we had coming up.

Pivac, who would see his side leak 15 tries in losing 0–91 to the All Blacks seven days later at Albany's North Harbour Stadium, says the match highlighted the difference between playing Fiji at home, compared with playing them away.

'It was the biggest game we'd had in Suva for quite some time', Pivac says.

'Fijians are right into their rugby, and they see the New Zealand guys on television all the time playing Super rugby, so it was a great opportunity for my guys to get out there and show what they could do.'

Not that the Fijian players were cowed at all, as they appeared to be a week later when lined up against the All Blacks and all their reputations.

'There was a real expectation leading into the Maori game, and we were pretty pleased with how we'd played, albeit while realising that it was a game we could have won', Pivac says.

'It was a hot day and the game was played on a hard ground. Those conditions are difficult to play in, and it appeared to me that a lot of the Maori guys were struggling with that for a fair while.'

As it was, the Fijians created enough scoring opportunities to win, but were left to lament their poor handling – most notably when winger Sireli Bobo inexplicably grassed the ball 70 metres out from the goal-line, but with no defenders in front of him, while fellow winger Vilimoni Delasau lost control of possession as he attempted to scoop it up and dive for the line.

'They were key misses. We certainly had our share of chances, but we probably cost ourselves just as much on defence on occasion, as we did by not finishing off those try-scoring opportunities', Pivac says.

The most critical defensive lapse led to one of the New Zealand Maori side's four tries, when Fiji was down a loose forward who was having an injury attended to, during a defensive lineout. The visitor's read the situation superbly to make the most of the gap, through which No 8 Angus MacDonald scored a try.

'It was a bit soft, but they made the most of the situation and should be applauded for that', Pivac says.

'While we were disappointed that we didn't win, it was generally felt that we'd given a good account of ourselves. We'd known that we'd needed to, to gain a bit of credibility prior to taking on the All Blacks.'

With Fiji subsequently losing to New Zealand 0–91, cynics would say that their 'credibility' didn't last very long, although Matt believes the Fijians' subsequent Test result against the All Blacks may have played a significant role psychologically in the mental approaches of both his side and the Lions, to their contest.

I remember, after watching that, thinking to myself that it had certainly highlighted to our players how much they were going to have to step up,

> given that we'd only just beaten Fiji ourselves and six of our forwards from that game were also starting against the Lions. The flip side was though, while I thought it might have given our guys a bit of a rev, the reverse could have been the case for the Lions. They could have been forgiven for thinking: 'if they can only just beat Fiji, who have then lost 91–0, how good are they really going to be, especially in the forwards?' In that way, perhaps Fiji's thrashing in the Test turned out to be a little bit of a blessing in disguise for us.

New Zealand Maori had gone into 'Lions mode' from the moment that the team session following the Fijian game had finished.

While the squad to play the Lions had remained in Fiji an extra day, not returning to New Zealand until the Sunday night after having played the Pacific Islands' Test on a Friday, thoughts of the task ahead were never far from the players' minds – even amidst the background of their Pacific Islands' paradise.

> We'd spent the day after the Fiji Test relaxing on the other side of the island, but arranged to get back to our hotel about the time the coverage of the Lions' first tour game against Bay of Plenty was set to start. There was a big television screen in the bar of the place we were staying. After we got off the bus, most of the players gravitated to the television to watch, virtually straight away. Most of them didn't even bother to take their things up to their rooms first. As team management, we took that as a good sign. It told us that their minds were already focused on the job ahead.

As well as the valuable on-field time, the Fijian trip also allowed All Black flanker Marty Holah to be introduced to the New Zealand Maori environment for the first time, while the sometimes wayward but talented North Harbour midfield back Rua Tipoki had returned after a stint playing overseas.

> I'd had my eye on Marty ever since he'd made his debut for the Chiefs in 2001. We'd had him checked out then to see if he had any Maori heritage. That had come back in the affirmative, but then we never got to select him because the All Blacks got in first. This was the first time he'd been available to us, and we were delighted to have him in the squad. As it turned out, he made some crucial turnovers for us against the Lions, and generally had an outstanding game.

> *Rua's return was the result of a lot of hard work. I was really proud of him for overcoming his demons, and the change in his maturity that had clearly taken place. When we were looking at the selection of the team, we'd identified leadership qualities in Rua, in terms of our environment. He knew the team set up, and had a lot of respect among the guys. We knew that he'd serve us well, which he did. The Maori team was special to Rua, he was like many of the players we'd had, in that playing for New Zealand Maori was almost like his All Blacks. He certainly never let us down, and this time was no different, although we were all also pleased when he went back to North Harbour later in the year and captained them into the semi-finals of the NPC. That, again, highlighted the leadership qualities we'd always known he had.*

While Tipoki added leadership to the group, the side's official captain caused a few problems in the run up to the Lions.

Although he'd played against Fiji, Gibbes was battling with a painful foot injury, which made his participation touch and go right up until the game kicked off.

'He'd torn tissue on the bottom of his foot. It was painful in its own right, but there was always the potential that, by playing on it, he could make the injury much worse', veteran New Zealand Maori physiotherapist Mike Stewart says.

'We treated him three-to-four times every day that week in the lead up, but it was only by the Friday that we were in a position to make a call on it. In the end, we declared that he was as right as we could get him in the timeframe allowed, but that the final decision had to be made by the player himself in conjunction with the coaches. Only Jono was in the position to say whether he was up to it or not.'

> *Jono hadn't trained with the team, but we named him when we released the team to the media and the public the day before the match. I spoke to Jono and asked him how his foot was. He said it was about 85 percent. I told him that was good enough for me because we needed his leadership out there. I needed him to lead the guys onto the field and get them through the all-important opening stages of the match. If we'd had to make a call to get him off after 20 or 30 minutes, then we'd have made it, but I still felt that it was absolutely essential we had him out there for that amount of time, at least, because he was the leader, and the one all the players looked to. As it was, he played the whole game and kept growing and growing right through it!*

With Gibbes's participation confirmed, Matt's biggest concern prior to kick off was in terms of hoping that the player combinations, who had trained well off the field, would click as effectively on it.

> *One of the biggest problems with the tight nature of the schedule, like we had for the Lions, was that we hadn't really had a chance to play together. Sure, we had a lot of relatively settled combinations already there, like the back three: Leon MacDonald, Rico Gear and Caleb Ralph, from the Crusaders, for example, but they still had to put it all together out on the field, bearing in mind that they were operating in a different environment from what they had been previously. The primary focus of our build up was about managing that, while also controlling all the hype that was associated with the game, which was obviously bigger than what we would normally have had to deal with.*

There was also the emotion factor, with it being Matt's last game. While he tried to hide that, his players weren't fooled.

'We could tell in the preparation, by the type of things that Matt was saying, that he really wanted this one', winger Caleb Ralph says.

'He was usually pretty well organised, but for this game he was really prepared and totally focused, and that rubbed off on all of us. We knew how important it was to him, and we all wanted to do the best we could by him.'

One change, from the normal pre-match build up, that Matt introduced for the Lions was subtly done by inviting in former All Black and New Zealand Maori No 8 Arran Pene to hand out the jerseys, two nights before the match.

Previously, this task had always been the role of the kaumatua (team elder), who blessed the jerseys before handing them over to each player, although Love had attended to the duty, and had passed on some of his experiences, before the match in Fiji.

In Pene, Matt could not have selected anyone more appropriate for the occasion of the match against the Lions.

Not only had the former Otago No 8 beaten the Lions playing for his province 12 years earlier, he'd also featured in the New Zealand Maori side that lost 22–20 to the Lions during that tour. Along with the team's technical adviser, Stu Forster, who'd also played in that match, Pene provided the current players with a visual link to the New Zealand Maori team's past.

'That was new for Matt, bringing someone in like that, but Arran spoke really well', Rico Gear recalls.

'He talked about how matches of this significance only come around once in a lifetime. How we only had one shot at it, and how he would have loved to be out there with us. The boys all knew he wasn't kidding either, you could see his passion for it. That made a big impression. He also really put it on the forwards, telling them that if they didn't sort out the Lions forwards, we'd lose. I guess you could say that the forwards all paid close attention to that, because they certainly sorted the Lions guys out!'

> *We'd spoken about the need to go for the full eighty, because the Maori sides of '81 [against South Africa] and '93 [against the British & Irish Lions] hadn't, and that's how they'd ultimately been found out. We also talked about being able to defend a lead, which is another thing those two sides hadn't been able to do. Having Arran there to talk to the players was part of that. It put a face to the words, and, in its own way, made the guys that little bit more accountable.*

As was to be expected, the early exchanges with the Lions were tight, with the capacity crowd at Waikato Stadium still being kept in suspense at halftime, which arrived with the scoreboard showing the two combatants locked together 6–6.

In the New Zealand Maori dressing room, Ralph wasn't surprised that a victory was well within his team's range.

'Despite all of the hype, we'd built up for the game in the same relaxed manner that we always had in Maori teams that I'd been involved in, and while the guys were excited, they all knew what they had to do, and that showed when we got out on the field. For all the publicity they'd had, we'd seen enough in the provincial games to know that we could beat the Lions, and nothing they showed in that first half had forced us to change that view.'

Gear concurs. 'I always felt that we were in control, even though it was pretty close', he says.

'There wasn't any stage in the match where I didn't believe absolutely that we would win, although it wasn't your typical Maori game. We played to win rather than to entertain as well, so it was a lot tighter, in terms of our approach, than most of the other New Zealand Maori games that I've played.'

One factor that did come into play in a big way after the break was Spencer.

> *As we headed into the sheds, I said to Donny [Stevenson] 'this game is in the balance, and we need to inject something special into it straight after the break because the first 15 minutes after halftime are going be crucial'. Clearly, it was time to play the Los card, and no disrespect was meant to Dave Hill, who'd done a splendid job in the first half, guiding the team around the park from first-five-eighths. In a way, we got the best of both worlds: Dave steered us around and followed the game plan to the letter while it was structured, Los came on after halftime and broke things up a bit.*

Prior to giving Spencer his instructions to warm up during the halftime period, Matt asked his experienced talisman for his views on how the game had panned out to date.

> *He felt that we were trying to go wide too early, and needed to suck a few more of their defenders in first, before we looked to open it up. I said to him 'fine, go do it'. With that, and the team talk out of the way, he left the changing room to warm up so that he was ready to go on with the rest of them when the halftime break was over. Our basic message to the team was that we'd taken their best shots and that if we could get quality ball, we could have a real crack at them. Good quick ball was the key because the Lions had been slowing the delivery of a lot of our possession down up until that point.*

Although the victory achieved was about more than one man, Gear says Spencer's 40-minute contribution was impossible to ignore.

'He made a huge impact when he came on', Gear says.

'It was just his unpredictability. The Brits didn't know how to handle it, and it caused them huge problems. No wonder he's gone so well since he's started playing club rugby over there. But as well as tying them in knots, having him on the field also gave us a huge lift. We all knew that he could create something out of nothing and that spurred all of us on.'

With Spencer at the helm, New Zealand Maori made their winning break after halftime, forging to a 19–6 lead thanks to twin penalty goals by Luke McAlister and a converted try from fullback Leon MacDonald, before steeling themselves for a gripping Lions riposte.

Time and again during a frantic finale, waves of red jerseys were hurled back from the New Zealand Maori line.

Holah earned his keep, securing vital break-down turnovers to relieve some of the pressure, while a number of individuals came up with big plays at one point or another.

Such was the pressure, as the Lions sensed a morale-crushing defeat was near, a break was finally made for tour skipper Brian O'Driscoll to scoot through a gap to score. The conversion closed the gap between the sides to just six points, at 19–13, and left Matt agonising over the past.

> *When O'Driscoll scored that try, I did wonder whether it was history repeating. If you go back to the '81 game against the Springboks, or '93 against the Lions, that's how it had happened. We'd taken our foot off the throat for a moment and it had been enough to turn the tide.*

History wasn't to repeat. With the coaches' demand to go the full eighty at the forefront of their minds, and a historic first-ever victory over the Lions in the offing, there was no way that the players were going to let this result slip.

Nor was the enormity of the moment totally lost in the inevitable adrenalin release after referee Steve Walsh blew for no side with New Zealand Maori still leading 19–13.

'Normally, as players, we don't really worry too much about a game we've just played, but this was a bit different', Gear says.

'I think we all appreciated the significance of what we'd just achieved, although the realisation as to its magnitude probably only grew in the days and weeks that followed the game.'

That was certainly the case for a number of the players, including experienced Canterbury prop Greg Feek, who was still fielding the praise and thanks of well-wishers weeks afterwards.

'I'll never forget walking along the road heading away from the park after the first Test, and someone drove past and wound down their window and shouted, "Go Maoris, you little beauty!" And that was after the All Blacks had just beaten the Lions. That incident on its own said a lot about how much our performance had meant, which was just amazing. You expect that sort of reaction after an All Black game, but it was something new and pretty mind-blowing for the Maoris. It was certainly a game that will be talked about in Maori teams for a long time to come.'

Feek was among a group of senior players who provided a touching tribute to the team's farewell pair, Matt and Spencer.

Both were, in their turn, hoisted on the shoulders of the two props Feek and Carl Hayman.

'It wasn't something he was prepared for, and he resisted for a little bit, but it was our way of showing our respect for all he'd done', Feek says of the team's impromptu tribute to their coach.

For his part, Matt admits it was a first, because he'd never been on the field before, now that all the halftime lectures are delivered from inside the changing room.

Feeky and Zarg [Hayman] were both members of our senior group of players, and after the game there is always a bit of a regime change, and you come under their jurisdiction for the post-match team session. That being the case, I figured that I'd better follow orders when they summoned me, although I wasn't really sure what they wanted. I initially thought they just wanted to say something to me. The next thing I knew, I was getting a view of the stadium and its surroundings from altitude! It was a special moment though, and one I'll never forget ... it meant a lot.

Not that all of the post-match festivities were so sentimental.

It was perhaps fitting, given the nature of the New Zealand Maori environment, that at least some of the celebrations should be touched by a bit of mickey take.

'It was quite hard case', Ralph says.

'Jono, Los and I were walking around the edge of the field in one group, clapping the crowd, who'd been awesome, and had stayed on to cheer afterwards. So we were wandering around clapping the crowd back to say thank you for all the support, then Jono leans over and says: "that's us. We're not the bloody Crusaders! Let's get into the room!" I just cracked up. It's a great memory to have.'

A great memory, on a night filled with memories, but one almost a world away from the earlier years and experiences in Matt's life.

2

Beginnings

'A life less ordinary'

The names of Makuini and Rerekau Te Pou won't feature anywhere if one was to go looking for a list of the major influences on modern Maori rugby in New Zealand, but the two ladies certainly played a significant role, if judged by the values they passed on to their mokopuna (grandchild) Matt Te Pou.

The future coach of the New Zealand Maori team was born into the Tuhoe tribe, one of the most traditional of all of the country's native tribes, in the Eastern Bay of Plenty town of Whakatane in 1950.

Like many young Maori of the time, Matt was initially raised by his grandparents as a result of the whangai system that was prevalent among Maori families, with Matt being brought up alongside the 20 other cousins his grandmother, Makuini, had in her care.

> *When you were whangai, you effectively had two sets of parents. While my parents still had all of the parental rights that you would have today, I lived with, and was predominantly brought up by, my grandmother.*

Makuini was one of the first Maori to be educated in the English system, having attended Auckland's prestigious Queen Victoria College.

That experience helped prepare her for the task of watching over so many young ones while her husband, Matt's grandfather, Hoani Te Pou, was away working on the many dams that were being built in the Whakatane, Atiamuri and Matahina districts during this time.

> *Work in the district was hard to find so Hoani, like a lot of people back then, had to travel to where the work was. A large majority of the Maori families we knew were involved and employed in manual labour at the time. As a result, we would often only see my grandfather about once a*

> *month. I suppose it was pretty hard on my grandmother, having so many kids running around that she was responsible for, but we, as kids, knew nothing different so we thought it was wonderful. It also meant that my grandmother had a major influence over my formative years. She was an outstanding lady, and someone I probably learnt more off than any other single person alive. A lot of the values I have in my life came from her.*

If Makuini wielded the most influence over Matt's early years of learning, his aunty, Rerekau, also had a key role to play. Rerekau, who'd married a local minister, Warren Foster, lived at Nuhaka, Wairoa, in the Hawke's Bay. Over the years, the young Matt had grown close to his aunty; so much so that Rerekau asked the family if Matt could live with her after she got married.

> *It might seem a bit strange to some people, especially Europeans, being shuttled around like that, but it was actually quite common in Maoridom. The family knew that there was a close bond between Rerekau and myself, so there was no major issue with me going to live with her. Rerekau, like Makuini before her, had a huge influence over me. In many respects, the leadership skills I learned that served me so well in later life – both in the New Zealand Army and in rugby coaching – came from those two women.*

Matt moved to Wairoa during his form one and two school years, gravitating towards rugby where he played for the local school, Nuhaka, and then for the Wairoa district in the prestigious Hawke's Bay Ross Shield schoolboys' competition.

Rugby had already become a big part of his life since he'd first started playing the game in Whakatane at the age of five.

> *A lot of the teams in Whakatane after the war were formed under the banner of the Returned Servicemen's Associations. Over time, these evolved into separate clubs like the Marists and the Pirates of today, but that was where most of those clubs we see now started. Back then, the RSAs even used to outfit all the kids with their playing jerseys. It was a system very much based on loyalty, though, in terms of who you played for. You went where your uncles and other elders had played. There was no argument or debate over which club you played for, as you might get today. Loyalty was a much bigger factor then than it is now, at club level anyway.*

While Nuhaka was 20 minutes out of Wairoa, the school, like the rest of the district, was infatuated with legendary stories of the district's most famous rugby son, the great Maori and All Black player George Nepia.

This was definitely 'Nepia country' although, as with all legends, some of the yarns relating to the great fullback were rather exaggerated in the telling down the years.

> There was a tale told by one of our teachers at school about how George had once kicked a ball from the local rugby grounds and broken the school window. Being young and eager to latch on to any information we could about our local hero, we, of course, all swallowed that and held it to be true.
>
> I went back to that school a few years ago – and looking at it now – I reckon old George would have had to have kicked that ball 200 yards! So our teacher's story was stretched just a little bit, but that's how big George Nepia especially, and rugby in general, was to us. It was everything. We'd play ourselves, and then watch the older ones play.
>
> Back in Whakatane around that time, and a bit later, the local club derbies could attract 5,000 people! All of the farmers would come into town and watch – the games were a major event. When All Black loose forward Red Conway was playing in Whakatane in 1965, he was the star of the show and everybody would watch everything he did.

While Conway only made the All Blacks for one season from Bay of Plenty, having previously made it from Otago, his impact on the district was such that Matt's club, Whakatane Marist, has its home ground named in his honour – Red Conway Park.

But while Matt's association with Whakatane Marist was to be a long one, his memories of playing for Wairoa in the Ross Shield have stayed with him, especially attending the tournament, which was held in Taupo – nowadays part of the King Country union.

> There were a lot of youngsters who were whangai in the district around then, and we all gravitated to rugby. I guess, growing up alongside our cousins, it was only natural that we would opt for team sports. I was used to having a lot of people around me, so team sports and a career in the Army were probably the obvious choices that I was going to make. Working in big numbers, being flexible, giving and taking and, particularly, giving

> *away your individual outlook at times for the betterment of the collective – that was all second nature to me, and a lot of other young Maori who grew up in that sort of environment were the same.*

Because team sports came naturally to the young Matt, it is no surprise that he, like many of his peers, showed an aptitude for rugby. While Nuhaka was a small school within the Wairoa district, it provided two boys for Wairoa's Ross Shield team of 1964, Matt among them. Matt returned for a reunion of that Ross Shield side in 2004, there meeting up with Huriwaka Rore, who was the team's best player.

> *Huriwaka was the greatest player I ever played with. He was our Jonah Lomu, and I coached Jonah at the Chiefs, so I know what sort of influence he had on all of the other players. We were a lot younger, of course, but Huriwaka was the same ... he was our Jonah. Whenever we were in trouble, we'd get the ball to him and he'd smash through and win our games!*

All but two of Wairoa's 1964 Ross Shield side attended the reunion, and Matt is happy to report that Rori is still happily living in Nuhaka, where he spends much of his time playing golf!

> *It – rugby – had a monopoly on young boys back then. The influence of the great All Blacks who were running around was even greater on our generation than it is today, and that was despite us not having the blanket media exposure that the top professional players now get. Even so, the All Black heroes were so real to us as boys. We all wanted to be just like them.*

Not that Matt believes the game's influence over young Maori has lessened with time. It is still as strong today, if not stronger, he believes, although now not as many are sticking with rugby after their junior years.

> *We did a lot of research in this area during my later years, when I was involved with the New Zealand Maori side, and the data told us that the numbers are definitely there. If anything, in rural areas particularly, and at schoolboy level in general, the numbers of young Maori playing rugby are even greater than in the past. The problem is that we lose a lot of them from about the age of 19 on. We need to find out why we are losing them at that point, and investigate ways and means of reversing that trend.*

Even with the losses, data compiled in 2005 indicated that 21 percent of New Zealand's registered rugby-playing population were of Maori decent, which is an over-representation given that Maori make up just over 14 percent of the country's entire population. At the professional level, among the Super 12 players contracted for the 2005 season, 34 percent claimed Maori heritage.

> *Maori youth take to team sports. We tend to struggle as individuals, which is why Michael Campbell, with his success in winning the 2005 US Golf Open, is such a great role model. The inner strength he showed, and the determination to be selfish and work on his game to achieve the success he has, is fantastic, but it is a bit of an anomaly among Maori. Because our thinking tends to be more towards the collective, rather than ourselves. As a race, we generally struggle in individual pursuits. It possibly explains why so many Maori battle in business.*
>
> *As far as our rugby losses go, perhaps the extended family ties are not as tight as they once were. That would explain why we are losing so many Maori players from the game in their late teens. Certainly, when I was growing up, all of my closest mates were my cousins – and they all played rugby.*

After his experience in Wairoa, Matt returned to Whakatane to attend high school. His first year back in his hometown, however, would provide him with a significant turning point in his life when his grandfather, Hoani, died before his eyes after suffering a heart attack.

> *It happened while he was in the bathroom. I was there with my grandmother. When my brother arrived, we were trying to get him out of the bathroom. It was the first time I had ever experienced death, and it really shook me. I was in the third form then but, by my fourth form year, I'd reached the decision that it was time to cut my own track. My time had arrived to grow up!*

On January 5, 1967, at the age of 16, Matt reported to the Whakatane office of the New Zealand Army, where he signed up as a regular force cadet. The cadets had been formed as part of the legacy of the Army's participation in World War Two, where the New Zealand force had experienced a chronic shortage of leaders. The cadet programme was designed to develop leaders for the future, with the preparation involving a majority of formal military training mixed in with some scholastic education.

> *I was like all young fellas are at that age – you've got both cowboys and indians in you! The idea of running around and blowing up bridges appealed to me enormously, but it didn't take long to get a reality check on that front. Our training was all hard yards!*

Initially sent to the Tauranga Area Army office, one hour's drive West from Whakatane, across the Bay of Plenty, Matt was among 15 baywide recruits in that year's cadet muster. Some of the training was conducted further down the line at the New Zealand Army base at Waiouru, where 250 cadets were assembled for mentoring.

> *The base was built along boarding school lines, except obviously it had a very strong military side to it. We carried the same weapons and gear that all of the regular soldiers in the Army were equipped with.*

Matt spent 18 months in the cadets, becoming a regular army soldier midway through his second year, in 1968. With the rank of corporal, he was in charge of nine other cadets, and quickly noted the large Maori percentage among the volunteers.

> *It also showed when I went to Vietnam, where nearly half of the New Zealand troops who served were of Maori upbringing. The numbers highlighted the fact that the Army, like team sports, promoted the collective outlook and focus that many young Maori were brought up with. Guys really responded to the enforced discipline of the Army. It changed a lot of people, and, in many ways, was similar to the situation I'd deal with later in my life when in charge of a group of professional rugby players. In both professional rugby, and the Army, you need good discipline, and to adhere to the systems that are in place if you are to survive and excel.*

The similarities between the military and professional rugby are not just related to overall team discipline.

> *The Army gave me another family, like rugby does when you are involved within the team environment. A lot of the disciplines that are required are similar: you've got to have self-discipline, consideration for others in the group and the group as a whole, have planning skills, be organised and, most importantly, have individuals offering leadership within the*

group. In many ways, as an individual, you've got to be able to adapt and remake yourself. A professional coach will sometimes ask a rugby player to do all of these things. The Army does it as well.

But while Matt played, and later coached, rugby during his military career, on the global stage a more serious 'game' was just around the corner. After being posted to the National Service Training Unit as an Instructor of Conscripts in 1968–69, Matt was then sent, midway through 1969, to Papakura Military Camp (16 Field Regiment). From there, he found himself pitched into the serious business of a proper shooting war within a year, when he volunteered to serve as part of the New Zealand Forces sent to South East Asia to fight alongside the Australians, Americans and other allied troops defending the sovereignty of what was then known as the Republic of South Vietnam. His role was as a radio operator posted to 161 Field Battery RNZA, stationed at Nui Dat in the Republic of South Vietnam.

3

Into the 'Nam

'Where boys became men'

The New Zealand Army's role in the South Asia conflicts, which stretched from the 1950s through until the early 1970s, is all too easily forgotten today.

Unlike the first and second world wars, there was no easily identifiable dividing line between right and wrong, and no clear claim of victory with which to justify the actions that took place.

Yet, for all the political issues, Matt remains extremely proud of the job he and his comrades did in South Asia, with the year-long service in South Vietnam still rating, 36 years on, as one of the real achievements of his life.

> *The New Zealand soldier was well trained, and it showed in Vietnam. Our military people who served there acquitted themselves exceptionally well. We had a lot of respect for the Viet Cong [Communist guerrillas], but they were not the supermen that they have often since been built up to be. Politically, that war was won and lost in the dining rooms of the United States, where public opinion was gradually turned against the war, and the American sacrifice that took place. In some ways, you can see the odd similarity to what is going on now in Afghanistan, and Iraq especially. If there had been a straight-out invasion of North Vietnam, like there would have been anywhere else, the place would have pretty quickly collapsed. It was just never to be like that. After Korea, where the Chinese had come in on North Korea's side after invasion in the 1950s, the Americans just weren't prepared to risk the threat of direct confrontation with another nuclear power again.*

Matt had headed to Vietnam after a period of training at Papakura, where his other pursuits had included a spot of rugby, playing as either a centre, winger or on the openside flank. Although the soldiers were very much part-time players, even when compared with their Saturday club counterparts, Matt recalls this as being a time when their participation was more important than their results.

> We were just happy that we were allowed to play the game. It wasn't like a normal set up where you trained all week and then played at the weekend. We spent the week running around in the bush training for war, so there was no time for rugby preparation as well. We'd come out at the end of the week, usually knackered, and then line up the next day against all of the club teams. Of course, we'd usually get hammered, but somehow that didn't matter so much. We were pretty realistic – we were only playing because we loved the game!

Rugby, however, went on hold once Matt shipped out to Vietnam in 1970, finding himself stationed at Nui Dai, 30 minutes from Vung Tau and a couple of hours from the South Vietnamese capital, Saigon. As a radio operator, Matt was part of a field battery that was attached to an Australian brigade. His job was to communicate with a wide range of parties to help ensure that the gun battery's barrages were directed as accurately as possible.

> One of the strange things about that war, when compared with conventional conflicts like World Wars One and Two, was that there was no real front line. There was a demilitarised zone supposedly separating North and South Vietnam, which had been set up after the armistice when the former French colonial rulers withdrew from the country, but that wasn't really the flash point of the conflict. The shit could hit the fan at any time because the Viet Cong had the South so infiltrated, they could pop up anywhere!

While the mass communication tools of the time were nowhere near as powerful and widely accessible as they are now, the New Zealanders serving in Vietnam were aware of the unpopularity of the war – both at home and further a field.

> We knew. A few of the guys were getting papers sent over from New Zealand, so we knew that there had been protests back home questioning what we, as a country, were doing being involved in the Vietnam conflict. No one really talked about that much though, because to do so would be

> *to undermine overall morale, and we were all too professional for that. We had a job to do, so we shut that aspect of it out. We all had pre-conceived ideas about why we were there before we went over. Perhaps the biggest impression I gained during the whole experience was how unpopular the war was – not just with our own people back home but with some of the Vietnamese themselves.*

Not that this was even allowed to get in the way of the job the Kiwi soldiers had to do.

> *It was very professional. I was involved with a great bunch of guys who were like family to me by the time we'd finished. The bonds were always strong with my players later in life, when I coached the New Zealand Maori team, but these were stronger again. I guess that is natural in a time of war.*

Nor did the Kiwi soldiers involved return with anything less than total respect and admiration for their primary allies, the Australian and American soldiers.

> *I personally worked with Thai and American soldiers in Bear Cat. The Americans were part of a gunship [helicopter] unit. I found them to be really top guys. Some of them were conscripts for sure, and didn't want to be in Vietnam – and understandably so; but we were all volunteers and regular soldiers, and we respected them for the job they did all the same.*

There was also respect for the South Vietnamese Army or ARVN (Army of the Republic of Vietnam), who inadvertently saved Matt's battery from a potential catastrophe during a deployment, when an ARVN patrol wandered into an ambush that had been set for the unsuspecting Allied troops and their field guns.

> *We were deploying, with our guns being pulled by Armoured Personnel Carriers, which is a time when we were always very vulnerable, when all hell broke loose a little further up the trail we were travelling on. An ARVN unit had walked straight into the Viet Cong trap that was waiting to be sprung on us. If they [the South Vietnamese] hadn't been there, and hadn't gone in first, the outcome could have been horrendous, because we had no mobility at all on that track, and would have had nowhere to go. As it was, the South Vietnamese did take a few casualties, but we didn't see any of the fighting because our convoy was pulled over until the Viet Cong were cleared from the area.*

While that was the closest Matt came to the front line of the battle, he was at Bear Cat Fire Support base on the Vietnamese coast at one stage, when the casualties were brought in from a nearby action.

> *There was always the possibility that you might find yourself in the wrong place at the wrong time and be wounded – or worse. But you couldn't think about that. If you did, it would have prevented the proper execution of your job, and that was probably our biggest fear of all. No one wanted to let down their mates.*

Matt's service in Vietnam ended in May 1971, with the soldiers returning home to a warm welcome, which included a march down Auckland's Queen Street in the central area of the city.

Thirty-five New Zealand servicemen lost their lives in the Vietnam conflict. A further 150 were wounded, yet the return home of the troops that Matt served with did not go off without a hitch.

> *As the parade was going down the street, there were a few anti-war protestors throwing red paint, and a few more who tried to lie down in front of the columns in the middle of the road. Those actions really hurt, and certainly didn't honour the servicemen who had died or been wounded, or the efforts of all of the rest us, who had gone to a war-torn country at the command of others to do our job. Having protests like that going on so blatantly in front of us did make you question whether it was all worth it. Their actions also put a sad tinge on everyone else who had turned out to cheer us and thank us for the job we'd done, and it seemed, at the time, like half of Auckland was there to pay their respects. I suppose it's sad in a way, that it is the minority of malcontents who you always remember the most!*

Fortunately for Matt, happier times were just around the corner. He met his future wife, Ida, who was flatting with one of his cousins while she attended teachers' training college in Hamilton, soon after his return from Vietnam, with the couple marrying during Labour weekend 1972 at Te Puke. After returning from the war to Papakura, Matt was soon posted to Waiouru as an instructor, and spent the next 15 years moving between bases and appointments as his military career continued. During this period, there was also time to rekindle his passion for rugby, which left a lasting memory around the birth of his first son, Thomas.

Thomas was born in 1973 on the same day that Matt, injured during the previous day's rugby game, was forced to drive through the

Paraparas to Wanganui Base Hospital from Waiouru Camp in order to get a dislocated shoulder attended to. The following year, the couple's second son, Matthew, was born in the Waiouru Maternity Hospital, while third son, Alamoti Sione, was later born in Papakura Maternity Hospital. Although injuries and age curtailed Matt's playing career, he was soon showing an aptitude as a coach. While at Papakura, and by now a Sergeant Major, Matt coached the 161 Battery team to become the best side on the entire base, taking out the regular Wednesday afternoon competition that attracted up to 10 teams.

> *It wasn't skilful rugby, but it was hard. You had SAS guys, men who were professional soldiers and quite ruthless in their attitudes. They weren't always great players but they were certainly tough. Often, it came down to who was the last man left standing!*

Further success followed when Matt coached the 16th Field Regiment side to win the Harding Cup, the Ranfurly Shield of corps rugby, before he was selected to take up an appointment training potential officers at the prestigious Duntroon Officers' camp at Canberra in Australia in 1986.

While in Australia, as well as grooming future officers, Matt continued his own development as a rugby mentor by coaching a team that won the Monaro division of Australian Capital Territory rugby competition.

> *There was a lot of trans-Tasman banter around that time, especially when it came to rugby, because the Wallabies beat us in the Bledisloe Cup that first year. Interestingly, I didn't hear so much out of the locals the following season when the All Blacks won the first Rugby World Cup and then got the Bledisloe back, but that's Australians for you! I made sure they knew that I was around ... when we were winning of course!*

> *In military terms, though, going to Duntroon was like graduating from provincial, or Super rugby, to Test rugby – you had to step up. There was a level of professionalism there that was similar in its own way to the All Blacks I had around me in rugby teams later. Both the trainee officers and the international rugby players were highly motivated. They wouldn't have been there otherwise.*

> *My philosophy was always to treat them the same. Integrity and commitment was important in the Army, and I expected the same of my players later on. They were only cheating themselves if they didn't put in, and also letting down all of their mates.*

Interestingly, it was the military that taught Matt the folly of operating a climate of fear in sporting circles. This was an old-school style of coaching that he later came to realise was still in vogue in New Zealand rugby in the 1990s, with two of its leading disciples being the high-profile coaches Laurie Mains and Graham Henry.

> *In coaching, you can't talk down to people like we did on the parade ground. You've got to let every individual be themselves. There is no rank when you are part of a team. I might be the coach, but I'm still a team member. My contribution is simply as the coach. I always felt that part of my role as a coach was as a facilitator, in terms of encouraging the players to get the best out of themselves by creating the right environment in which they could excel.*

> *There was no point in me telling All Black locks what they should or shouldn't be doing in the finer points of lineouts because they quite clearly knew a lot more about that than I did. A lot of the old-school style coaching I found that was still prevalent in New Zealand in the 1990s was based on fear. We operated that way on the drill ground. If I was doing that all day in the Army, why would I want to be doing it that way again on the weekends when I was coaching rugby? While the Army taught me all about leadership, it also taught me that there are different ways you can lead.*

The philosophy – in terms of the balance that had worked so well in the military – quickly showed that it did cross over to the civilian world, and to sports teams, when Matt decided to end his 23-year military career after he returned to New Zealand from Duntroon in 1989. After virtually discharging himself from the service on the trans-Tasman flight back to New Zealand, Matt returned to Whakatane where he and Ida settled on a farm.

> *The Army had taken up such a huge chunk of my life; it was time to do something else. Outside of the farming, I probably wasn't sure what exactly that 'something else' would be at that stage, but I knew it was time for a change.*

It didn't take long for rugby to start filling the gap that the military had left. By 1990, Matt was coaching his old club Whakatane Marist, trying to build the senior side up again after a few lean seasons. His timing was excellent, in terms of the rebuilding process, because the long-overdue

Marty Holah had to wait five years to debut for New Zealand Maori but made the most of it when he did. Here British & Irish Lions halfback Matt Dawson finds the All Black flanker a handful. © PHOTOSPORT

'King' Carlos Spencer kept the Lions guessing all night. © PHOTOSPORT

Hooker Corey Flynn keeps the attack alive as the New Zealand Maori side rampages against the Lions. © PHOTOSPORT

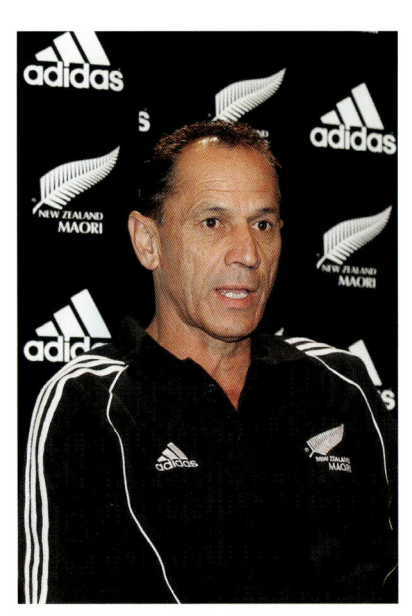

Matt fronts up to the international news media as the New Zealand Maori team's date with the Lions approaches. © PHOTOSPORT

The guitar was never far away when kaumatua Whetu Tipiwai was on the team bus. Mike Stewart collection

Rua Tipoki leads the formation as the team polishes up its performance of 'Timatanga', the New Zealand Maori side's haka, at Waikato Stadium. Mike Stewart collection

Winners are grinners! The New Zealand Maori team brains trust (left to right) of kaumatua Whetu Tipiwai, manager Peter Potaka, technical advisor Jim Love and Matt (at right) are joined by the Minister of Maori Affairs, Parekura Horomia (second from right), after the win over the Lions. Mike Stewart collection

The job done, it's time to celebrate. Matt and his assistant coach Donny Stevenson (right) relax on the team bus after the win over the Lions. Mike Stewart collection

The morning coffee as a team was an important part of the New Zealand Maori side's pre-match preparation. Here the players relax in Hamilton on the morning of their historic match against the British & Irish Lions. Mike Stewart collection

Deacon Manu (left) and Corey Flynn with the spoils of war. Mike Stewart collection

It is a tough life, this touring! Jim Love (left) and Matt make themselves at home in Fiji in 2005. Mike Stewart collection

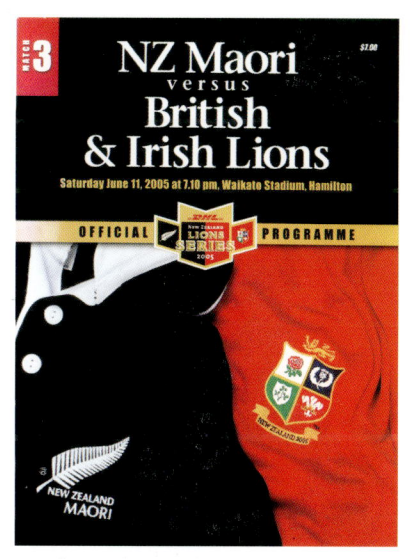

British & Irish Lions–New Zealand Maori match programme, 2005.

The Nuhaka School rugby side in 1963. Matt is on the far right in the top row. Matt Te Pou collection

Communication was a vital part of Matt's role in Vietnam. Matt Te Pou collection

Wherever you went in Vietnam, helicopters and machine guns were never too far away. Matt Te Pou collection

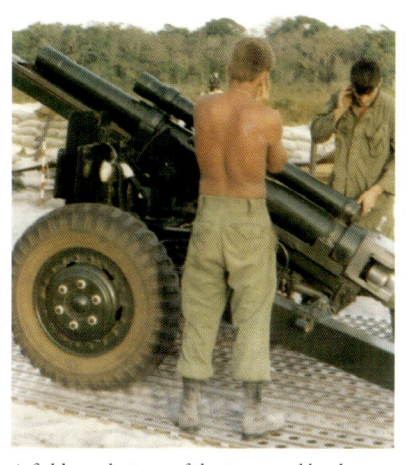

A field gun battery of the type used by the unit Matt served with in Vietnam. Matt Te Pou collection

Allied troops on the move in Vietnam. This was a time where the visiting forces were at their most vulnerable to attack by the Viet Cong. Matt Te Pou collection

Helicopter forces were used to move both men and machines around Vietnam during the Allied occupation. Matt Te Pou collection

Matt (far right, second row) with the Whakatane Marist Rugby & Sports Club senior side – the Baywide Senior A Championship winners for 1992. Matt Te Pou collection

advent of a Baywide Bay of Plenty club competition arrived in 1990, and Whakatane Marist was included in the top echelon. Just four Eastern Bay of Plenty clubs were admitted alongside the traditional Bay of Plenty power houses from the more populous Tauranga and Rotorua districts, and the competition was fierce, but Matt's men held their place for the following year.

While Marist proved competitive in Matt's first season, and lost by just four points to the eventual champions, Waikite, during the first round, and by five points to the other finalist, Ngongotaha, in the second, the club's overall tally of just seven wins from 17 matches reflected a lack of confidence that only comes with experience. Six of Marist's losses that year were by margins of 10 points or less.

A year later, with the bulk of the previous season's squad wiser from the knocks they'd taken in 1990, Marist made a flying start to the second Baywide club competition by winning its first five matches, including a 24–15 success over champions Waikite. Significantly, Marist also beat Rotorua club Eastern Pirates, the club of the famous Stone brothers – Arthur and Darrin – 26–12. Pirates, however, were to prove Matt's nemesis when his side made it through to the championship semi-finals. Eastern Pirates beat Marist 20–11 on the day when it mattered the most and went on to take out Waikite in the final. While getting to within a game of the title and not being able to close out the deal was disappointing at the time, Marist's top four finish, coupled with a strong performance in making the finals at the North Island Marist clubs' annual Spillane Cup tournament, told Matt that his side was headed in the right direction.

> *That year, 1990, was about survival for us, being a smaller club, as far as the Baywide competition went, but we made steady improvement in the second year. Doing as well as we did at the Spillane tournament in 1991 also gave the players a huge boost. While that first year had been all about fighting to stay in there, the players grew in confidence as a result of achieving that goal. And the confidence and self-belief continued to grow as the second season progressed, to the extent that, by the end of the competition, we were right up there and mixing it with the bigger clubs in the championship semi-finals. While we weren't quite good enough to go on and win it, we'd set a standard. By the end of that season, I was confident I had a team that would go on to be a force to be reckoned with the following year.*

Matt hit the jackpot. Not only was Marist a major player in the third Baywide club competition, the team ran away with the prize in just his third season in the job.

Spearheaded by Bay of Plenty representatives: centre Jason Spanhake and flanker Brett Sinkinson, the latter of whom would, later in his career, have the misfortune to get caught up in an unholy row when used by Graham Henry with Wales, even though he wasn't actually eligible; Marist opened the season with eight straight wins. Not even a 14–21 loss to their conquerors from the previous year's semi-final, Eastern Pirates, could slow the Whakatane club's momentum as it went on to win the first round, thereby earning home advantage in the play-offs that followed the second round of the competition.

Marist started the second round as it had finished the first, stringing a further three wins together in a row, before being edged out 26–25 by Mount Maunganui. That afternoon proved significant because it was to be the last defeat Matt's side suffered in the season. After bouncing back to beat Waikite 22–0 and neighbours Opotiki United 23–0, Marist took out Te Teko 36–7 in a one-sided semi-final to set up a showdown with arch rivals Eastern Pirates in the championship decider. This time, the pride of the Eastern Bay sub-union was not to be denied, and they ended up winning the final by a comfortable margin, 26–7. The victory capped off a season where Marist had won 16 of the 19 competition matches that the team played.

> *We'd all grown as a group from the previous year, and learnt from our mistakes. That showed by the fact that we were able to finish up that year so strongly in the matches that mattered at the end of the competition, winning them all by clear-cut scores. The club was on a real roll. The pleasing thing was, not only were we winning, the players were starting to get their rewards. By 1993, 13 of our senior players were in Bay of Plenty representative sides. They were starting to make it.*

They were not the only ones!

Bay of Plenty or bust!

'Rebuilding a province's pride'

The Bay of Plenty Rugby Union has long been a difficult beast to manage.

Unlike the majority of New Zealand's provincial unions, which are centred around one major metropolitan area, Bay of Plenty has two – Tauranga and Rotorua; while the Eastern Bay of Plenty sub-union, which is focused around Matt's home town of Whakatane, often finds itself sandwiched in the rivalry between the power brokers of the two more populous areas.

That was certainly the case in 1993, when Matt inherited a Bay of Plenty representative side that was still battling two years on from a season that is undoubtedly remembered as one of the most disappointing the union has endured in the modern era.

Despite winning five of its first six games in 1991, which included two wins on a short tour of Fiji, and a 22–21 success over that year's surprise World Cup quarter-finalists Western Samoa, the Bay folded up badly towards the end of the season.

The side, which was coached by John Brake, won on just four more occasions in its remaining 12 matches. It finished an NPC campaign that it had started with high hopes of cracking the top four, with the ignominy of having to play in a promotion-relegation match.

Worse still, Bay of Plenty lost that match – being beaten 22–13 by then second division champions King Country, which saw the union's much smaller southern neighbour replace it in the top echelon for the following year.

The saga of 1991 was to have long-term repercussions for Bay of Plenty rugby, both in terms of losing a lot of promising talent from the region to other teams over future years, but also with regard to its national status.

It was not until 2001, a full decade on from its demotion, that Bay of Plenty, which is the sixth most populous New Zealand union (with more residents than the likes of Otago, Taranaki, Northland and Southland), was finally readmitted to the top division of the NPC.

By that time, professionalism had arrived, and Bay of Plenty found itself in a subservient relationship to its neighbour and Super rugby host union, Waikato, as part of the Chiefs franchise.

In 1992, Bay of Plenty had a new coach, future New Zealand Sevens guru Gordon Tietjens; but even he couldn't provide a quick fix.

Although the union scraped into the semi-finals of the second division, thanks to a last-minute try by future New Zealand Maori fullback Adrian Cashmore, which allowed it to edge out Southland 14–9 in the decisive preliminary round game, there was to be no miracle.

Despite a valiant effort away to Counties Manukau in the semi-finals, Bay of Plenty lost 29–31, and ended the year with a disappointing five win, eight loss record, while a further match was drawn.

That was far from acceptable, as Tietjens found out to his cost, with his first tenure as the Bay of Plenty coach lasting just a year. Ironically, such was the manner of the wheeling and dealing behind the scenes in Bay rugby politics, Tietjens was to end up returning to the position again two seasons later, with his second stint lasting from 1995 until he finally called it quits when the union was safely back in the top flight at the end of 2001.

For 1993 and 1994, however, Tietjens was sidelined because it was to be the turn of the Baywide championship-winning Whakatane Marist coach of 1992, Matt Te Pou, assisted by a former Bay of Plenty fullback Brett McKillop, from nearby Opotiki.

Politics is always a big factor with Bay of Plenty rugby, and I knew that when I took on the representative job. It was probably how I got it in the first place!

The Tauranga versus Rotorua thing never really dies, but it was probably bubbling away even more actively than usual in my first year with the rep team. The fact that I was independent, having come in from Eastern Bay of Plenty after we'd taken out the Baywide the year before with Whakatane Marist, may have helped me a little bit with the politics, but not much! There was still a lot of internal squabbling going on.

> *What added to the political chaos of the time, and made things even worse, was that we were a team with no money. A fair bit had been spent on the side in that last year, when it was in the first division, with a few new players having been recruited to the area, but that all quickly dried up once the team was relegated. It was definitely a year of rebuilding.*
>
> *While the goal was obviously to get back to the first division if we could, we realistically weren't good enough at that stage ... we were definitely a second division side.*

By the way Matt's first season had started, Bay supporters could have been excused for thinking the good times were back. His first match at the helm, a non-championship contest against first division North Harbour, saw the Bay prevail 36–21. While a heavy defeat against Waikato followed, King Country was put in its place when Bay of Plenty won 32–24, giving Matt two victories over first division opposition from his first three matches in charge.

> *There was a lot of talent in the side in that first year, but it was quite raw. We lacked a little bit in experience and leadership when the heat went on. Given a bit of freedom to express themselves, the guys could play, and that showed in some of our results, especially in the early part of the year, when there was no pressure. Once that came on, towards the tail end of the NPC, however, some of our weaknesses showed.*

Prior to the start of the NPC, Matt experienced a bizarre week where his side thrashed lower division neighbours Thames Valley, 76–17, but were then outclassed 93–5 by an All Black-strength New Zealand XV, which was warming up for a game against Samoa at Rotorua, which it ended up winning 37–13.

> *It was part of the learning curve. Being on the end of a score like that was probably akin to being run over by a tank. Most of the players in that team were All Blacks, and that showed when they went on to beat the Samoans by a slightly bigger margin than the All Blacks did in the Test, but it still didn't do much for the confidence of my side. It was an experience that certainly left me with a greater understanding of what it would be like to be the coach of an international side that the All Blacks had creamed!*

With that 'experience' tucked away behind them, Matt's side made a confident start to the second division programme, wracking up consecutive wins against Wairarapa-Bush, South Canterbury and Southland.

The South Canterbury match, which Bay of Plenty won 53–15 against an opponent that would also go on to reach the semi-finals, was an especially pleasing moment for Matt, because the game was played in front of 'his' people in Whakatane. There was merit also in the 27–26 win over Southland, which was achieved after the long trek south to Invercargill.

As is often the way, with the excitement steadily building, the big bump was just around the corner. In the Bay's case, it came in the form of a 10–37 whipping from Sid Going's North Auckland side in Whangarei, which was to take on an even greater significance later when Matt's side ended up drawing them in the semi-finals.

That defeat was one of just two that Bay of Plenty sustained during the round robin phase, with the other being an 11–30 loss to Counties at Pukekohe. However, the side only qualified for the semi-finals in fourth place on a congested ladder behind North Auckland, Counties and surprise semi-finalists South Canterbury.

> *Back then, the rule for the playoffs, which had only been introduced the year before, was that you played at the alternate venue from where the first round match had been played. That meant we got North Auckland back at Rotorua, which was a real bonus for us, but something that Sid wasn't too pleased about, given that his side had finished top of the table. I certainly sympathised with his position, but only after the final whistle, once we'd beaten them!*

While a North Auckland forward pack, featuring current or future All Blacks, locks Ian Jones and Glenn Taylor and prop Con Barrell, took charge in the first spell, the visitors only turned with a 16–14 halftime advantage, and that was nowhere near enough for the amount of energy they had exhausted. Once the game opened up after the break, Matt's side ran riot, finishing with five tries in a commanding 41–26 victory.

> *Looking back, we probably played our final a week too early, but it was certainly enjoyable sitting back and watching the guys take Sid's boys to the cleaners. Our strength was in our speed, so we ran them around as much as we could. A couple of the tries we scored were long-range efforts and you could see the heads of their forwards drop as they had to trudge*

back. When that's happening to your side, and you're playing in the tight five, it can be a pretty tough game.

Tough indeed, but rugby is also a game where fortunes can change quickly, as Matt and his side found out a week later in the final against Counties.

Although the Bay had reversed an earlier away loss to North Auckland in the playoffs, and also had home advantage for the final, Counties learned from North Auckland's mistakes and controlled possession too well to deny Bay of Plenty even the sniff of an opportunity.

Coached by Ross Cooper, who Matt would later act as assistant for with the Chiefs in Super 12, the Counties forwards were well led by two men who would also end up having a close and successful association with Matt in the New Zealand Maori team: No 8 Errol Brain and lock Jim Coe. Samoan international flanker Junior Paramore had shocked the home side in the second minute by scoring a try, but then came a valuable lesson that was to stay with Matt for the remainder of his coaching career, when a Bay backline ploy misfired spectacularly.

The boys were trying hard to get back into the game, but we tried a double miss in the backline and it went horribly wrong. Counties had a Fijian winger, Luke Erenavula, and he got in-between our guys, intercepted the ball, and was gone 80 metres up field to score. It was a 14-point turnaround, because we probably would have scored at the other end, and that knocked the stuffing out of our players. But, it also highlighted to me the fact that you never try anything too fancy playing against Fijians because of the danger they represent. That knowledge came in pretty handy over the years when I came up against them coaching New Zealand Maori.

By fulltime, Counties were home 38–10, with the defeat reducing Bay of Plenty to a 10-win, six-loss record from Matt's freshman season in charge. Results wise, it certainly represented an improvement on the previous year, while making the final also meant taking a step further than the 1992 side had managed.

It was disappointing to lose the final for sure, especially in the manner in which we did, but we were pretty happy with where we were at when we looked back over the whole campaign. Realistically, we'd probably over-

achieved in terms of our pre-season expectations, so that was a positive and it gave us something to build on the following year.

Cashmore, who played fullback for Bay of Plenty that year prior to shifting to Auckland the following season, says the team relished Matt's calm demeanour and relatively relaxed style.

'Everyone really respected him', Cashmore says.

'Pretty much all of the guys knew of his military record, which in itself commanded their respect, but also what he had done at Whakatane Marist, so it was a pretty happy environment. The key thing with Matt, aside from the open way in which he dealt with everyone, was the level of his organisation. It was a feature of his coaching, even in the early days, and was the same during my two stints with New Zealand Maori. We might have still been in the amateur days when he started, but the same things that were being appreciated by the amateur guys back in those early Bay of Plenty days were also being appreciated by the professional players at the end of his time with the Maori team.'

In many ways Cashmore, who played two Tests for the All Blacks in 1996 and 1997, typified the quality of playing talent being lost from the Bay of Plenty during the union's years in the second division wilderness. His was a departure that was keenly felt the following year, when Matt's side managed just seven wins from 15 games, although it did, at least, make the NPC semi-finals again. Another future All Black, then Tauranga Boys' College lock Royce Willis, made his representative debut as a replacement during one of Bay of Plenty's NPC matches that season, but he, too, would later leave the district. Willis ended up starring for the Blues and Chiefs in Super 12, as well as Waikato and the All Blacks, before continuing his career to Japan.

Bay of Plenty has huge potential as a provincial union, and it's pleasing to see that it is starting to be tapped into.

Winning the Ranfurly Shield in 2004, and then making the first division semi-finals later that year, was a big step forward, especially in terms of the union's credibility in the eyes of the players. There's a lot of money in the Mount Maunganui area especially, which is important because you can't go forward in the professional environment without it, but the playing talent is starting to come back into the region as well. That's a promising sign. Not only are guys who have been away filtering back,

> *some of the younger ones are staying, and that will serve Bay of Plenty well in the future, if things are managed properly.*
>
> *We'll always lose the odd player to other provinces here and there, especially if they can't get a go in Super rugby through the Chiefs, but we need to keep the core of the team together if we can. The 2006 side is a good example – most of the Chiefs' tight forwards were from the Bay! So if we can keep those guys together, it's a good base from which we should be able to build up a pretty competitive Bay of Plenty side.*
>
> *The two things Bay of Plenty needs to do is to keep beating Waikato, which will make sure that we continue to get our fair share of players in the Chiefs. The other thing is to take a leaf out of Taranaki's book. They've been upsetting the odds for years, and demand the respect of everyone they play. Taranaki always take a few of the bigger guns out every other year, and we need to mirror ourselves on that by also lowering a few of the bigger teams on a more consistent basis.*

While Matt's second season in charge of Bay of Plenty was notable for a match against the touring Springboks, which the Bay lost 12–33, the five wins it collected in the NPC was only good enough for an away semi-final against Hawke's Bay, which turned out to be a nightmare. Not only did Hawke's Bay win, they did so 65–18, running in nine tries to none against an opponent that had held the Magpies to a 27–38 score line during the round robin match eight days earlier. Seven of the Hawke's Bay players from the semi-final would go on to feature as professionals in the Super 12 when it kicked off two years later.

> *They were a strong side, but the heads dropped. Once they got away on us, there was nowhere to hide and the tries kept on coming. It was a disappointing way to end, but it probably showed what a strong competition it was that year, especially given that Hawke's Bay then went and lost to Southland in the final in Invercargill the following weekend. I was a bit surprised by that result, but given that we'd fallen away so dramatically, having a romp like they did in the semi-final probably did them no favours in the long run.*

Nor did the result do Matt any favours, with the manner of Bay of Plenty's semi-final defeat probably being the final straw, as he was removed as the union's representative coach in favour of the man he had earlier replaced, Tietjens. Not that this proved a hindrance to Matt's coaching career. If anything, it freed him up to devote more time to the area of the game to which his name has become synonymous – Maori rugby.

Matt the Maori: 1994

'Welcome to my world'

While the task of restoring Bay of Plenty's flagging fortunes provided Matt with his main mission for the 1993 season, an even more significant chapter of his life opened up after he was invited to prepare the Northern Maori side for the annual Prince of Wales Cup clash against Southern Maori.

The prestigious trophy, which dates back to 1928, was competed for on an annual basis by sides representing the top half of the North Island (now the region of the Blues and Chiefs Super rugby franchises) against the rest of the country, to reflect a fair representation of the spread of the Maori population throughout the land.

The 1994 match, Matt's second, proved to be the last time the trophy was contested. A three-way zonal format was toyed with for two years in 1995–96, and formal New Zealand Maori trials played for two more years after that, before any official lead-up to the New Zealand Maori team's annual programme was totally dispensed with in 1999.

Prior to Matt's introduction, Southern Maori had won the previous two contests, and started the 1993 match at Levin as hot favourites, too, because of the inclusion of seven current All Blacks in their lineup.

Matt's Northern Maori side, meanwhile, was without all its eligible Auckland players, who were in South Africa trying to win the inaugural Super 10 final that was being contested at the same time.

> We were up against it. No doubt. Southern Maori had all of the names, while my side had only four players who would go on to be All Blacks in their time – Adrian Cashmore, Eric Rush, Mark Cooksley and Kevin Boroevich. We knew that we were the underdogs though, and that probably helped us, although the game itself was a close-run thing.

After trailing 9–6 at halftime, the northerners had worked their way into the lead with time running out. At that stage, Rush recalls, the side's most experienced campaigner and captain, Boroevich, called the team together and told them not to try anything stupid.

'Boro got us into a huddle and said: "nothing fancy. No more of those 50-50 passes. We'll just play it cool and grind it up the middle until the end". Well, no sooner had he laid down the law then the next thing we see is Boro, with us hard on attack, chucking out one of those 50-50 passes he'd been telling us not to throw! Of course it was 'Murphy's Law'. His pass was intercepted by Sam Doyle who ran virtually the length of the field to score, and suddenly we were behind again!'

The Southern side's joy didn't last for long. While Doyle's try had given them the advantage, with just five minutes left on the clock, the Northern side continued to press, and Rush, himself, bagged the match-winner – his second try of the game – with just over 30 seconds remaining.

> It was a brilliant try. You don't get a lot of time together as a team before those type of games, but we'd rehearsed a couple of backline moves quickly, and the guys pulled that one out of the bag to work Rushy over. It was incredibly satisfying, both because they'd had the confidence to back themselves and try it, and, naturally, because it had worked!

But while his try might have spared the captain's blushes, Rush recalls that the hard-nosed veteran front rower, who'd played 26 matches but just three Tests in his All Black career between 1983 and 1988, was unrepentant.

'As we were walking off after the game, and then in the dressing room, all of the boys were giving Boro heaps', Rush says.

'He was getting it left, right and centre about what he'd said, and then the pass he'd thrown, but he just took it all in, smiled and said: "it's a team game boys!" Everyone just cracked up laughing.'

The Northern player's joy at their skipper's discomfort, and their own success, was quickly muted when the squad to play the British & Irish Lions seven days later was released.

Rush was among just five of the victorious Northern side who featured in that game, which New Zealand Maori lost 20–24, with second-five-eighths Rhys Ellison, locks Mark Cooksley and Jim Coe and Boroevich, himself, being the others.

When the side was named, and most of our players missed out, you could see all their heads drop. They'd worked their butts off to achieve something quite special, and here they were being overlooked. For a fair few of them, players like Errol Brain and Adrian Cashmore, their time would come, but it was still disappointing for us as a group. I always suspected afterwards that the Maori team to face the British Lions must have been pre-selected, almost before that match, because the Prince of Wales game didn't seem to have much of an impact on who was chosen. This was a time when Laurie Mains, as All Black coach, and his fellow selectors did seem to have a lot of input into nearly everything.

If the selection of the Maori side to play the Lions left a sour aftertaste to Matt's first experience of the Prince of Wales Cup match, the 1994 edition was to show that his initial effort had been no fluke, because the Northern side again prevailed 36–32.

The 1994 game was played at Oamaru's Centennial Park at the end of May, but the New Zealand Maori side had already been active to that point of the season, having earlier made a historic four-match tour of South Africa in March to participate in that country's invitation M-Net Night Series alongside Western Samoa, Eastern Province, Transvaal, Western Province, Free State, a South African Development XV and Namibia.

'The initiative for that tour came from South Africa, from Louis Luyt [South African Rugby Board President] and Johan Prinsloo [the chief executive of the Transvaal Rugby Union that hosted the tournament at Ellis Park],' the then New Zealand Rugby Union Maori representative on the New Zealand Rugby Union (NZRU) Council, Mattie Blackburn, recalls.

'Louis and Colin Meads, who was also on the council at that time, had become good mates. I think their links went back to the days of the Cavaliers' tour in 1986. Anyway, Colin was always a very good friend to Maori rugby and so Louis and Johan came to New Zealand and met with myself, Colin and our council chairman, Eddie Tonks, and the invitation was issued from there.'

Blackburn, who'd previously coached the New Zealand Maori team on its world tour in 1988, had been appointed to the NZRU Council in 1990 as its Maori member. He also became the first Maori in 75 years to hold the chairman's seat on the Maori Rugby Board Whakapumautanga (now known as the New Zealand Maori Rugby Board), and went on to be Matt's manager with the New Zealand Maori team up until the year 2000. Blackburn's six-year stint as the Maori representative on the NZRU

Council ended in 1996, when he was replaced by Tom Mulligan of Hawke's Bay.

'That was an exciting time for Maori rugby in general. The tour to South Africa was just part of it', Blackburn says.

'We also made major progress at a lower level by being able to introduce the regional Maori tournaments at that stage, securing NZRU funding to make them viable. The influence those tournaments have had, and continue to have, on player development is incalculable.'

Blackburn's term also saw the introduction of a kaumatua, or spiritual leader, to travel with the New Zealand Maori team, with Dennis Simpson of Wainuiomata near Wellington filling the role first, when he accompanied the side on the South African tour.

'It had always been the plan to raise the cultural element within the team and allow the players to explore their Maori roots', Blackburn says.

'The introduction of the kaumatua was part of that, and they generally led the process to start with, although it's fair to say that Matt Te Pou then picked up the ball and ran with it. The cultural aspect of the New Zealand Maori team had been a sleeping giant, but the introduction of the kaumatua awoke that giant. Matt then skilfully adapted the cultural aspect into the established team processes.'

Among the players involved in the 23-man touring squad was future All Black second-five-eighth Mark Mayerhofler, who was 'over the moon' to gain his first selection in any adult New Zealand national team, having previously been an age-group representative.

'I was 21 at the time, and had just moved to Christchurch from North Harbour. I hadn't even been in the city a month, having signed to play for Canterbury, and, suddenly, I was off and away with the New Zealand Maori team. It was an awesome feeling', Mayerhofler recalls.

The trip itself proved quite an adventure, with the South Africa of 1994 being a relatively unknown quantity as a destination, having just returned two years previously from the era of apartheid-inspired isolation, compared with its status now as a frequently visited rugby venue.

'Certainly, we didn't really know what to expect. Most of the guys in the team had never been there before', Mayerhofler says.

'Even so, that was a tour that ran along old-school lines. I was one of the young pups. The only player younger than me in the team was Carlos

Spencer, who was just 18, so we buddied up and tended to keep quiet and follow what we were told by the older fellas.'

The tour opened with a run-around against a Vaal Triangle XV at Sasolburg, which proved a light introduction, because New Zealand Maori romped to a 119–3 win over the out-classed locals.

As much as anything, the afternoon was memorable for being the debut first-class match refereed by Jonathan Kaplan, who was to go on to become the most prominent South African referee of the modern professional era.

After the first-up rout, the New Zealand Maori side then discovered the rugged side of the Afrikaans' nature during a 16–16 draw with Free State in their opening M-Net series game, a result that still qualified the visitors for a competition semi-final against Eastern Province. Before that match, however, came a 'friendly', if one can call any rugby match in South Africa by that definition, against the Griqualand West province in the mining town of Kimberley.

Having been injured against Free State, Mayerhofler sat out the Griquas match, which New Zealand Maori lost 21–30, but recalls being uncomfortable as he watched from the sideline.

'I got hit by a flying beer can during the game that someone had thrown, and there was a fair bit of racial abuse directed at us, but I suppose we had to expect that, being in heartland Afrikaaner territory', he says.

'The reaction of the locals during that game really only confirmed what I had suspected after the night before the game, where I had to attend a dinner representing the team, along with some of the management. That was a very strange evening because much of the official speaking was done in Afrikaans and it did sound, at various times, like they were making jokes at our expense. You'd hear what sounded like the word "Maoris" mentioned in a sentence, and shortly after the guests would all erupt with laughter. It wasn't altogether a totally pleasant experience!'

New Zealand Maori ended the tour with a 24–26 loss to Eastern Province, with the tournament itself eventually being won by the hosts Transvaal. While the coach, North Harbour's Chas Ferris, had had All Black assistant coach Earle Kirton as his offsider for the South African trip, Kirton was back on All Black duty by the time the New Zealand

Maori side's mid-year programme came around, which opened up the opportunity for Matt to come on board as Ferris's new assistant.

The New Zealand Maori team had never really had a proper full-time assistant coach prior to that year, so it was probably a fortunate thing that I got my timing about right! Winning two years in a row with the Northern Maori team probably helped my cause, although I already had the job by the time we won the second game.

As well organised and methodical as always, Matt did his homework prior to entering the New Zealand Maori team environment for the first time, studying up on the history of the side.

One of the things I'd always experienced growing up in Maori communities was that there were two main areas of Maori pride – the Maori Battalion and the Maori All Blacks. It was only once I prepared to become involved with the team that I studied the historical results and came to appreciate that they weren't all that good. In the past, we'd been getting bowled by provincial sides!

Part of the problem, Matt believed, was a lack of credibility, which manifested itself in leading players not wanting to make themselves available for the side.

There were obvious reasons for that. Playing for the Maori team represented more games, and if they were just run-arounds against the provinces, it was understandable why some of the All Black guys would perhaps want to give them a miss. It was also still the amateur era as well, so they weren't being paid, and couldn't be directed that they had to play.

There was also the dynamic of the provincial union coaches, who were no doubt putting pressure on their top players not to play, so that they would be that little bit fresher for their own provincial campaigns later in the year in the NPC. So there were a lot of pressures there, but I knew, with things changing in the game so rapidly at that time, that the Maori team would have to change too, if it was to guarantee its survival.

The key thing that Matt identified was the restoration of Maori pride.

We had to get that back. We had to turn the situation around so that the players all wanted to play for the New Zealand Maori side and were competing strongly against each other for the shot. If we didn't have that competition, there was no way we were going to change things, and it all came down to putting some pride back into the jersey. That was where we came from. By the time we finished in 2005, the pride was back, guys were desperate to play for the team and we had players literally queuing up for the jersey and very proud to be Maori.

To inspire such a revolution was always going to take time, however, and the first steps were inevitably small ones. Following on from the South African tour, the New Zealand Maori team's domestic programme for 1994 was hardly earth-shattering in its intensity, with a mid-week game against third division Mid-Canterbury at Ashburton to be followed by a 'Test' against Fiji at Christchurch.

There are places for the New Zealand Maori team to go, and places where it shouldn't, and the South Island probably fits into the latter category, unless we play a really big game there that is going to attract plenty of attention. The situation in 1994 typified the level that the team was at, in terms of its status. For those two games, we had small crowds at each and literally no profile at all. It would be like Manu Samoa playing a home game in a city like Invercargill, where there are very few Samoans! You just wouldn't do it, but the New Zealand Rugby Union did it to the Maori team that year.

For all that, Mid-Canterbury proved a starting point in a number of ways. Not only did the game represent the first step of a 21-match first-class run that would see the New Zealand Maori side go unbeaten through until 2001, the third division part-timers also managed to score a try through their hard-working No 8 and captain John Smitheram, even though they were eventually crushed 58–13 by a Maori side featuring seven players who had been or would be All Blacks.

I was really proud of the way Mid-Canterbury played against us. The final scoreboard probably didn't do justice either to the way they approached the game or the effort their players put in. Nothing came easy and they really ripped into us, although, to be fair, it wasn't the sort of game that was going to earn our team bigger games and greater respect. We could only get that by achieving results and beating every team that was put in front of us.

Mid-Canterbury went on to win the third division that year, but long-serving New Zealand Maori hooker Slade McFarland, who debuted for the side at Ashburton, and ended up playing more games for the Maori side under Matt than any other player, insists that the South Islanders also played their part in the renaissance of the Maori team that was to follow.

'We had to start somewhere, and that was the starting point. It was probably a good thing in a lot of ways, especially because it provided a measuring point as to how far we'd come, later on', McFarland says.

'Personally, that tour was a big buzz for me, getting the opportunity to meet and play alongside established All Blacks like Arran Pene and Jamie Joseph, because I was only 21 at the time, so it was a huge step forward in my career.'

Not that the team environment was quite so all-embracing of Maori culture, as it would develop to be during Matt's reign.

'In 1994, the atmosphere was still quite relaxed', McFarland says.

'There was the odd song sung on the bus, but we didn't have the strong profile around the cultural element. That started from a year later, when Matt became the head coach. Even so, you could sort of feel his determination, in those early days, to change things.

'At that stage, the Maori side was stuck in a situation where it was basically given a schedule on a take it or leave it basis, but Matt took it on himself to turn that attitude around. He basically said to the players: "You're either with me, or I'll find some other players!"

'In that way, he was just what the Maori team needed, because he instilled the belief back into the players and reintroduced an identity – both into the team, and the players as individuals – that had been lost for a while.'

Mayerhofler, who was one of only eight survivors from the South African trip earlier in the season to also feature in the mid-year squad, remembers the difficulties associated with the Mid-Canterbury and Fiji games.

'We had small crowds for both matches and it was freezing cold each time, so you probably couldn't blame the public for staying away', he says.

'I suppose I should have been disappointed, being one of only a couple of Canterbury players in the team, that more people didn't come along and watch us against Fiji, but I still didn't really feel like a Canterbury player at that point. While I'd played a couple of games for Canterbury by then, I suppose I wasn't really viewed yet as a local.'

In a nice touch, Mayerhofler donated the New Zealand Maori jersey he wore in the 34–3 win over Fiji to his club, Christchurch, and reports that the club officials were delighted to add it to the collection at the club-rooms, where it is still displayed.

'It was nice to be able to give something to the club, even though I was still relatively new, and you could say it was my first 'Test', or certainly first international, jersey', Mayerhofler says.

'But while playing Fiji was an international, collectively we all aspired to play games in the Maori jersey against the bigger nations. The experience of playing Fiji, for example, was certainly dwarfed by some of the major games, like Australia and the Lions, that the team got to play later on.'

While the Test produced three tries, all scored by the New Zealand Maori, future Maori skipper Errol Brain recalls it was a player on the Fijian side, by the name of Joeli Vidiri, who captured most of the attention afterwards.

Brain had been called into the Maori side as a replacement, and watched with interest from the sidelines as his future Counties Manukau and Blues team-mate caused the home side plenty of bother.

'Joey could be as quick as lightening when he wanted to be – and he really turned it on that day', Brain says.

'Fortunately, a few of the Counties union guys were there, and they were probably just as quick to get down and talk to him afterwards.'

One was former Counties and All Black prop Rod Ketels, who ended up as Vidiri's manager when the flying winger joined Counties, and ended up going on to win an All Black jersey in 1998, as well as winning two Super 12s with the Blues in 1996 and 1997, and helping Counties to the first division final of the NPC in both of those years.

'It was certainly good to have him in a Counties jersey', Brain notes.

'It sure beat playing against him, although I'm not certain some of our Maori team-mates, who were from provinces other than Counties, would have been that pleased to see him pop up playing against them again!'

Although the week-long assembly concluded with two wins in the bag, importantly, it finished with Matt having had a taste of the New Zealand Maori team environment. The experience left him even more determined to put the team back on the pedestal on which he believed it belonged, which was a lofty goal to take on as he succeeded Ferris as head coach.

That first year showed me just how much work there was to do, in order to get the pride back into the jersey, while also getting the team back up where it deserved to be. With Chas deciding to step down, I was asked if I would like to take over, and I was quite keen to take up the challenge.

So the Matt Te Pou era as head coach of the New Zealand Maori team had begun.

6

Night of the snow queens: 1995

'Hitting the ground running!'

'It's all about whenua boys. We try to take their whenua and they try to take ours. The team with the most whenua at the end wins!'

So re-tells Eric Rush, of one of Matt's sermons to the New Zealand Maori side during his initial years as head coach.

'That was Matt', Rush says.

'The guys all respected him for his humility and loved all of his army sayings. He's just got that mana about him. It was the way he held himself, and the guys really responded to that. I can always remember him saying, just because we're the Maori team, that doesn't mean that we have to be slack.'

A renewed sense of collective purpose wasn't the only difference the players noticed once Matt took charge.

'Matt made it clear from the start that the All Blacks were the pinnacle', North Harbour hooker Slade McFarland recalls.

'He saw half of his job as one of promoting his players, and I guess the number of All Blacks who emerged out of our environment speaks volumes for the job he did on that score, but he was also about building the team up again and restoring its place – both within New Zealand and internationally, while also reaffirming the New Zealand Maori team's role for the Maori people.'

The restoration of the Maori team as a threat on the international stage was the key part of a vision Matt put in place, in company with members of his management team and key senior players, during his first year in charge in 1995.

Undaunted by the fact that his side's only two outings, in what was a Rugby World Cup year, were to be against provincial teams, Matt openly shared his long-term aim, to establish New Zealand Maori as a side that won at least 50 percent of its matches against the top nations of the world, within the group.

There was also, McFarland says, another aspect of the team's focus that received a major lift in profile under Matt's stewardship. That was the team's position as a flagship for its people – an entity they could be proud of, and one that younger rugby playing Maori could aspire to, one day, be part of.

'Matt was very passionate about promoting Maoridom, both within the team – in terms of introducing and driving the cultural aspect – but also in terms of exposing our culture and heritage to the wider community', McFarland says.

'The role-model aspect was probably not something most of us were aware of to start off with, but just by playing footy and being successful, we were raising the team's profile, and so positioning ourselves as positive role models. We were enjoying ourselves along the way and that came through, too – people could see that.'

Not that Matt hid from the social problems dogging the Maori community, McFarland says. In fact, he was quite the opposite.

'We do have a dark side to our persona. You only have to look at a film like *Once Were Warriors* and the domestic issues depicted in it among the Maori characters to see that. The events that were portrayed in that film do happen in New Zealand. There are a lot of social problems prevalent among the Maori population, in higher proportions than you get among the country's European people. The crime rate among young Maori is also higher than it should be, unemployment is too high, and there is a lot of other bad news out there.

'What Matt gradually taught us as players, was to see the team as a beacon of light for our people. The New Zealand Maori team was a great public relations opportunity for us to redress the tide of negative news about Maori and provide something positive. And the great thing was, we could do that just by being ourselves and doing what we did best – playing rugby.'

From 1995, the emphasis on the cultural aspect of the Maori side became a major focus, and Errol Brain says there was little resistance to this change.

Brain, who'd been playing for New Zealand Maori since 1990, says the novelty that the cultural injection gave to the team environment – with the collective singing, the waiata and the kapa haka sessions – quickly became an added attraction.

'It was refreshing', Brain says.

'For a lot of the guys who'd been around for a while, like I had, it was something we really responded to. Most of us had never been exposed to it to any great extent in our lives before, so it became a major point of difference that the Maori team now offered.

'Playing for the team suddenly became a completely different experience to anything you could get anywhere else, and word of that quickly spread. Suddenly, we had a lot of high-profile guys wanting to be part of it. When I'd started off a few years earlier, most of the All Black guys had largely made themselves unavailable, unless there was a big match like the Lions to aim for.'

For all of Matt's lofty ambitions, however, 1995, like the season before, was primarily about doing the hard yards. With the early season action at a premium, because the third Rugby World Cup was being held in South Africa throughout May and June of that year, the New Zealand Maori team was restricted to another two-match programme in the space of a week at the start of July.

It was to be an inauspicious start to Matt's decade-long tenure as Maori coach, although the tour opener against King Country on a cold mid-winter's Tuesday night in Taupo was not without its amusing moments.

One of my lasting memories of the lead-up to that game was how one of our players, who also played for King Country, voluntarily handed over all of their lineout calls before the game – so much for my faith in provincial loyalty!

As the years went on, that was something I found would happen quite often when we came together. Guys would get talking, and the next thing you would hear the cunning senior players in the team quizzing some of the younger guys about moves their provincial teams operated, and so forth. This wasn't happening accidentally. They were gaining a bit of intelligence to take back to the respective provincial sides to use later in the year! It was always interesting to see which players fell for it, and which ones were wise enough to see through what was going on!

The intelligence gained on King Country's forward operation certainly didn't hurt the Maori side as they fashioned out a hard-fought 44–28 win, scoring six tries to three.

> It was an extremely physical battle on a very cold night at Owen Delany Park. We hadn't been able to spend a lot of time together beforehand, so the inside 'information' we had on them certainly helped us.

There was other 'information', however, that the players had opted not to share with their new coach. As Matt was later to discover, the official after-match function was not the only one that was happening at the hotel in Taupo, where the team bus headed following the match. The venue was also playing host to the annual mid-winter Taupo 'Snow Queen' Festival.

> The cunning buggers certainly hadn't mentioned that beforehand, although I'm sure that they all probably knew about it! I didn't have a clue. The first inkling I had, as to what was going on, was when the official part of the after-match finished and they announced that the competition was starting up to find Taupo's official Snow Queen for the year. Then they started rolling out all these attractive young ladies!

With the Maori team based in accommodation on the outskirts of town, the team leadership had met earlier in the day and agreed on a 10.00 pm departure from the after-match, given that they had a recovery session to perform the next morning in readiness for the match against Waikato on the following Saturday. By the time 10.00 pm came around though, Matt found only one player had reached the bus on schedule alongside himself and the team manager, Mattie Blackburn. The rest of the team were all still at the function, and revelling in their role as the competition's unofficial judges.

> We'd made an agreement that we'd all go at 10.00 pm, and it had reached that time, so I said to the bus driver: 'Away we go', even though there were only three of us on the bus. The next morning, our recovery was to be held at a gym in town at 8.00am. A few of the players who were down at breakfast asked me whether we were still starting at 8.00am, or if that was the time they had to be on the bus. They got a bit of a shock when I told them that was no longer what was happening. When they asked why, I said to them that had been the arrangement when they had needed a bus, but, because they hadn't needed it the previous night, they didn't need it now!

The result was that a number of the players, who'd streamed back to their lodgings at all hours of the early morning, paid heavily for their sins. The gym, where recovery was to take place, was located 5 kilometres away from where the team was staying, and the players were left with no choice but to run that journey in order to make it to the session. The unanticipated exercise found a lot below their best in terms of performance.

'It was quite hard case, and there was plenty of dry retching going on. Quite a few of the guys were really struggling during the last bit of the run as they staggered down to the gym', Brain recalls.

'It was important that Matt had stood his ground, though. If he hadn't, the boys would have lost a lot of respect for him. We all knew that we'd crossed the line!'

> *It was the old Sergeant Major coming out in me, but I said to them: 'Guys, we've got to be straight with each other. We've got to be fair. If we make a team call, it is a call we're all bound by, and we've got to stick to it'!*

If the King Country post-match experience had left a few of the players feeling a little worse for wear, a boost for the whole team was just around the corner when All Black lock Robin Brooke joined the side in camp ahead of its Saturday match against Waikato. Just back from South Africa, and the agony of a World Cup final surrendered to the hosts in extra-time, Brooke was desperate for a game, even though just two weeks had elapsed since the All Blacks' 12–15 defeat.

> *Rob had really felt the loss in South Africa and just wanted to get a game in. Because we already had two top-quality locks in Jim Coe and Mark Cooksley, and hadn't planned on factoring Rob into our side, I had to find another position for him. The only option was to play him on the blindside, so I told him that he would have to play loose. He replied: 'I feel loose already!' As it was, he then went out and played a blinder.*

The All Black lock scored one of the New Zealand Maori side's nine tries as they blew Waikato away 60–22. He also left a lasting impression on his coach.

> *That was the only time I ever had the opportunity to coach a side that Rob was in, but I've got so much respect for what he did that week, because he did it for the right reasons. He wanted to play to leave the memory of*

the final behind, and I'm just glad that we were able to provide him with that opportunity. What he also did, perhaps unwittingly, was to raise the bar of everyone else around him. Having an established All Black of his stature showing that attitude, and giving his guts for the team, was of enormous benefit to the New Zealand Maori side in the longer term. Robin Brooke showed the pride in the jersey that we wanted all of the guys to have.

In doing so, he also set the tone for Matt's era as New Zealand Maori coach, during which time the pride in the team returned.

Into the Pacific: 1996

'Of frogs, kings and collapsed scrums'

Playing an international for a national team for the first time is a big moment in any rugby player's career. Being appointed as captain for that occasion is rare, but such was the honour accorded to future All Black skipper Taine Randell when he led the New Zealand Maori team on his international debut against Samoa in 1996.

While Randell was just 21 at the time, and had only made his debut as a mid-week All Black during the previous year's end-of-season tour of Italy and France, Matt was happy to accommodate the wishes of the new national coach, John Hart, by handing the newcomer the leadership armband for the first part of that season's programme.

I had a good relationship with John during his time as All Black coach. There was lots of communication, and we always knew where he was coming from in terms of his suggestions, which was important. Sure there was a lot of pride in our jersey, but while some people might suggest that allowing the national coach to impose a captain on us went against that pride, we were also about helping to promote Maori players into the All Blacks. If we could do that by playing guys that the All Black selectors wanted to see, that was great – and it was hardly going to weaken our team having them!

That's how it was with Taine against Samoa, and I was proud of the way our senior players responded to that situation. Rather than seeing it as an imposition, they all supported him. Such was the level of the leadership Taine was surrounded with in that match, he was largely free to concentrate on his own play, and that showed because he had a fine game.

Errol Brain, who would assume the leadership of the side on a regular basis later in the year, says Randell's instantaneous appointment as skipper above team regulars didn't ruffle any feathers.

'There were no problems with it', Brain says.

'We all knew the pecking order. The guys understood that the All Black selectors wanted to have a close look at Taine, both as a player and as a captain. The good thing about it was that he didn't let the team down. Taine had a stormer against the Samoans!'

For his part, Randell admits the situation of his elevation was unusual, although he says the captaincy was an extra. His main delight was at being able to play for the New Zealand Maori team in the game against Bay of Plenty, and, especially, the 'Test' against Western Samoa.

'It [the Western Samoan game] was a big moment in my career, both personally and for my family', Randell says.

'I gave my jersey from that game to my grandmother, Moetu. She was extremely proud of it.'

Originally from Hawke's Bay, before he headed south to Otago for his university education, Randell was a product of the same boys' school, Lindisfarne College, in the Hawke's Bay's, that had recently produced All Black and New Zealand Maori team wing and fullback John Timu.

'I qualified for the Maori team through the heritage of my father Mike', Randell says.

'He had played a bit of rugby for the Maori Agricultural College in the Hawke's Bay during his own playing days.'

While having a player of Randell's quality available was a nice situation for the New Zealand Maori team to be in, Matt acknowledges that the coming and going of the various All Black players from the team environment always had the potential to cause problems.

It wasn't always ideal having them come in for one game and then disappear for the next. We had our own challenges to face and needed consistency in the area of our team leadership if we were to be successful. And we weren't always going to have access to players like Taine because they had been ear-marked for bigger things. That's why we were extremely fortunate to have a core of seasoned provincial guys like EB [Brain], Jim Coe, Deon Muir and later on players like Jono Gibbes. Having that experience gave us a constant and consistent leadership presence, so we didn't have to start again from scratch for every new campaign.

He might not have been able to play for New Zealand Maori as much as he'd have liked, and had to wait for another five years for his next appearance after the match against Samoa, but Randell still treasured the opportunity.

'Everyone I ever spoke to always loved playing for the Maoris', Randell says.

'In professional rugby now, with so many games and different competitions that you play in – whether they be club, provincial or international – it can become a bit of a chore at times. It can be almost like another day at the office, no matter what the colour of the club or provincial jersey is. The Maori team was never like that. It has an important point of difference.'

Randell says a lot of the difference was because of how the team was run.

'Matt and his management team pulled on the old emotional heart strings a bit. That was how they set up the team environment. You don't get a lot of that in professional rugby now, but they showed it was still an effective way to motivate players.'

Not that emotion was allowed to get in the way of the ultimate objective.

'Not at all', Randell says, 'while it was a refreshing change from the approach you would find in other teams that you played for, the result still mattered. In some ways, it was probably even more important for the Maori team to do well than the other teams I played for, because there were less matches, which made each game we did play that much more significant. The pressure to achieve the good results the team had was just handled differently.'

Nor was Randell the only player to relish the differences, especially with professionalism having been introduced earlier that year which meant, for the first time, the players were fully professional when they assembled for the New Zealand Maori team's programme. They were also all coming out of the first-ever Super 12 competition. While that competition had proved demanding, Chiefs hooker Slade McFarland says the taxing Super 12 schedule hadn't dulled the players' enthusiasm to be part of the New Zealand Maori scene again.

In fact, the opposite was occurring.

'The thing I remember most about that time is that you could see how Matt's influence was growing on the players by their attitudes', McFarland says.

'A lot of the guys had been bashed about a bit in that first Super 12 because they simply weren't used to as demanding a schedule as that, at such an early stage of the year, but all of the players were still putting their hands up to play for the Maoris. Whenever you ran into guys on your travels, they were talking about the Maori programme, and this started a long time before the games came up. The anticipation was definitely there, and that hadn't been the case before.'

Part of the reason for that, McFarland believes, was the introduction of a more testing programme. Not only was 1991 and 1995 World Cup quarter-finalists Samoa on the menu, there was also the prospect of a trip to France to play the French Barbarians at the end of the year.

> *There was discussion around that time about the possibility of playing the French Barbarians in Europe. It was definitely a carrot, and word pretty quickly spread among the players that a tour might be in the offing. Unfortunately it didn't eventuate, which was a huge pity because a game between the French and the Maori team would have been a great spectacle that would have brought together two like-minded philosophies on how to play the game.*

Mark Mayerhofler for one, recalls feeling 'dudded' when he discovered that the proposed tour of France at the end of 1996 wasn't going ahead.

'When we were together earlier in the year for the Bay of Plenty and Samoa games, all of the talk was about France at the end of the year. The boys were really keen on that! Then we played the NPC and suddenly the story was that France was off, and we were going up to Fiji and Tonga for three matches instead. I was like: "Stink one!" All the other boys were the same. We were all asking: "What happened to France, man?" I'm not being disrespectful to the Pacific Islands, but going up there wasn't quite the same.'

While Mayerhofler didn't ultimately have France to focus on, he did have the job of helping to make new team-mate Daryl Gibson, also of the Crusaders, comfortable in the Maori team environment, after Gibson was selected for that year's domestic series.

'Playing for the Maoris first really introduced me to the culture so I was able to help Gibbo along with that side of things', Mayerhofler says.

'I was a lot like Daryl, and some of the other boys, in that regard. Growing up out in West Auckland, I was a city boy and not really exposed to my Maori roots. Mum was quite proud of her Maori heritage, but she never pushed it onto myself or my brother or sister, and never spoke the Maori language at home. That might have been a legacy of her own school days, where they got the cane if they spoke Maori!'

Yet Mayerhofler says, as his time in the Maori team continued, he came to appreciate the responsibility as a role model that selection carried with it.

'I always felt bad because I couldn't speak Maori, but playing for the team brought out a personal pride in my family's heritage. My family were certainly proud about my involvement with the team, especially so in 1997 when my brother Chris and I got to play alongside each other for the Maoris. It was only once I'd made the team and then caught up with a lot of my relatives in the time after, that I really appreciated how much my selection had meant to my wider whanau.'

Gibson, who attended a white middle-class secondary school, Christchurch Boys' High, says he'd always aspired to make the New Zealand Maori side, but admits to feeling 'something of a fraud' once he got there.

'I'd watched the Maori team play as a young kid and always thought that, while it would be great to be an All Black, it would be just as special to be a Maori All Black', Gibson says.

'It was around the time where a lot of the top Maori players were also All Blacks.'

But, although Gibson had studied up to stage three of the Maori language while attending Canterbury University, he says the depth to which Maori culture played a part within the team environment still came as a real eye-opener.

'I'd heard about what went on a bit from other players, but coming out of the Crusaders Super 12 environment, where we hadn't had a great first season as professionals, it was totally different', Gibson recalls.

'Matt was totally new to me, but I quickly came to appreciate that he was the heart and soul of the operation, and that didn't change over the years that I was involved with the team. He was always the driving force, regardless of who the players were he had around him, and whether they were All Blacks or not. He always drove the importance of learning and understanding our culture. For someone like me, who hadn't really been exposed to it as much as I would have liked to have been when I was younger, it was a blessing, and a great education. I learnt so much.'

Gibson's mother hailed from Dargaville, but was the second youngest of 16 children. How she came to lose contact with her heritage was systemic to the circumstances experienced by many young Maori as their communities became more and more integrated with the largely European world.

'By the time it came round to her time to learn about the culture, her father felt it wasn't that important. He felt the future was learning to speak English, and learning about European ways', Gibson says.

'She still regrets that she never learnt her native tongue. Her elder sisters are all fluent in Maori, which makes some of us feel a bit dumb when we attend family reunions.'

Even as a bona fide New Zealand Maori representative, Gibson says it still took him a little while to feel like he 'belonged'.

'I might have been brown on the outside, but I had to learn a bit before I really felt that I deserved to be part of it.'

At least Gibson's slightly tanned skin made him feel like he identified with his Maori team-mates. For the blonde-headed southerner Tony Brown, who also debuted for the Maori team in 1996, his outward looks only served to raise questions over his credibility and right to be part of the team.

'I found myself explaining to a fair few people a lot of the time, right from when I first started playing for the New Zealand Maori, how I qualified to be involved', Brown recalls.

'I guess blonde-headed Maoris are quite rare, so we stand out a bit. Having that situation turned out to be quite advantageous for me, though, because it encouraged me to learn about my Maori heritage so that I could explain to people my background – and how I qualified for the team.'

For the record, Brown's family traces its roots back to some of the earliest Maori chiefs, with the hapu still claiming native mutton birding rights in coastal Otago to this very day.

To reinforce the Otago first-five-eighth's sense of belonging, however, his mischievous Maori team-mate Glen Osborne came up with a novel way of expanding Brown's knowledge of his culture – he appointed Brown as the team's official 'Interpreter'!

This role required Brown to stand up on the team bus after visits to marae, and other official Maori functions, and explain to his team-mates what had been said during the welcome speeches, which were all in Maori. He was also required to decipher Maori terms for the benefit of his teammates, giving a lesson on new words every day while the bus travelled to training.

'Oz [Osborne] knew that I knew little or no Maori, so the whole thing was a bit of a set up, but I guess it gave a few of the boys a good laugh', Brown recalls.

'I got one quick lesson from Oz after our first team meeting and then I was pretty much on my own. I had to interpret the welcomes, as well as come up with three new Maori words every day, and explaining what they meant.'

Naturally, Brown winged it a fair bit, with often hilarious consequences.

He told a few pretty tall tales, but the boys loved it. We all learned a fair bit from him. None of it was true, but everyone had a good laugh all the same!

For his part, 'The Interpreter' admits to having often come out with the first thing that came into his head.

'Matt did help me with one word – 'kotanga'', Brown says.

'At first I thought he was being serious, but then I realised he was talking about a 'coat hanger' – a head-high tackle!'

While Brown's antics as the team's official decipherer of Maori terminology provided hilarity on an almost daily basis, the team's 1996 programme started with a deadly serious threat looming in the background. Matt made sure that the players were well aware of what was at stake.

With professional rugby starting up, we were faced with a whole new ball game, and it was obvious that something would have to give from the old pre-professional environment. Richie Guy [NZRU chairman] had already admitted as much. By that stage he'd said publicly that some things from the past would have to be sacrificed, and we knew damn well that we could be on the chopping block – if we didn't perform and make ourselves too important to do away with.

In 1996, the Maori team was realistically in similar territory as the New Zealand Universities. Both had played touring teams in the past, both had their own advisory boards, outside of the NZRU Council, running them. If you look at New Zealand Universities now, they're gone. They don't play major international teams anymore, don't really have a public profile and only rarely get to field any of their top players.

That could just have easily been us, too, if we hadn't performed well enough to ensure that it didn't happen. But it wasn't enough to just talk about it. I could talk about it all I liked, the team had to come together and do the job.

That's why we spoke about it quite openly with the players and let them know where things stood. It gave our programme an extra edge for sure, but it also showed me that the issue of pride in the jersey had been successfully addressed, in terms of how the players responded – by taking ownership of the team. They knew what was at stake, but they did their talking on the field!

The programme for 1996 started with a homecoming of sorts for two Bay of Plenty old boys, Matt and fullback Adrian Cashmore, as the New Zealand Maori side faced their former provincial union in preparation for the Test against Samoa.

The match marked Cashmore's debut for the Maori team, and fell just 11 days before he played the first of the two Tests he would play for the All Blacks, coming on as a replacement during the second Test against Scotland at Eden Park.

While he returned to the Maori environment for the Pacific tour later in the year as a fully fledged All Black, Cashmore says that status didn't lessen the prestige he felt about his role with the Maori team.

'I'd always had a huge regard for the Maori team as a result of growing up in Tokoroa where my father had played for Tokoroa Pirates, which is a predominantly Maori club', Cashmore says.

'My Maori heritage comes from my mother's side of the family. They were all from the East Coast, but having that linkage there meant that I collected my share of 'information' about Maori culture when I was growing up – although I always regretted not knowing more. Dad was coaching at Tokoroa Pirates when Paul Koteka, the big prop, made the New Zealand Maori team from the club. I didn't know any All Blacks, so knowing him was a huge deal for me at the time, and probably heightened the significance with which I've always held the Maori team.'

While the pair's return to Rotorua proved to be successful, with the Maori side running out 48–28 winners, the locals didn't fall over easily. The Bay of Plenty players, seven of whom had been coached by Matt in

Into the Pacific: 1996

the side two years previously, made their presence felt by scoring four tries against the Maori team's seven, three of which went to future All Black Norm Berryman.

> *They fired a few shots. They made it a hard game for us, but that was good. It was what we needed to get us ready for the Samoans. On a personal note, I did find it a bit difficult playing against what had been my own team, but I was pleased that Bay of Plenty had given us such a stern work out. We got a lot more out of that game as a team than we would have if we had run up a bigger score and won by a wider margin.*

With such a limited preparation time, all but two of the Maori starting lineup fielded against Bay of Plenty backed up three days later against Samoa, although Matt says match fitness, at least, wasn't a problem, thanks to the arrival of the Super 12.

> *Beforehand, we might have had guys coming together who hadn't played too many hard games over the previous four or five weeks, but that all changed with the advent of professionalism. Instead of coming to us out of club rugby, the players were coming in match hardened as a result of the Super 12.*
>
> *By 1996, we were also in the position where our senior players were all in place from the previous couple of seasons, so the environment was a lot more settled.*

As for Samoa, Matt acknowledges they represented 'a step up' on the calibre of the opposition the Maori team had faced in the previous two seasons, with the game effectively forming the opening round of a Pacific Islands' title fight.

> *We certainly saw it that way. As quarter-finalists from the last two Rugby World Cups, the Samoans were a confident team. And so they should have been – they possessed class individuals right through their playing roster. They were also probably after a bit of redemption, having copped a bit of a hiding from the All Blacks at Napier the week before. So we knew they would be well motivated. But so were we. As another Polynesian team, we saw playing them as though we were playing for the unofficial crown as the King of the Pacific. Beating them would also show that we had stepped up from where we had been at previously, where we were mainly stuck playing against provincial teams. It was a 'Test' match for both of us, and both teams certainly approached it that way.*

The other factor that set the contest aside from the Maori team's most recent experiences was its placement as a night game, which was something still relatively new to the players at that time.

> We talked a lot about how we'd fill the time in during the day before the game. We probably spent as much time working out how we'd cope with that, as we did sorting out our game plan. Night rugby is something we all take for granted now, but it was a big deal back then. We were all still experimenting, in terms of trying to find the best ways to prepare for night games.

Even though the scores were always close, the Maori side's supremacy was seldom in doubt on a cold Friday night at Auckland's Mt Smart Stadium, which had recently become the home base of rugby league's Warriors. This was largely due to the fact that their forwards dominated, which enabled the Maori side to enjoy the majority of possession throughout the game.

Although the 28–15 score line accurately reflected the competitive nature of the contest, New Zealand Maori scored four tries to two – with two going to Brain – and always looked to hold the upper hand, save for one scare when Samoan skipper Pat Lam was hauled down by New Zealand Maori flanker Dallas Seymour beneath the shadow of the home side's goal posts. Had Lam scored, his try would have set up a nerve-wracking finish. As it was, the New Zealand Maori side replied with a try by Brown to close out the game.

> There is an interesting history to the rugby when it comes to Polynesian versus Polynesian. It's a lot different to any other rugby that the guys play. Those games are always hard, and Samoa was no different.

Nor would the away matches in Fiji and Tonga that followed in November that year prove to be any easier. With the trip to play the French Barbarians not having eventuated, a three-match, eight-day programme was put in place for the New Zealand Maori team, with a Test against Fiji followed by two matches in Tonga. Prior to the trip, Matt was offered the valuable opportunity to bring the bulk of his touring side together on an unofficial basis for a match against a Fletcher Challenge Invitation XV at Kawerau, which was used to mark the fortieth anniversary of the Tasman Pulp and Paper mill operation.

> Fletchers approached us about the possibility of staging the game. We were only too happy to accommodate them because it worked in well for us as a preparation for our tour. The company flew in all the players,

and we were put up against a strong invitation side that Gordon Tietjens coached. The invitation side was so strong, and went so well, that one of their players – King Country lock Dion Waller – played his way into our squad for the tour! Both teams got into the spirit of it. It was a festival game, with marquees on the ground's perimeter where there were spits set up with meat being cooked, while there was also the odd hangi cooking away, too. Both teams had agreed beforehand that we would run at each other – and the players sure did that. We ended up winning 51–49, so the spectators that came along to watch sure got their fair share of entertainment!

The tour of the Pacific was the first undertaken by Oamaru-based physiotherapist Mike Stewart, who'd come on board with the Maori team that year to replace Barry Donaldson, after he'd moved on to the All Blacks. Stewart, who'd been the North Otago provincial team's physiotherapist for the previous seven years, had first met Matt when he acted as the physio for both teams during the Prince of Wales Cup game in Oamaru in 1994.

'Even then, Matt was well organised, and very clear about what he wanted', Stewart recalls.

The pair worked together well. So well that Stewart was a constant presence throughout the rest of Matt's time as the New Zealand Maori coach, and even outlasted him by a year, attending the Churchill Cup in North America with the side in 2006.

'To say the Maori environment was hugely different to what I had been used to with North Otago almost feels like an understatement', Stewart says.

'It was like a different world … totally professional in every way, and a real eye-opener coming from an amateur background like we had back then in North Otago. And that's without even considering the cultural aspect of the Maori side, which was something completely different for a white European from the middle of the South Island!'

Stewart might have had a very different background to his coach, and a number of the players, but it is a testimony to his skill and work ethic that he quickly became such an important part of the team and remained with the side over such a long period.

One of my regrets is that I wasn't able, during my time as Maori coach, to push Mike on into a role with the All Blacks, like we were able to propel forward so many of the players. He was held in the highest regard by the players – you don't survive in a job like his for as long as he did without having that respect. He was also an incredibly dedicated member of our management team. If it wasn't for him, and all the hard work he did working constantly on Taine Randell's hamstring and calf all week in the lead-up to that Samoan game, Taine wouldn't have been able to play. He could only jog lightly on the morning of the game and was only able to start running after lunch – which shows just how massive the job was that Mike did! And Taine was not the only player that owed his place on the field to Mike's diligence at various stages during my time.

The shame of it was simply that the team jobs at the Rugby Union just aren't allocated based solely on someone's experience, which would probably be a better way to do it than how it's handled now. While there is an employment process for team management positions, it's usually a done deal – especially at All Black level, merely rubber stamping the personnel that the All Black coach has already ear-marked.

I know Mike applied for the All Black job on at least a couple of occasions, but didn't get the nod. That was a shame, and a bit of an indictment on the appointment system they use, because he is as good as any of the physios around – the players will tell you that. I guess it was just a case of him being from a small town, and so not having the big 'friends' some of the other physios had.

Stewart recalls that the first game on tour against Fiji was played in driving rain, which led many of the locals to arrive at Suva's National Stadium wearing cardboard boxes on their heads to keep out the wet weather.

'It was certainly unusual and pretty quickly highlighted the fact that we were no longer in New Zealand', Stewart says.

Another aspect of the Fiji Test, which New Zealand Maori won 25–10, that lingers in the players' memories is the fact that the sodden ground was covered in frogs.

'They were leaping around all over the place, revelling in the wet, although one of them made the mistake of getting too close to Fijian hooker Greg Smith', Maori captain Errol Brain recalls.

Brain played on the blindside flank against Fiji to allow Waikato's Deon Muir, himself a future Maori captain, to make his debut for the side at No 8.

'It was quite tense at the time, because the scores were quite close, and Smithy was getting ready to throw the ball into a lineout, when this frog jumped out from underneath him. As quick as a flash, he lashed out with his boot and stomped on it. Everyone from both sets of forwards just cracked up with laughter!'

While Smith's swift action served to lighten the mood, the abrasive approach taken by the Fijians helped to snap the Maori out of the relaxed attitude that had prevailed since the players had learned about the demise of the French tour.

'At the time, it's fair to say most of the guys thought of the Islands trip as a bit of a booby prize. As an after thought, because the trip to France, which we'd all been looking forward to, hadn't got off the ground', Brain says.

'The Fijians made a real game of that first match, though. It turned out to be a pretty tough tour.'

Brain says the key to the Maori team's success on that trip, as always against the Island teams, was in not allowing them to get on the front foot.

'We were always very cohesive and direct with the way we played against the island sides, especially up there. Matt always told us to run straight at them, not off to the side. If you went to the side, there was always the chance that they'd stick their arms out and coat hanger you! The other thing about playing in the Islands was that it was vital to get away to a good start. You couldn't ever let them think that they had something over you because, if they did, it would spread like a disease and you'd pretty quickly find yourself in big trouble!'

A drama that was played out within the confines of the overall match-up between the two teams, was the individual clash between Sevens specialists Eric Rush and Waisale Serevi. Although the pair didn't mark each other, with Rush on the wing for the Maori while Serevi played at first-five-eighths for Fiji; their long-standing rivalry as the two best known names on the international Sevens circuit captured the imagination of the good-natured Suva crowd.

'It was like a game within a game', Brain recalls. 'Every time Serevi got the ball, the crowd would go mad with excitement, while they booed or jeered every time Rushy got it.'

The locals also found cause to get excited when future Highlanders winger Aisea Tuilevu scored a thrilling individual try, running through and past a fair few of the Maori players in the process, after breaking out from inside the Fijian 22-metre line. It was a movement, Brain recalls, that got the better of some excited patrons, who invaded the field before Tuilevu had even reached the goal-line to place the ball for the score.

'By the time the spectators came onto the field, Aisea had already run through all of us, and the fans chased him all the way to our line', Brain says.

'It was a bit of a shame for us that none of them could tackle!'

Tuilevu's try aside, the Maori generally had the better of the game, scoring four tries en route to the win Although it came at a cost, with Cashmore being forced out of the rest of the tour after suffering a sprig through the leg.

'It was quite painful. We could have had it treated up there, but there was no way I was going to allow that', Cashmore says.

'We'd all heard plenty of stories of people with punctured skin wounds in the Islands getting all sorts of bad infections as a result. I was probably being a bit paranoid, but there was no way I was staying. Fortunately, the team management was fine with me coming home.'

After Fiji, the Maori side moved on to Tonga, where it was matched up against a star-studded Tonga Barbarians combination in a mid-week contest.

The locals had brought in a number of New Zealand-based players of Tongan upbringing or heritage to bolster their ranks, including future All Blacks Carl Hoeft, Charles Riechelmann, Kupu Vanisi, Pita Alatini and Doug Howlett, who'd just finished his schooling at Auckland Grammar at that stage. Another player who featured was Matt's oldest son, Thomas, who qualified through Ida's Tongan lineage.

> It was a hell of a team that we played against. Probably as strong as the two Test sides we played on that tour. Because it was a mid-week game, though, and we only had a four-day turnaround before the Test in Tonga, I played a lot of the guys who wouldn't be playing in the game the following weekend. Their job was to go out there and win to set the Test side up.

The 'mid-weekers', with just five players backing up from the previous weekend's match in Suva, achieved that goal, but not without a tough struggle before they eventually prevailed 26–19. The win was secured thanks in no small part to some accurate goal kicking from Hawke's Bay fullback Jarrod Cunningham, who landed six from six to complement the Maori side's two tries. Among the players who'd completed the mission successfully was another of Matt's sons, Matthew, who'd made the touring squad after a strong season playing for Thames Valley. The Tonga Barbarians match represented the only time Matthew would wear the New Zealand Maori jersey, although he later went on to appear for Tonga, playing against the Maori side on the Pacific Island team's New Zealand tour in 1998.

Aside from the physical nature of the way the Tongans play the game, matches in the Pacific Island Kingdom have another dynamic attached to them, in that they are generally always attended by Tonga's king, a renowned rugby fan.

'The King would come out to do his exercise while were we training', Stewart recalls, 'but such was the protocol over there, you had to stop what you were doing while in his presence. He would go around the running track accompanied by his body guards while we were training out in the middle of the field. But if anyone kicked a ball anywhere near to where he was, we had to leave it until he'd gone past before we were allowed to retrieve it.'

Naturally, this caused its share of frustration.

'He was a great big pain in the arse', Brain says emphatically.

'Every time he came near us, we had to stop out of respect for him and, because he is such a big rugby fan, he took his time and hung around for a bit. It made for a very stop-start training!'

The other dynamic to the royal presence came on match day, in terms of charging up the home side, as McFarland remembers.

'Everyone got introduced to him before the game started, and you could just see in the Tongan guys' eyes what effect the royal seal had on them', McFarland says.

'That game was one of the hardest physically that I have ever played. I can remember at one point the Australian referee [Peter Marshall] trying to explain to the Tongan players: "When I blow the whistle that means you stop!" We were a bit lucky to get away with that game in the end. Bubs [Mayerhofler] probably won it for us. We were certainly happy to get out of there once it was over.'

After Matt had implored his side to make a good start, the team promptly conceded a try from the kick-off, and found themselves under pressure for much of the rest of the game.

'It is hard case playing up there, especially with the King around', Mayerhofler says.

'We'd been told beforehand that if the King needs to go to the toilet during the game, they stop the match until he's ready to resume watching it again! Fortunately, he didn't have to have a pit stop on the day we played there.'

The King's bowel movements aside, the visitors had plenty of other issues to deal with.

> Tony Brown got concussed early, although he later recovered to kick an outstanding dropped goal, but we were under the pump well and truly for most of that match. About the only area where the Tongans were struggling to handle us was in the scrums, where they kept getting in trouble with the referee.

Indeed, the Tongan scrum was under so much pressure that experienced Australian referee Peter Marshall finally lost his patience and warned the home side, after they collapsed a New Zealand Maori scrum near their own goal-line, that a penalty try would result if they committed the same offence again. Shortly after his ultimatum, another attacking Maori scrum was collapsed although, unbeknown to Marshall who was on the other side of the formation, this time it was pulled down deliberately by the experienced King Country prop Phil Coffin, who'd been a mid-week All Black during the South African tour, earlier in the year. Exasperated by the Tongan's apparent refusal to take heed of his earlier warning, Marshall duly awarded the New Zealand Maori team a critical penalty try.

> It was a huge play in the game – one of two key turning points, but Phil took a hell of a risk doing what he did. If the referee had worked out what had actually gone on, we'd have been penalised and a primary attacking opportunity would have been lost. Not that Phil was at all worried. When I challenged him later on that night about the risk he'd taken, he just smiled at me, tapped the side of his head and said: 'It's all up here, brother!'.

While an element of subterfuge yielded the visitors' one of their tries, brute force provided the other after Mayerhofler literally ran over the top of his unfortunate opponent before steaming through the gap that he'd created to score a brutal solo try.

> They had been smashing us before Bubs scored that try. Not only did he bowl his marker out of the way, I think he might have knocked him out. That act certainly gave our guys a huge lift, while telling the Tongans that they had a real fight on their hands.

The game finished up falling the New Zealand Maoris side's way 29–20.

Mayerhofler also recalls an amusing act involving an unfortunate member of the crowd, as much as he does his own decisive scoring play.

'Every time I think back to that match, it's usually the first thing I think of. It happened while all was quiet because Tonga was having a shot at goal', Mayerhofler says.

'There is a track around the National Stadium in Nuku'alofa, and all the people sit behind it. You also get plenty of people on the fences surrounding the stadium, and a lot of kids climb the trees outside the stadium perimeter to get a better vantage point. Anyway, during this kick, everyone was quiet, then all you could hear was this branch breaking and then this big thump as a kid fell out of a tree. The whole crowd just burst out laughing. I remember telling my Dad about it once I got back home. I don't think he believed me at first, but then they showed some of the game on television, and you could hear in the background the branch snapping and then all the laughter.'

8

An Apia afternoon: 1997

'When an island went to war'

If the 1996 New Zealand Maori programme had indicated to the players that the team was back on the international map – the schedule put together for 1997 reinforced the fact.

Not only was the team included on the New Zealand itineraries of the touring Ireland A and Argentinian sides, it had also been invited to Apia for a re-match of the previous year's battle with Manu Samoa.

As he assessed the programme, and began the early stages of his planning for the year, it was clear to Matt where the biggest threat to the New Zealand Maori side's still unbeaten record (under his charge) lay.

The Samoans were going to be gunning for us in a big way – there was no doubt about that.

The invitation to go up there came in pretty much straight after we beat them, which said a lot on its own. But we also knew that they had a proud record playing at home and had taken out a lot of strong provincial and international teams up there.

Our assignment was going to be difficult, of that we had no doubt, but we weren't going in blindfolded. We had a fair idea what we were going to be up against, and I knew we would have to be well prepared.

The Samoans hadn't lost a match at home since 1989. That put a huge onus on Matt to get his preparations, which started with the Maori trial in early June, right.

The trials we were able to put together back then were extremely valuable to us, not only for sorting out which players were going to make the

> team, but also in terms of allowing us to try out a few of the positional combinations that we were looking at using.
>
> Because we didn't have the extended preparation time before our campaign that a side like the All Blacks had, we had to maximise every opportunity we got, and the trial was one such opportunity. That often meant putting up a shadow side against the rest.

The Rugby Union phased out the Maori trial after 1998 to cut costs. While Matt was happy to go along with that decision, astutely assessing that it was unwise to rock the boat while his side was being consistently delivered a substantive programme, he acknowledges the lack of a preparatory trial did make the task of his selectors that bit more subjective in future years.

> The biggest problem was that we had guys who weren't playing Super 12 coming into our ranks. The All Blacks obviously didn't have that, so whether they had a trial, or a warm up game against the A side, it really came down to what suited John Hart and his successors. They weren't ever going to be in the situation of selecting players straight out of club rugby, but we were.
>
> While Super 12 provided the bulk of our players, and we could assess their merits and form in that competition, there were always a few who came in from outside. In the cases of those players, once the trial was gone, we effectively had to judge them on their NPC form from the year before, because we didn't really get to see them play again prior to selection.

The Maori trial of 1997 was held in Tauranga, two days before the All Black selectors held their national trial in Rotorua. With a number of potential New Zealand Maori candidates involved in the All Black trial, which effectively took on the form of a shadow XV against the rest, the full Maori squad wasn't able to be assembled in Palmerston North until just the day before the side opened its campaign with a night fixture against the touring Ireland A side.

That situation, and the unorthodox way Matt handled it, caused New Zealand Maori captain, Errol Brain, to wonder for the first and only time whether his coach was placing too much stock in the cultural side of the team's preparations.

'Time was really at a premium by the stage we had the full squad together in Palmerston North. Matt then made the call that we would spend the first day doing waiata and singing songs to bring all the guys into the team properly. I couldn't believe it and certainly didn't agree with it', Brain recalls.

'But, it turned out to be a stroke of genius. What Matt achieved by doing it that way was to bring together, as one, the whole squad, including a few of the guys who'd had disappointments from the All Black trial and had then come down from Rotorua to join us.

'After that session, those disappointments were left at the door, everyone was on the same page, and it was all about the team rather than any individuals.'

Mark Mayerhofler, who'd had the huge delight of being invited to participate in the All Blacks trial, only to then suffer the deflation of being told by All Black coach John Hart – before the match had actually been played – that he wouldn't be selected, and would be going on to play for the Maori, confirms that Matt's innovative approach did the trick.

'It was my first-ever All Black trial, but any excitement got taken away from me before we'd even played when John [Hart] called me to a meeting and, among other things, told me I'd be playing for the Maoris and wished me luck', Mayerhofler says.

'A lot of other guys who weren't in the shadow Test team got told the same thing. Having had that let down, I was grateful that I had somewhere to go, in terms of the Maori team, and something else to concentrate on. It would have been terribly disappointing if I'd had to go back home to club rugby with my tail between my legs!'

As an added bonus for Mayerhofler, his elder brother Chris, who played flanker, had also made the team. The pair represented New Zealand Maori for the first time together during the mid-week match in Samoa against a Western Samoan XV.

'The environment was just always so welcoming, and being thrown into a waiata and kapa haka session straight away on arrival was a great way to leave all of our other baggage behind', Mayerhofler says.

'It was almost a case of Matt saying to us: "Right, you're with the Maori team now. It's time to behave like a Maori and think of the collective rather than dwelling on individual issues".'

Seven players joined the Maori camp after the All Black trial, including established All Black hooker Norm Hewitt, who was none too impressed after being overlooked by John Hart for a role in the first internationals of the year in favour of Otago youngster Anton Oliver.

> The condensed nature of our programme always required a lot of planning, but we also had to be prepared for the fact that we had players who would be coming in with disappointments, having missed out on the All Blacks. The best way to get them over that was to remind them what they were now part of within our team.
>
> One of the advantages we had then, in terms of the playing ability at our disposal, was that professional rugby had really fine-tuned the skill sets of the country's top players. They were bigger, fitter and stronger than they had ever been before, which allowed us, in the early years anyway, to get away with cutting a few corners in preparation, if we only had a day or so to get ready for matches.
>
> What worked for us, in terms of that Ireland A game, might not have worked in later years, though, because the skill level did drop a bit. With so many experienced players leaving the country, and the All Blacks having the first pick of all the guys, some of the younger ones we got – who had been fast-tracked through to replace the players that had gone overseas – were not quite as skilful as their predecessors. They had the same professional attitude for sure, but they weren't as well rounded as players, simply because they hadn't yet done the miles.

Ireland A was coming towards the end of a taxing seven-match tour by the time it struck the New Zealand Maori. While the A side effectively represented the next best players Ireland possessed behind its top XV, and was prepared by current England back attack specialist coach Brian Ashton, the Irish were simply ill-prepared for the pace and skill of the New Zealand sides they encountered. By the time they reached Palmerston North, Ireland A had already shipped 69 points against Northland, 74 against a New Zealand Rugby Academy XV and 52 against Matt's old province Bay of Plenty. Their only win had been achieved against Thames Valley at Paeroa.

> We couldn't really worry about them. That night was a starting point for our campaign, so the game was all about what we could do. Setting out a statement of intent and starting as we meant to continue, as it were. The Irish might not have been as strong as we probably expected them to be prior to their tour, but they were still an international side and an opponent that we had to take out.

An Apia afternoon: 1997

Ashton fielded his strongest XV for the match, sending a clear signal to his players when he dropped the under-performing captain Garry Halpin, but the Irish were still only able to hold back the tide for a while.

In the second half, the match was largely one-way traffic as the New Zealand Maori side coasted home 41–10.

'It was satisfying to go out there and get the job done, especially given the lead up we'd had', Brain, scorer of one of the team's four tries, says.

'Even though the Irish had taken a bit of a pounding by the time we got to them, with a programme of four internationals in place, for us, we felt like we were hitting the big time as a team to some extent. While one of the games was a mid-weeker in Samoa, the rest were all against major international sides, which placed the acid on us to prove that we were worthy of the opportunity we had been given.'

From Palmerston North, the New Zealand Maori side moved on to Napier four days later to greet Argentina, who'd arrived in New Zealand with a familiar face guiding their coaching regime – former Canterbury and All Black coach Alex Wyllie.

> With Grizz [Alex Wyllie] as their coach, and given the way the Pumas traditionally played, we knew that Argentina would really come at us up front. It was going to be a huge test of our forward pack, but the guys really fronted up. If anything, we probably took the sting out of their forwards a little bit, ahead of their first Test with the All Blacks the following week. Norm [Hewitt] was outstanding. He'd always added value when he came into our environment – he got a real bounce out of wearing the Maori jersey – but he also probably felt that he had a point to prove at this particular stage. Anton Oliver was emerging, and Norm was quite clearly starting to worry about his future in the All Black jersey.

Although the unfortunate Pumas dropped their bundle completely against the All Blacks a week later, being massacred 93–8 in the first Test at Athletic Park, the New Zealand Maori side had done its bit to undermine the tourist's confidence. Rocked by two first-half tries, and unable to gain any supremacy against a rugged opponent up front, Wyllie had nowhere to turn when his side trailed 3–20 at the break. Three further second-half tries by the home side, and two by Argentina, at least gave McLean Park patrons a look at a bit more ball movement, but there was no doubting that the New Zealand Maori side had been well worth its commanding 39–17 win.

'We'd talked about the power of their tight five in the lead up to the game. Argentinian forwards are generally big, strong men, so we knew we at least had to match them, and we did', Brain recalls.

'Dale Atkins [assistant coach] didn't overdo the scrum training, but he did put a lot of responsibility on the shoulders of our front rowers: Norm, Paul Thomson and Phil Coffin, and those three really responded.'

Mayerhofler says the grand platform that was laid up-front made it easy for the backs to enjoy themselves.

'The big fellas were doing all the hard work. Once the ball got out to us, we were able to chuck it about a bit, run their bigger guys around and have some fun', he says.

'Everyone was playing with plenty of confidence, and the quality of the ball we were receiving was such that it encouraged us to back our skills and have a real go at them.'

While the Pumas represented just the second leg of four games that the New Zealand Maori team would play in an 11-day period, Mayerhofler says the way the players were managed off the field helped to keep them fresh.

'There was never the intensity off the field with the Maori side that you got with the All Blacks, or even in Super 12 sometimes', Mayerhofler says.

'Matt allowed the guys to relax after games, be themselves and have a few beers if they wanted to. Those that did simply ran off the affects of the alcohol the next day, when preparations began for the next game. While we worked hard on the field, Matt recognised it was important that everyone was able to enjoy themselves as well.'

The enjoyment factor was particularly important post-Napier, as the team faced a gruelling road trip by bus to Auckland the next day, in order to make the flight to Samoa.

> *It was hard to escape the feeling that we were still second-class citizens sometimes! The day we had to drive from Napier to Auckland, it probably would have been quicker if we'd had to fly from New Zealand to Sydney, in terms of the time spent travelling.*
>
> *We turned that situation to our advantage, though. On the bus, the guitars came out and we used the time for an additional kapa haka bonding session.*

An Apia afternoon: 1997

The attitude of the players was always great, so additional hurdles like that never affected morale at all. They recognised the issues we faced, but we were sure to put everything on the table in front of them and trust in the guys. That covered what they were allowed to do when they were out socialising after games as well. They were allowed downtime. The players knew when that was, when they could go out and socialise, and when they had to pull their heads in.

There was never any politics. We either stood united, or we fell.

While a travel schedule that required the team to bus the seven hours from Napier, and fly out to Samoa that night, and all happening the day after an international match, would be considered unacceptable by top professional players now, Brain says there was no grumbling.

'It was a come-down from what our expectations probably were, and certainly wasn't something the Rugby Union would ever ask the All Blacks to do, but Matt was very up-front with everyone about it beforehand. So we knew that was the way it was. We just had to get on with it, although it was probably a good thing that no one was breathalysed when we got to Auckland. Everyone had kicked back on the road trip, sung a few songs and had a few beers, so the air inside the bus would have smelt pretty rank by the time we got to Auckland airport!'

The difficulties provided by the team's travel schedule soon paled into insignificance once the New Zealand Maori side arrived in Apia. From the moment the team touched down on Samoan soil, it was clear to every member of the party that they were well and truly on enemy territory.

'Because Samoa had been unbeaten at home for eight years, we realised that, not so much the Samoan team, but the Samoan people were going to do everything they possibly could to inconvenience us and put us off, to help their team's chances of beating us', Brain recalls.

If the local indifference to being the perfect hosts wasn't a challenge enough, there was also the heat factor.

'It was blisteringly hot', Slade McFarland says.

'I went for a run that first morning we were there. I set out just before the sun came up, but I reckon the temperature went up from about 15 degrees when I started, to 30, just during that run!'

The atmosphere within the Maori camp was spiced up even more following the side's 40–8 win over a Samoan XV in their lead-up match after Counties Manukau halfback Michael Scott was invalided out of the tour courtesy of a broken jaw.

The injury occurred as the result of a dramatically late hit.

'He passed the ball from halfback and it had got as far as our centre by the time the 'hit' took place. Even if you say it was just late, you're probably being a bit generous', physiotherapist Mike Stewart recalls.

'It was pretty blatant, and the incident certainly added to the feeling, although the tensions had already been running fairly high. The player concerned, who made the tackle, was no thug off the street either. We found out later that he was an accountant by trade!'

> *The mid-week Samoan side was definitely sent out there to soften us up and try to intimidate us. There's no doubt about that. In a way, it was a shame I didn't have Jim [1998–2002 assistant coach Jim Love] there with me at the time. He'd played a lot of rugby up in the Islands during his own time as a New Zealand Maori player, and always said that the golden rule when you passed the ball was you then counted to three, and then you ducked!*

The advice came too late for Scott. It also came too late to prevent Brain, his close mate and provincial captain at Counties Manukau, from inadvertently fuelling the animosity by lashing out at the Samoan's rough-house tactics in the newspaper.

'I was fuming about what had happened and told the local rugby writer, who I knew, that I was livid with how they'd played', Brain says.

'It was all in the emotion of the moment. With hindsight, it wasn't the smartest thing I could have done, and I regretted it later. What it did, by telling them that we were annoyed, was emphasise to the Samoans the fact that they'd got to us. And that only served to encourage them further.'

The Scott incident did, however, also have the effect of pulling the visiting side even more tightly together.

'It was important that we stuck together, because we had a few younger guys in the side that year who could have been put off by it all', Brain says. 'So we had to show our collective bottle and make sure no doubt crept in.'

Caleb Ralph, who was in his second year in the Maori team, but was still only 19, recalls how intimidating the atmosphere leading up to the game had become.

'The hit on Scotty was absolutely blatant, and things sort of sky-rocketed from there', Ralph says.

'They [the Samoans] were definitely up for it, both the team and their people. And both the players and the local people quite clearly expected Samoa to beat us. It was out of it. It was like we were playing against the whole island. The older guys had talked about how tough it would be before we got there, but you don't really appreciate stuff like that until you're caught in the middle of it. The senior guys really held us all together before that game. And you could see by their reaction after it was all over, how much it meant to them.'

Yet for all the pre-match tension, Adrian Cashmore reports that Matt remained remarkably relaxed.

'Everything was full-on leading up to that game. We'd prepared well for what we knew would be a huge challenge, but Matt was just the same as he always was', Cashmore says.

'Totally relaxed and calm, yet thoroughly organised. That's just the way he is. You could see why he would have been such a good man to have in the Army. He'd be great in a crisis, that quiet dignity and considered argument or instruction. That's what he was like that week.

'It was one of the reasons why the guys were so respectful of him, and so desperate not to ever let him down. Matt always repaid the guys' efforts by allowing them to do what they wanted off the field – things weren't so regimented like they tended to be with the All Blacks. When it came time to train and play, Matt asked that you were 100 percent committed and the players all responded to that.

'Maybe it was a legacy of his military career, but Matt's time-management skills were superb. His training times were always exact, and he stuck to the times he'd given us before training, whether the session had gone well or not. He was the only coach I ever had who was like that, and it was an aspect of his leadership that we, as players, really admired him for.'

From Matt's perspective, nothing that was thrown at his players in the lead-up to the 'Test' really surprised him.

> *Deep down, we probably all knew what to expect. They were defending a long and proud home record. The fact that we'd beaten them back in Auckland the year before only added to their motivation to get back at us. We knew we were up against it just playing them, and then there was the heat factor to consider, as well. It was unbelievably hot there!*

The Samoans tried to take advantage of the conditions by scheduling the game for a midday kick-off, a time when the sun was at its hottest. The visiting side travelled to Apia Park in an open air bus, which Daryl Gibson reports resulted in most of the players having worked up a huge amount of sweat prior to them even setting foot on the match field.

Stewart recalls there was also a lingering doubt among the players over the potential for the crowd to become involved physically, if things went against the Samoan team. This prospect had been heightened by memories of the New Zealand Divisional side striking off-field trouble, albeit in entirely different circumstances, when they'd visited Samoa in 1993. On that occasion, a flare up between locals and players at a hotel caused the tour to be abandoned one match prior to its scheduled completion.

'A few of the boys were aware of what had happened to the Divisional side and the potential for something nasty to occur again', Stewart says.

'While there was never any official 'escape' plan discussed at management level, a few of the players had gotten it into their heads that we would all bolt to the team bus and high-tail it out of there if things got out of hand!'

The off-field events had steeled the resolve among the players, producing a pre-match intensity that Brain says was generally uncharacteristic of the New Zealand Maori environment. Although it produced an impressive result as the visitors jumped to an early 15–3 advantage on the back of tries by halfback Rhys Duggan and flanker Craig Glendinning. Ironically, the latter would switch camps later in his career to play for the opposition, turning out for Samoa at the 1999 Rugby World Cup.

Stung by the early Maori onslaught, the Samoans struck back with tries by their Super 12 wingers, Brian Lima (Blues) and Afato So'oalo (Crusaders), with Lima's score delivering his second jolt to the Maori side after he almost forced Brain from the field with his first tackle of the game.

'Brian hit me so hard in a tackle from the kick off, it turned my eyelids inside out', Brain recalls.

'I honestly didn't know what had happened to start with. I was totally dazed. Whether it was a deliberate ploy by them to target the opposing captain or not, I'm not sure, but it certainly told our guys from the start that it was going to be a case of sink or swim.'

By halftime, New Zealand Maori had clawed its way to a slender 21–20 advantage, despite the concession of a 60-metre intercept try to Samoan first-five-eighths Earl Va'a, after a move between Maori inside backs Rhys Duggan and Eugene Martin went horribly wrong.

'We'd decided before the game that we had to play it reasonably tight to nullify their counter-attack from general play, and the intercept try we conceded only served to confirm that our policy was the right one', Brain says.

'Our scrum worked really well on their ball to reduce the threat of their loose forwards attacking from first phase. Keeping the ball in hand like we did also limited their opportunities from turnover.'

As the second half progressed, the pressure exerted by the New Zealand Maori forwards gradually took its toll. For the second year running in the Islands, the side benefited from a penalty try awarded by Australian referee Peter Marshall, this time for a deliberate off-side by flanker Junior Paramore when the visitors were threatening the Samoan goal-line.

'That was a Test in everything but name', Mayerhofler, who became an All Black the following year, says.

'It was certainly far more of a Test contest than, say, the All Blacks against Italy might be. Winning in such difficult circumstances made it very special.'

By fulltime, the New Zealand Maori side had pushed out to a convincing 34–20 win, handing Samoa its first defeat in Apia since Queensland had won there during the 1989 Super 10 series.

'The key to playing up in the Islands is in the mind set. You have to front up, and that's what we did against Samoa', Mayerhofler says.

'I think the Island players respect you more if you run as hard at them as they do at you. It might not be the most scientific way to play the game, but it's the way you have to play if you want to be successful up there.'

For Matt, the result represented a triumph, both in his planning, and in the commitment of his players to carry out their assigned tasks and play to the game-plan provided.

We knew the Samoans would be extremely disciplined. They hadn't achieved their great international record without it, so we had to match them in that area if we were to be successful. Having said that, the guys also had to stand by their mates. We prepared for a punch up if there was to be one [which there wasn't], and told the guys to stick together. If it happened, it would be a case of one in, all in. You couldn't just throw one punch and walk away like often happens in games in New Zealand. Things are a bit more full-blooded up in the Islands!

Perhaps the most pleasing thing for me, from the game, was how we managed to shut them out totally in the second half, keeping them scoreless. That was a hell of an achievement against an international side as good as they were – in the top eight on world rankings, and probably higher than that again if they played the other seven at home. To blank them in a half of rugby on their home track, in front of their people, showed just how well my guys had played.

It was a performance worthy of the New Zealand Maori team's traditional post-match victory haka although, given the pre-match tension, Brain wisely checked with opposing skipper Pat Lam before giving his team the go ahead. The match had pitted the two close mates together as the rival skippers, with Brain having been the best man at Lam's wedding.

'The guys were pretty jubilant, and were talking about doing a haka, so I asked Pat what he thought the crowd response would be', Brain says.

'He told me to do it, and that they would stay out on the field with us while we did the haka, just to keep the crowd calm.'

The haka marked the beginning of some memorable post-match celebrations, which included a huge party by the swimming pool back at the team hotel. Mayerhofler celebrated the success by swimming fully clothed in his team No 1s (team suit) after being pushed into the water by his elder brother, Chris.

'It was sheer exhilaration', Gibson says.

'After all of the tension in the build up, the guys just let rip. The sight of Bubsy [Mayerhofler] and Norm Maxwell doing bombs in the pool in their '1s' is not something I'll ever forget, but it summed up the excitement we all felt.'

There was one part of the 'celebration' that a member of the Maori team would prefer to forget, however, after he was sighted by his team-mates later that night getting dangerously well acquainted with a fa'afafine (Samoan trans-sexual).

'Quite a few of the boys had a fair few beers after that game, and I guess it's fair to say that a couple of them might have had a few too many', Brain says.

'It [the fa'afafine] had been spotted hanging out with some of the Samoan players earlier in the night. Then it turned up where the remainder of our guys were.'

Eric Rush recalls trying to warn his unfortunate team-mate that all was not what it seemed with his newly found 'friend'.

'He was fairly intoxicated', Rush says, laughing, as he recalls the incident.

'I tried to tell him, and kept at him for a while, but he kept telling me to: "Go away!" In the end, he was resorting to threats, so I left him to it.'

The incident of course, quickly spread like wildfire through the team the next morning, which resulted in the player concerned confronting Rush, pleading to hear that he was being had on.

'He was desperate for me to tell him that it was all a have, and that it hadn't happened', Rush says.

'I don't think I'll ever forget the look on his face when I told him: "I'm afraid it's all true bro!"'

While the unfortunate player would prefer to leave the memory of that part of the celebrations back in Samoa, Matt took great delight in how the younger members of the team, Ralph and lock Norm Maxwell, had responded to the intensity that the Samoan experience had provided, while teaching them a valuable lesson in the process.

> Both were still very young guys, really only at the start of their careers in the big time, and it's probably fair to say that it took a little while before they were both comfortable with all aspects of our environment.
>
> I remember Norm, especially, was a little indifferent at first, worrying I think about whether he really was a Maori. All that changed after the 1997 tour, though, and especially after the experience in Samoa. He came to me at the end of that trip and told me that, going forward, I should just pick him. I didn't have to worry about ringing him first to make sure that he was available, I should just put his name down – and he'd be there!
>
> That incident told me we were getting the balance within the team right, but it also helped me to understand that there was still a little bit of resistance to the cultural side of things, probably because some of the players were worried about being embarrassed by their lack of knowledge of the Maori culture.
>
> I took from this, that we had to take it slowly and develop, not just rugby players, but Maori rugby players – and there was a definite way to do it. I also took from the situation with Norm and Caleb encouragement that we were doing the right thing in educating the players about their heritage. We owed it to them to develop their Maori culture, because they were great rugby players already, we wouldn't have selected them if they weren't, but if we didn't develop their understanding and knowledge of their culture, then we were just another Saturday rugby team!

That was something, the Maori side that departed Samoa on June 22, 1997 most definitely wasn't, having established themselves as the undisputed kings of the indigenous Pacific Island teams by completing a run of home and away victories over Fiji, Tonga and Samoa, respectively.

Five of the players who featured in the 34–20 victory over Samoa would advance to the All Blacks in the next two years, while the stakes would be raised for the New Zealand Maori side too, with a home match against England the next year, to be followed by a three-match tour of Scotland at the end of the 1998 season.

> *The Samoan game signed off our environment. The team had come a long way in the four years since I'd become involved, but it was really only after we beat Samoa that I felt we'd developed to something like our full potential. The achievement of that result, in such adversity, said to me that, if we prepared well, the New Zealand Maori team could beat any side in the world.*

In 1998 the team would get the chance to prove it!

The England massacre: 1998

'Remember the Treaty!'

The game might have gone professional two years earlier, but by 1998 Matt was just only catching up with that development. Having essentially coached fully professional players in the New Zealand Maori team for the previous two seasons, while effectively still an amateur coach, Matt finally joined the professional era; although it was as assistant coach of the Chiefs that he first 'cut his teeth' as a pro.

> *I suppose my appointment to the Chiefs came about primarily because of the success I'd had with the New Zealand Maori team. I was excited by the opportunity, but it was a step into the unknown. Not only had I never experienced a Super 12 campaign before, and I'll admit here and now that I was surprised at how big the commitment actually was, I also didn't really know the head coach, Ross [Cooper], all that well. I'd never been an assistant coach before either, so I was pretty much starting from scratch for the whole thing.*

So too were the Chiefs.

After placing sixth then eleventh in their first two seasons under the regime of former North Harbour coach Brad Meurant, the side was starting afresh for its third season, with the former All Black selector, Counties and Thames Valley coach Ross Cooper at the helm. Matt was brought in as 2IC, the Chiefs' third assistant coach in as many years after Sid Going and John Boe had held the role during the inaugural years.

> *The difference between being the main man and being the assistant is huge, and it took a bit of getting used to. For starters, as the head coach,*

> *you can speak your mind and be totally up front. You are, after all, the boss. The assistant coach has to be a little more guarded, so as not to undermine the head guy. Effectively, as an assistant, you are a supporter of the world whether you agree with what is going on or not. If you don't agree, you really have no choice but to shut up and go with the flow!*

This is not always easy when the side is not performing.

While the Cooper–Te Pou partnership made a winning debut when the Chiefs beat eventual competition winners, the Crusaders 25–23, first up at North Harbour Stadium, the season's early promise ultimately amounted to little.

Week two saw the Chiefs 28–25 winners over the Queensland Reds in Brisbane, but a 19–22 loss at home to the Hurricanes in the next round knocked the confidence out of the side, and it never really returned.

Although the Chiefs wound up winning six games and losing five, the same record that was achieved in 1996, their seventh placing – five points astern of the semi-final positions – was considered disappointing, especially because they'd beaten two of the eventual semi-finalists in their first two outings.

The programme was a major learning curve for Matt in more ways than one. The exposure to the political wrangling between the Waikato and North Harbour unions over control of the franchise left him convinced that the amalgamation of the two first division provinces would never properly work.

> *The set up we had for the team was very good, even though there was a lot of travel involved to satisfy the demands of all of the provincial stake holders.*
>
> *The political overtones, and the North Harbour versus Waikato thing, was always there, though – you couldn't escape it. While it wasn't an issue within the team amongst the players, as such, it did create uncertainty. We didn't have one home base, for example, having to play at both North Harbour Stadium and Rugby Park [Hamilton] for our home matches.*
>
> *I guess that made it just that bit harder for all of the supporters to identify with the team, when compared to, say, the Hurricanes or the two South Island teams, where the core of the sides were drawn from the Wellington, Canterbury and Otago provincial teams respectively.*

The England massacre: 1998

The issue of the Chiefs' franchise make up was settled by Matt's second year. The New Zealand Rugby Union sensibly returned the North Harbour and Northland provincial unions to their more geographically logical location within the Blues, while Counties Manukau and Thames Valley realigned with the Chiefs.

Although that decision took the political heat off the team, the 1999 campaign was virtually all over for the Chiefs, even before it started, after they were hammered 3-48 by the Crusaders on the opening night of the competition in Christchurch.

It took another five weeks, and four more losses, before the Chiefs finally dug their way out of the hole by recording a courageous 16-13 win over the ACT Brumbies in Canberra. That result boosted confidence to such an extent that the Chiefs finished with five wins from their last six matches, and a sixth placed finish – equal to the franchise's best.

The trouble was: the expectations for the season had been higher than that.

It was a difficult year. Starting like we did put the pressure on everybody, and it was obvious to me, long before the end of the competition, that there would probably be consequences, and that I could be looking for another job!

Ironically, Matt says the best week of his two-year stint with the Chiefs was his last, in South Africa, where he was able to get back into what he did best, taking charge and organising success.

Ross's mother had died, so he returned to New Zealand after our loss to the Stormers at Cape Town. That put me in the chair for the week leading up to our final game against the Bulls. The players were all disappointed with how things had gone for us, but they were determined to finish with a flourish. We prepared well for that game and played pretty well. Pleasingly, from my perspective, looking ahead to the New Zealand Maori campaign, four of the players who scored tries for us at Loftus Versfeld were Maori players, so they were going to take confidence out of that leading up to our programme.

While the Chiefs beat the Bulls 39-31, with Bruce Reihana (two), Rhys Duggan and Glenn Marsh contributing four of the side's five tries, the performance was not enough to save Matt's neck. He returned home to a review from the New Zealand Rugby Union and the franchise, suspecting that his fate had already been determined.

> *Perhaps the thing that surprised me a little bit was that Ross survived. They shot the sergeant! I suppose I could always say that I'd bowed out with a 100 percent record after we beat the Bulls! Realistically, though, it was always going to be tough to retain our positions. Ross just obviously had more friends higher up the political food chain than I did, and that's often the way in rugby unfortunately. That's life in the fast lane. We hadn't delivered, and there are always casualties in that instance.*

While Matt would go on to bigger and better things with the New Zealand Maori, it didn't get any better for the Chiefs. In fact, things got worse, with the side winning just three matches the following season, which saw Cooper resign after a tenth placed finish. The Chiefs finally made the semi-finals for the first time in 2004, the last of the New Zealand sides to do so, but have since fallen back into a similar pattern of promising more than they've delivered during the last two seasons.

> *I always enjoyed the buzz of getting together with the Maori team during my time, but especially so during those two years with the Chiefs. With the Super 12 not having gone as well as I would have liked, it was important to be able to 'get back on the horse' as soon as was possible, and the Maori team provided me with that opportunity. Importantly, also, it put me back into an environment I knew well, was confident in and had a greater measure of control over. It was also one where I was surrounded by people with whom I had a successful track record. Because of that, the trust was absolute, and we were always confident in what we were doing.*

There was one significant change to the New Zealand Maori management team for 1998 as the side prepared to pick up from where it had left off in Samoa the previous year. That was in the assistant coaching position, where Jim Love, having previously having been involved with the New Zealand Maori trial teams, took over from Dale Atkins.

Although there was plenty of excitement within the ranks at the start of that campaign, with England to play, and a three-match tour of Scotland looming on the horizon at season's end, the New Zealand Maori side first had to negotiate a potentially tricky assignment against Tonga.

The Tongans, who just about didn't make it to New Zealand because of funding problems, forced everyone to sit up and take notice when they

The England massacre: 1998

beat Counties Manukau 22–15 in their tour opener on a Friday night at Papakura.

While Counties hadn't been at full strength, as the beaten finalists in the 1996 and 1997 NPC first division finals, they had been comfortably expected to beat the tourists. Their failure left New Zealand Maori skipper Errol Brain fuming.

'With all due respect to them, they were basically only a bunch of New Zealand club players, so to lose was embarrassing', Brain says.

'We were probably a little bit guilty of under-rating them [Tonga]. Once they got a sniff, we just couldn't seem to get back into it. We simply didn't play well enough on the night to deserve to win.'

Given that England was the main feature of the New Zealand Maori team's domestic programme, there had always been the danger that the Tongans would sneak in under their radar as well.

The shock win over Counties Manukau ensured that wouldn't happen.

I couldn't admit it to my players, but privately I was quite delighted when Tonga beat Counties. My son, Matthew, was playing for them, so obviously I was pleased for him, but I also felt it would be a blessing in disguise for my team, in terms of our preparation leading into that match. Three of the players [Brain, second-five-eighths Tony Marsh and prop Lee Lidgard] who played for Counties in that game were coming into our squad, and I knew they'd all be desperate for a bit of payback.

The family dynamic, with Matthew on the Tongan side, only spiced the pre-match atmosphere up further, especially as the youngster couldn't resist a bit of good natured ribbing of his father.

He was giving me a bit of lip. Matthew rang me on the Tuesday before our Friday night game and told me how they were going to get into our guys. The next thing I know, here he is on the television news one night saying the same thing! I thought to myself: 'not wise young fella, giving out ammunition freely to the opposition like that. I think you've still got a bit to learn!'

Te Pou junior and his team-mates did learn, but only after infuriating the New Zealand Maori players even further by snaring an early try to take the lead, after centre Fepikou Tatafu latched on to a loose Tony Brown pass.

Standing under his goal-posts at Whangarei's Lowe Walker Stadium, Brain read the riot act to his troops.

'The Tongans were all high fiving and jubilant. You'd have thought they'd won the game', Brain says.

'I told the boys, as we stood there waiting for the conversion, to have a good look at what was going on. It's fair to say, after we'd finished, the Tongans weren't high fiving anymore!'

With places for the plum match against England at stake, the New Zealand Maori response was swift and destructive.

The forwards took control up front, denying the Tongans any further opportunities to break up the structure of the match, as they had previously with the intercept.

The momentum was then capitalised on ruthlessly by the Maori backs, who wound up contributing eight of the nine tries in an eventual 66–7 rout.

'One of the pleasing aspects of it was that we never loosened up, as can sometimes happen when you are running away with a game', Brain says.

'Maybe it was the fact that they scored early that fuelled our rage. The lure of playing against England was probably there, too. Either way, the team concentrated for the full eighty. We certainly felt by the end of it that we had put them away like we should have!'

International rugby has no time for sentiment, and one of the side's victims during their sustained assault was the son of their coach, who, playing on the openside flank for Tonga, wound up more battered than most.

Such was the physicality, Matthew was replaced before the final whistle, and was still nursing scars from the battle when sought out by his father during the post-match function an hour after the match had concluded.

> *Because of the position he was playing, it was obvious to me that Matthew was going to get 'sorted out' by our side at some stage. When I finally found him at the after-match function, he was with his mother and grandmother. When he looked up at me, I could see he was a bit scarred, so I just patted him on the head, smiled and said: 'Daddy's sorry!' His mother still reminds me of that quite often!*

Matthew went on to play for Tonga at the 1999 Rugby World Cup, enjoying a more memorable afternoon when the Pacific Islanders' opened that particular tournament against the All Blacks at Bristol. Matthew appeared as a substitute in a match where Tonga held New Zealand to a 16–9

No Snow Queens in sight here! The 1995 New Zealand Maori team. Matt Te Pou collection

The commitment Errol Brain brought to the New Zealand Maori jersey is clear for all to see as he engages the Western Samoan defence during the 28–15 win at Mt Smart Stadium in 1996. © PHOTOSPORT

Matthew junior with Ida after his selection for the New Zealand Maori side in 1996. Matthew went on to play for Tonga on the tour of New Zealand in 1998 and at the Rugby World Cup a year later. Matt Te Pou collection

No explanation necessary! 'The Interpreter' Tony Brown in action against Western Samoa. © PHOTOSPORT

Action from the 1996 match between a New Zealand Maori XV and an Invitation XV at Kawerau, prior to the New Zealand Maori tour of the Pacific Islands. Matt Te Pou collection

Norm Hewitt delivers the message to his team-mates during the New Zealand Maori trials at Whakatane in 1997. Matt Te Pou collection

Tony Marsh, who went on to play Test rugby for France, looks for holes in the Tongan defence at Whangarei in 1998. © PHOTOSPORT

The enigmatic Norm Berryman played some of the best rugby of his career in the New Zealand Maori jersey. © PHOTOSPORT

Waikato halfback Rhys Duggan leaves the defenders for dead as the English massacre of 1998 takes shape. © PHOTOSPORT

He might have been a Sergeant Major in his army days, but Matt never needed to rant on the training paddock to get his message across. © PHOTOSPORT

Matt with former All Black captain Wayne 'Buck' Shelford who remains an enormously respected figure, especially in Maori rugby circles. Matt Te Pou collection

Norm Berryman (left), Bruce Reihana and Adrian Cashmore relax with a young fan in the team room during the tour of Scotland in 1998. Matt Te Pou collection

New Zealand Maori players offer a few pointers to members of the Manutaki Trust during a buddy bonding session prior to the team's departure for the tour of Scotland in 1998. Matt Te Pou collection

If looks could kill! Norm Hewitt leading the haka and giving the opposition the evil eye.
© PHOTOSPORT

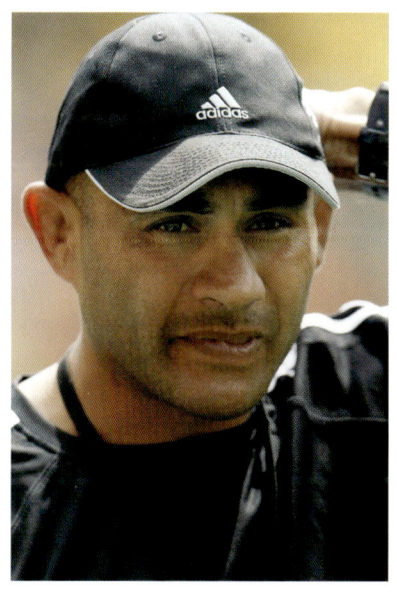

Eric Rush ponders life as Paul Simonsson's slave during the New Zealand Maori team's 1988 world tour. © PHOTOSPORT

The New Zealand Maori team visit caused much excitement throughout France in 1988.
© Peter Bush

Flanker Glenn Marsh, the outstanding performer in the New Zealand Maori team's 24–8 win over Scotland in 1998, was well restrained when the two sides met again in New Plymouth two years later. © Pro Sport Photos

Such was the tenacity of the Scottish defence at New Plymouth in 2000, clear space was difficult to find, as New Zealand Maori flanker Matua Parkinson discovers as he attempts to link up with fullback Adrian Cashmore. Parkinson was a try scorer, while Cashmore kicked the winning goal in the New Zealand Maori team's 18–15 victory. © Pro Sport Photos

The England massacre: 1998

halftime advantage and gave their more fancied rivals a fair old buffeting in the second half, as well, before the All Blacks finally eased out to a 45–9 victory. In that instance, Matt was in his son's corner, helping the Tongans on an unofficial basis with some pointers on the training field in the lead up to the match.

But, while the magnitude of their defeat in Whangarei a year earlier had left the Tongans licking their wounds, Matt and his new assistant coach faced a different problem. How were they to prevent the players, in their excitement from both the big win over Tonga and the now apparent fact that they would be facing a well below-strength English side, from getting carried away.

'We talked about it, and it fell to me to stir things up a bit', Love recalls.

'We had a lot of pretty experienced forwards in that side, and they'd played quite well against the Tongans. They'd done the job there very efficiently, but we felt they still needed a bit of a rev up, so I gave that to them at our next training. We just couldn't afford to start getting cocky. The rev certainly came as a shock to a few of them – a couple of the senior players gave me sideway glances, but I guess the proof was in the outcome. We smashed the English up front!'

While there had been much excitement when it was announced that the New Zealand Maori side would play England, the credibility of the 'honour' was thrown open to question after the future Rugby World Cup-winning coach Clive Woodward arrived for the tour minus 15 of the English players who'd performed so well for the British & Irish Lions during their winning series in South Africa the previous year.

So green was the English touring party, after the English club owners ruled that most of their star players must rest, 17 of the players who toured were uncapped, while the other 19 had amassed just 152 caps between them.

Predictably, in such circumstances, Woodward's men struggled, with the trip now popularly recalled in England as the 'Tour from Hell'.

Humiliated 0–76 by Australia during their first stop in Brisbane, England also lost 22–66 to the All Blacks in the first Test at Carisbrook, three days before their outing against the New Zealand Maori.

Yet, what is less commonly remembered about that tour is that England did have its moments. Not only had the tourists held a powerful New Zealand A side coached by Graham Henry to just an eight-point winning margin during their first game in the country, the All Blacks had led only 9–3 after half an hour in Dunedin, and looked to be in for a difficult afternoon until England lock Danny Grewcock got himself sent off.

Grewcock was marched for lashing out with his boot at All Black hooker Anton Oliver, and with his departure went any English hopes of credibility as they leaked nine tries in the final 50 minutes.

To complicate their preparation even further, Woodward had to rush back to England after the first Test because his father had died, which left his assistant, future All Black coach, John Mitchell, to watch over preparations for the New Zealand Maori match.

It wasn't a flash England team by any stretch, but they still had the English jerseys on. We had a lot riding on that night, both as the first really big game against one of the big five countries that we'd had since I'd had the team, but also with the tour of Scotland coming up. Not only did we want to prove our worth as a team, but the players were all out to impress, to make sure they got on that trip. Our forward pack had a lot of experience by then. It was a big stage for them. Fortunately, it all clicked.

'It always had to start up front', Love says.

'We could have the best backs in the world, and we certainly had some very good ones, but possessing them was no good if we couldn't get them the ball. We always aimed for parity at least, or better, and always knew – as a forward pack – that if we could achieve that, then the team would win.'

England's poor tour record to that point had created an expectation that they would be cannon fodder for the New Zealand Maori. Brain admits that is a factor the players were aware of.

'There was certainly pressure there to put them away', he says, 'but we never talked about winning margins or anything like that. The boys were definitely really tuned up for the game, though. They had some big boys up front, so we decided to keep the ball in hand as much as we could, knowing that if we did that, they wouldn't be able to live with our backs.'

The English couldn't.

Of the nine tries scored by the New Zealand Maori side during its exhilarating 62–14 victory, seven went to the backs. Three of the tries originated on the New Zealand Maori team's side of halfway, with the passage of play for Norm Berryman's second try covering 55 metres, Rhys Duggan's try-scoring sequence covering 85 metres, from the base of a defensive scrum, while Roger Randle ran 95 metres for his second – and the Maori team's ninth – try of the evening, after securing an intercept.

> *There were some brilliant tries amongst the nine we scored. While the English quite clearly couldn't handle it, I don't think too many sides would have lived with us that night. It was one of those games where things just went for us. I can remember Jim Coe [New Zealand Maori lock] nearly scoring from a centering kick – it was just all happening our way, and the players showed plenty of confidence and backed their skills.*

For Mattie Blackburn, Matt's manager, who'd been involved with the side for 19 years, the night is one he'll never forget.

'If you were looking for one game to epitomise everything that Maori rugby is about – the flair, the skill, the passion – then the England game is it', Blackburn says.

'It was an incredible night. Regardless of how good or otherwise the opposition was, the quality of the rugby the boys played was outstanding. It was the traditional Maori style of rugby played at its best.'

Daryl Gibson, who later went on to play alongside some of the beaten English players when he moved to the United Kingdom to play for the Bristol and Leicester clubs later in his career, says the lack of success secured by the visiting side on that tour didn't devalue the sense of achievement felt by the Maori players.

'That night was a huge opportunity for us. It was the biggest stage, internationally, that the Maori team had played on for five years, since the Lions game of 1993, in terms of the media coverage and global interest. We resolved beforehand to show the world what we could do, and what Maori rugby was all about.'

The key to the success, fullback Adrian Cashmore says, was in the team's preparation.

'You can say what you like about them now, but they were still an international side, and we treated them with the utmost respect in the build up', Cashmore says.

'It would have been easy to have relaxed a little, given the beatings they'd already had on that tour, but the guys were far too professional for that.'

Besides, Cashmore had already experienced the fact that the English had more to offer than they were being given credit for, having been at fullback on the wretched night in Hamilton where New Zealand A had laboured to an 18–10 win over the visitors.

Following the massacre in Rotorua, England went on to stretch the All Blacks for a long period again, before losing the second Test 10–40 at Auckland. They then completed their trip by holding South Africa, that year's Tri-Nations winners, to a 0–18 score-line at Cape Town.

'The thing about the Maori game was that everything was done so clinically. That highlighted how well we'd prepared', Cashmore says.

'The other thing I remember about that night was the aftermath. Once we'd played the game, then it was into the dressing room and the guitars came out!'

As the score mounted, it would have been understandable if the players had relaxed their grip and loosened up the game a bit, but physiotherapist Mike Stewart reports there was never any likelihood of that.

'I went out to attend to one of our guys with about 20 minutes to go, and there was still plenty of chatter going on among the players', he says.

'But it was all pretty intense, as if the result was still in the balance, which it wasn't. The talk was all: "Keep up the D [defence]. Don't let them score!"'

It was about the one objective the Maori side didn't achieve on the night, with England salvaging two late tries, although they were scant consolation given the magnitude of the defeat.

'They were unlucky', hooker Slade McFarland says.

'We didn't care individually who the players were – they were the England team, and we really wanted to turn it on!'

If any extra motivation was required, McFarland says it was supplied by a quick thinking comedian among the large Rotorua crowd, who supplied telling motivational advice to the home players while the two teams were forming up for a lineout.

'Here we were, in the middle of this international match, and some guy yells out to us: "Remember the Treaty!"' McFarland recalls.

'Some of the guys were laughing about it at the time. I think everyone saw the funny side of it after the game, but perhaps a few of the boys did see it as a bit of historical payback. As the match went on, there was certainly a ruthless attitude that developed among our guys to humiliate them by as big a score as we could. No one slackened off.'

The boys were all on a huge high afterwards. Our vision had been to mix it with the top countries, and we'd achieved that fairly emphatically. There was also plenty of humour, with the comment about the Treaty, and the Maori sense of injustice it referred to, going down well with the players. It was quite funny really, unless you happened to be English!

One person not smiling post-match was Mitchell, whom Matt would later have communication issues with when he returned home to assume the head coaching role with the All Blacks.

He was pretty quiet, as you would expect, and I felt for him a bit. It must have been hard, coming back to his homeland with a team depleted of a number of front-line players, and then having to face the music on his own against us, because the head guy wasn't available. John just congratulated me, shook my hand, and made mention of the superior size and speed that we'd had on the night.

Making for a double celebration, the evening's curtain-raiser had seen the newly formed New Zealand Maori Colts make a winning debut by out-classing Japan A 53–21.

The Colts team had been formed with a view to establishing a development pathway into the senior New Zealand Maori side, as a result of Matt taking a Maori development side away to the Cobra 10-aside tournament in Malaysia in 1997. Matt's side won that tournament, which lent its weight to the official establishment of a development combination to blood future New Zealand Maori players.

The Colts side was coached by Willie Hetaraka and Ray Falcon, with the star of the first edition proving to be, future All Black winger, Rico Gear, who totally bemused the Japanese with his hard running on the way to scoring two tries.

The Gisborne Boys' High School old boy had already played for the national sevens side in his first year out of school, the previous season, and for Poverty Bay in the NPC.

First-five-eighths Willie Walker was another player to star for the Colts who would go on to contribute usefully to the New Zealand Maori cause at senior level.

'It [the Colts side] was an awesome concept', Gear says.

'The environment within the team was very similar to how it was later on, when I made the senior side, so it was a real eye-opener for all of us young fellas. We were fortunate to have Whetu Tipiwai as our kaumatua, and he showed us the ropes. He was the person who taught me the haka, and it was great to link up with him again when I made the senior side three years later, by which time he was the kaumatua there.'

Gear had played in the New Zealand Maori trial prior to appearing for the Maori Colts, and would be involved again in 1999 and 2000 before earning his first senior spurs.

'Matt had explained to me that I was there to learn in those first couple of years, and it was a great experience having senior guys like Rushy [Eric Rush], and other players of his status, around to talk to and learn from', Gear says.

'I'd been exposed to our culture quite a lot when I was growing up in Gisborne and missed it when I moved up to Auckland to further my rugby career. Being able to go back into the Maori environment, both for the trials and with the Colts, was almost like going home in a sense.'

Gear, and his younger brother Hosea, who appeared for the New Zealand Maori side in North America in 2004, spent a lot of time with their grandparents during their childhood, where they became acquainted with their culture.

'Quite a few people back home in Gisborne spoke Maori, so I decided to learn to speak the language myself', Gear says.

'I wouldn't say I'm totally fluent, but I'm glad I learnt. Being able to speak and understand Maori has given me a sense of self-fulfilment, although I can certainly appreciate why many young Maori opt not to learn the language now. It is a big commitment to learn and it is, unfortunately, not something you end up using that much in everyday life.'

While Gear went on to debut for the senior New Zealand Maori side against a Wasps Invitation side in 2001, that year proved the last in which there was a Maori Colts side.

> *It was an important development opportunity that was lost when that side was disbanded after 2001. For the short while that we had the Colts side, it provided a great channel for developing up and coming Maori talent, both for the betterment of the senior Maori side but also New Zealand rugby as a whole.*
>
> *Rico got his start in that team and he went on to become an All Black. Once we lost the Colts side, it placed even more emphasis on the regional Maori tournaments and the lower divisions of the NPC as pools from which we could identify and develop talented young Maori players.*

The demise of the Colts was for the future.

The England massacre: 1998

With England conquered, and an end-of-year tour to Scotland, where every All Black player would be available, to come, Matt ended the night of June 23 a satisfied man. There was just one cloud on the horizon. It concerned his skipper Errol Brain. Brain was heading to Japan at the end of 1998 to continue his playing career with the Toyota club.

While the Japanese season didn't overlap with the dates for the tour, Brain was doubtful as to whether the New Zealand Rugby Union would allow him to take part.

'Matt took me aside and told me that he wanted to include me, but we both knew he probably wouldn't get the final say', Brain recalls.

'Because of that, I was fairly realistic. While I hadn't wanted England to be my last game for New Zealand Maori, I treated it like it would be and cherished it as such.'

Unfortunately for Brain, the England massacre was to be his final chapter as a New Zealand Maori player.

It was sad that he wasn't allowed to tour. It was also silly. I said to the Rugby Union officials: 'If you are running a business, and you're paying a guy to work for a whole year, surely you'd work him for the whole year!' Obviously they weren't business people! We wanted him, and there was a precedent already because the Rugby Union had allowed Zinzan Brooke to tour with the All Blacks in Britain the year before, even though he was leaving to go and play with Harlequins in London at the end of that tour.

I guess I just didn't have the sway down at the Rugby Union HQ in Wellington that [All Black coach] John Hart had!

Going on that tour would have been an appropriate swansong for EB – he'd done a lot for the cause of Maori rugby, but it wasn't to be. The Rugby Union said no, so I had to find a new captain.

It was time for the New Zealand Maori team to move on because a date with Scotland awaited!

10

Murrayfield Maori: 1998

'The tour with a difference!'

The best indication as to the success of the 1998 New Zealand Maori tour of Scotland can be gauged by the attitude of the players involved in the trip.

Talk to any of the tourists eight years on, and they will still tell you it was one of, if not their most enjoyable, touring rugby experience.

'It was one of the best tours I ever went on', All Black Caleb Ralph says.

'The guys still talk about it quite a bit. In many ways, the environment on that tour was a lot more comfortable than what you get with the All Blacks. It was just so different. There wasn't the outside pressure that comes with an All Black trip, where the players don't get a lot of time to themselves. With Matt, the boys knew that they had to work at training, but they could put in on the park knowing that there would be no other 'surprises'. The rest of the time was their own to do what they liked.'

Ralph, who first appeared for the All Blacks in 1998, and then became a regular in the side in 2002–03, describes the freakishly talented Norman Berryman as an example of the type of player who thrived under Matt's more relaxed leadership style.

'The thing with Matt was that he worked out what the right approach was to get the best out of all of his players. Norm was awesome on that trip, yet he never went as well when he played for the All Blacks. Matt just knew how to handle him.'

Berryman, who had debuted for New Zealand earlier in the year during the Tri-Nations, was one of five current All Blacks included in the 26-man squad.

A further 11 players from the touring party would later graduate into that category before the end of their careers.

> With the All Blacks all available for selection, it was a tough side to select. A lot of guys had put their hands up throughout the season at home, even though a fair few of the positions were fairly clear cut. Perhaps the hardest thing was that there were a few players who probably would have got on the tour at another time, but missed out because the All Blacks were available. Their time in the Maori jersey would come.

While All Black coach John Hart did consult with Matt, the New Zealand Maori coach and his selection panel were left to pick the players they wanted, with the notable exception of the Japanese-bound skipper Errol Brain.

> We ended up with a good blend. While we had a group of All Black guys, and a fair few younger players, who we believed were fairly quickly going to make it through to that grade, we also had a group of seasoned players who had been with us for a while – Deon Muir, Lee Lidgard and Jim Coe being the most senior names among that group. They were the backbone of the team because they'd done the hard yards with us, and knew our environment backwards. As a result, they set the tone for everyone else.

With Brain out of the running, Matt says Muir was the obvious choice to succeed the Counties man as his skipper, even though he'd still to captain his province, Waikato, at that point. Muir's sole leadership experience, to that stage of his career, was as skipper of the St Stephen's High School First XV.

> We'd been bringing Deon along, grooming him if you like, to step up when EB moved on. It probably happened a little bit earlier than we'd originally planned, but we had no doubts that Deon was up to the mark – and he proved it on that tour.

> Deon was a 'follow me' type of leader, in a very similar mould to EB. Although he probably said a lot less off the field, and wasn't as strategic as EB had been. But that wasn't an issue; we had other senior players who could carry the load there.

> In many ways, Deon was an old-school style New Zealand No 8 forward. He was hard driving and did the basics well, made the hard yards. There wasn't a lot flashy about his play, as you might get with someone like Zinzan Brooke, but Deon always got the job done.

> In another era, he would have been an All Black. It was disappointing for him, that the honour never came, but in a selfish way that was good news

for us – and we had to look at it that way. In Deon Muir, we had a player who would serve us well as a leader over the next few years.

The Scotland trip also heralded the arrival of another Waikato player, who would serve the New Zealand Maori cause well over the next few seasons, in the form of Te Awamutu winger Bruce Reihana.

While Reihana would go on to become an All Black the following year, when he was called over to the Rugby World Cup as a replacement, the now Northampton-based utility back credits his New Zealand Maori selection as a vitally important part of his development, both as a rugby player and a person.

'Making the New Zealand Maori team had been a goal, something I'd aspired to from the time I had first really got into rugby', Reihana says.

'When I was selected, it was a huge thing, not just for me but also for my family – and particularly my parents. They had backed me, and supported me, when my life could easily have gone off in another direction. By becoming a Maori All Black, I felt I had repaid their faith in me.'

Although he has since furthered his career overseas, heading for the English Premiership competition after the 2002 season, where he has excelled, becoming his club's co-captain; Reihana remains passionate about his Maori heritage. And, more particularly, about the plight of many Maori kids.

'Young Maori are easily misled', he says.

'There's so much potential in the Maori people, but a lot of that talent goes astray. A bit of direction, and the setting of a few goals can help so much, and I was exceedingly fortunate in that way.'

Hailing from a large family, with 11 step-brothers and step-sisters from the combination of his mother Nicole and father Lawrence, Reihana was raised playing both rugby league and rugby as a child, primarily alongside all of his brothers.

'It just shows what can happen', he says.

'Some of my brothers had real talent. They could have been stars, but things didn't go well for them. They got in a bit of trouble, and went to 'the other side of the road', and that was it. It could easily have been that way for me, too, I visited there a little bit as a youngster and got into my share of trouble. Fortunately, my father put me back on the straight and narrow, and sport gave me a lot in life to look forward too. It kept me out of trouble, while giving me some self-esteem, a good work ethic and a bit of mental toughness.'

Prior to scoring a professional contract with the Chiefs for 1998, Reihana had been working as a concreter. It wasn't the most glamorous occupation and was hard work physically, but the player says it taught him discipline.

'My danger period was between the ages of 16 and 18', he says.

'That is the time when so many young Maori go off the rails. I was lucky. I had my sport to focus on, and my father pushing me along, so I got through that difficult period, where a lot of others, including some of my brothers, hadn't. I was lucky enough to make the Waikato side at 19 in my second senior season, and then I was away. But the story didn't have to have a happy ending. I always look back on where I came from, in terms of my roots, and think how lucky I was. My life could so easily have gone the other way!'

Having endured such personal challenges during his upbringing, Reihana was only too aware of the New Zealand Maori team's importance as positive role models for Maori youth, during his four years with the side.

'That aspect made the honour of playing even more special', Reihana says.

'I looked at a lot of the young Maori kids we'd encounter during my time with the team and could always see myself in them, in terms of where I was at at their age. My main hope was that they followed our direction. That the team, through our success on the field and the positive message that sent, was providing them with something they could one day aspire to.'

If Reihana had any doubts as to whether his hard work to make the grade had been worth it, it only took the Scotland tour to dispel those.

'I'd spoken to a lot of the Waikato lads who'd been away with the team before, so I knew a fair bit about the environment. It almost sounded too good to be true, but once on tour, it lived up to my expectations', he says.

'Being selected to go on Deon's first tour as captain made it even more special, because he was from my club, and had been a bit of a mentor to me from the time that I'd first made the Te Awamutu senior team.'

If Reihana looked on his skipper as being 'the next thing to family' before the tour started, by its end he was viewing the whole team as kin.

'The Maori team had, by far, the best team culture and environment that I was ever associated with in rugby, and that includes my time with the All Blacks, with Waikato and the Chiefs, and then my time in the United Kingdom at Northampton', he says.

'And I'm not being derogatory towards any of the other teams that I've played with – I've been fortunate enough to have some wonderful experiences – but the Maori team was as close as I've ever been to being involved with a family, without actually being with your family.

'Touring with the team was almost like being at home; you were made to feel so wanted. That feeling is great motivation in terms of spurring you on to try and play to the best of your ability. That was probably the key as to why the side went so well during my time, even though we often had to come together quickly before games.

'All of the players were naturally talented, but it also came down to the motivation, and the bonds were just so strong. We wanted to succeed for each other first, then the jersey, then for everyone else out there.'

> *We had two main goals when we brought the team together before leaving New Zealand, and we were very clear on that. The first was to succeed by winning the three games that we had to play. But we also wanted the players to enjoy themselves and let that enjoyment express itself in the way they performed on the park. By the time we got home, I felt we'd achieved both of those objectives. The players were focused at every training after our first one, and gave 110 percent, but they were good tourists, too. We had a lot of laughs and some very good socials, including a great 1970s night, but we had no issues off the field, and we won the games as well.*

If there was one aspect of the tour that initially surprised Matt, it was the amount of media attention the side attracted when it finally made it to Scotland after an arduous 38-hour trip from New Zealand.

> *The British media were all over us. I guess it was the novelty factor of us being a racially selected indigenous team. I suppose it also had something to do with the All Blacks not touring that year, so we were it. But I've never seen so many cameras as when we arrived over there. I was looking around all over the place to see who the movie star was who had arrived on our plane!*

While the team didn't possess any stars of the silver screen, one of its number did earn himself notoriety on the tour's first night in Scotland. The player fell asleep in the lavatories at a hotel where most of the team had convened to ease their transition into the British time zone with a few quiet drinks.

Greg Feek was rooming with 'the lavatory sleeper'. Because he was on his first tour away with the New Zealand Maori side, the Canterbury prop didn't know what to think when his room-mate didn't return from the social outing.

Nor did the unfortunate player appreciate quite where he was when he awoke some hours later, finding himself alone and in cramped quarters. After working himself out of the toilet cubicle, the unwitting tourist came to realise that he was locked in a public hotel after hours, gaining a full appreciation of his position when he tripped off the premise's alarms as he attempted to make his way out one of the regular exits.

The embarrassed player was later returned to the team's lodgings by the Edinburgh constabulary, although that wasn't to be his last late-night escapade.

'It happened again two nights later in our room', Feek says.

'I heard this creaking noise and didn't know what it was, so I got up to investigate, and there he was fast asleep on the toilet again!'

Such incidents didn't detract from Feek's maiden tour with a side that was to become a major part of his life. The former Taranaki prop, of the lower Eastern North Island's Te Atiawa iwi, featured in every other New Zealand Maori team that Matt coached, apart from in 1999, when Feek was unavailable because of his elevation into the All Blacks.

'It was an awesome tour, with some great guys', Feek says.

"I was just a young fella then. I'd only had my introduction to Super 12 earlier that year, first as a replacement for the Blues, and then with the Crusaders. The attitude of the players on that tour was excellent. They went hard out on the field, but enjoyed each other's company off it. As a rookie, I didn't say too much to start with, but you quickly learnt that you had to stick up for yourself because everyone was trying to 'jerk' you in some way or another – the constant banter between all of the players was hilarious.'

This included battles between room-mates, with Mike Stewart recalling that flankers Troy Flavell and Glenn Marsh proved to be the oddest couple of the tour.

'One, Glenn, was an absolute perfectionist. Everything on his side of the room was neat and tidy and totally in order. The other, Flav, was a total mess. His gear was everywhere, and would have been spread right through the room had Glenn allowed it. So they weren't an especially compatible pair, but that's all part of the touring experience – you get by the best you can. In the end, with those two, though, we just about had to draw a line down the middle of the hotel room to keep them apart!'

Stewart also remembers the team's first session, on the morning after it had arrived in Scotland, being a blemish on their otherwise excellent record on the training field.

'Most of the boys had hit Edinburgh's Grassmarket the night before. The management were quite happy to let them blow out a few cobwebs and have a bit of fun before we all got down to work', Stewart says.

'They all had a pretty good time, but we paid for it the next day. I don't recall the ball getting past the first-five once in the whole session, before it was dropped. The only gain from that training was a good blow out!'

If the first session had been sloppy, the team quickly got down to the serious business of preparing to win its three matches.

Being in Scotland also provided another focus.

The itinerary took the side close to the Scottish village of Dunblane where, two years earlier, tragedy had struck when an unemployed man had gone berserk with a rifle at the local school. Sixteen primary school children were killed, along with their teacher, before the gunman, Thomas Hamilton, had turned the gun on himself.

> *The players were aware of the history. It brought out the wairua [spiritual nature] of the team, in that the players decided they should pay their respects to the fallen by visiting the cemetery.*
>
> *The back seat [senior players] made the call that we should take the time out from our schedule, and I was happy to go along with it. As a result, we held a karakia [prayer] at Dunblane Cemetery.*
>
> *While we were at the cemetery, and in the area that had been specified for the burial of the victims from the massacre, one of the players noticed a small black and white sign erected among the flowers which said 'Matata'. That is a village not far from where I live. Seeing that was quite eerie, but it certainly gave us all the feeling that our impromptu visit to the burial place had been meant to be.*

On the playing field, the New Zealand Maori team's first assignment was Edinburgh, one of Scotland's two professional regional teams that played in European competition. The game was played at Hawick just out of Edinburgh, where the team was hosted the night before at the same club that had hosted the 1888 Natives side, the first-ever touring side from New Zealand.

> *It was a great night, but the Scots were probably a little too hospitable as hosts and told us a bit too much of the history.*
>
> *I could see, as their historian was talking, that the players were all taking everything he said on board. And there were a few frowns on player's faces when he told them about how the Maori wing had been floored by the Scottish fullback after he'd got a try, because he'd waved goodbye to the Scot as he'd rounded him to score. His action was seen as unsporting by the Scots, our host had said, but I could almost see what our guys were thinking as he told us this story. I knew that I suddenly had some great ammunition to fire up the boys with before the next day's game.*
>
> *Sure enough, on the bus back to our hotel, all the players were talking about how the Scots had dealt to one of our old fellas and how they were going to make them pay for that. Needless to say, I brought that story up again briefly the next day while I was delivering them my pre-match team talk!*

The sermon had the desired effect.

While Edinburgh wasn't one of the strongest teams in Europe, they were made to look second rate as the New Zealand Maori side cut loose to romp to a 69–3 victory, bagging 11 tries in the process. Two were scored by Berryman, and two by Feek on his New Zealand Maori debut, while Reihana also marked his first game in the jersey by scoring a try.

> *While they were quite strong in the set piece, which we'd expected, we found that the Scots couldn't live with us when we started to biff the ball around. The skill set of our players was vastly superior, which gave us a lot of confidence looking ahead to the Test match.*

Among the supporters who had travelled over from New Zealand was the well-known kaumatua and minister Bob Schuster. Once Matt became aware of his presence in Scotland, he asked if Schuster could address the side prior to the Test.

> *That was quite special. Bob is a man of high standing in Maori society, so it was great to be able to get him, and the people he was travelling with, involved. They came as a group from Hawick, where they were*

staying, and joined the team in a karakia in our team room, which Bob conducted, prior to the match. During the karakia, Bob blessed all of the new Test jerseys as they were handed out to each of the players.

Unusually, the Test against Scotland was the middle match of the itinerary.

But, as impressive as the tourists had been in their opening match, the veteran Scottish coach Jim Telfer still felt that his side could win.

Telfer, who'd coached the British Lions in New Zealand in 1983 and had played for the Lions against the New Zealand Maori in 1966, had a warm regard for Maori rugby, although he admits that Matt's side surprised him.

'We knew we would be in trouble if their backs got too much ball, but we were quite confident beforehand that we might be able to hold an edge over them up front', Telfer says.

'Unfortunately, that thought turned out to be a bit misguided. While we were disappointed afterwards that we hadn't played so well, part of the reason for that was the physicality of the Maori pack. That came through as much as it does when you play the All Blacks, the difference being that you expect it against the All Blacks. We hadn't expected the Maori to be at that same level.'

We felt we'd done our preparation well in the lead up to that match. We'd had longer together than we usually had, and had selected a strong forward pack with a lot of experienced heads, because we figured that was the area where the Scots would try to attack us. The idea was that if we could match their set piece and bustle them at every opportunity, the class of our backs would give us the edge.

The plan worked almost perfectly.

After absorbing plenty of Scottish pressure in the first half, where Matt later felt his side had been guilty of trying to do too much with the ball too soon, the New Zealand Maori side gradually gained the upper hand in the second half, to draw out to a 24–8 win. The losing margin would have been even greater for the Scots had their fullback Derrick Lee not scored the only try the Maori conceded on the tour, in the final minute of play. The tourists scored two tries at Murrayfield, by fullback Adrian Cashmore and the flanker Marsh, with Matt saying the latter showed against Scotland that he would have been worthy had he ever been bestowed with full international honours.

His twin brother Tony, who we'd had with us earlier in the year but who had missed out on the tour because he'd headed off overseas, went on to play Test rugby for France. With a bit more luck, Glenn could easily have been a Test player too, because he was definitely good enough. He was one of the outstanding players of the tour; it was just his misfortune that the All Blacks had a player as good as Josh Kronfeld was, playing in the position at that time.

Even so, I was disappointed for Glenn that he was never given the opportunity. After the way he'd played against Scotland, if he'd been available for them, I'm sure they would have picked him!

While the Counties Manukau man was industrious throughout, the Scottish coach was bedazzled by the quality of the Maori team's back play in difficult conditions, with a wet ground and slippery ball.

'The quality of their back play was quite brilliant at times. It would have been a delight to watch if I hadn't been the opposition coach', Telfer says.

'Norm Berryman, in particular, was a menace. We couldn't hold him when he played against us for Northland on our 1996 tour, and he did the same job on us again. Their back three caused us a lot of problems right through the game.'

Although Berryman broke Scottish tackles just about at will, he also caused angst among his own team-mates, often ignoring supporting players in order to continue on himself.

'I was on the outside of him a couple of times after breaks, and I'm still waiting for the pass!' Ralph, who played centre against Scotland, says.

'It was like the ball was stuck to his hands … he just didn't want to let go of it.'

Despite failing to score himself, Ralph says the outing at Murrayfield meant more to him, on a personal level, than his Test debut for the All Blacks against England at Eden Park had, earlier in the year.

'It [his All Black debut] was just so rushed. Before we played England, I'd only had a handful of games at the top level and, suddenly, I was there. It all happened so fast, it was hard to take in', Ralph says.

'With the Maoris, I'd been in the team for two years, knew all the players I was playing with a lot better, and felt much more a part of the team. Because of that, playing a big match at a famous stadium like Murrayfield just meant that little bit more to me personally.'

On the other wing, Reihana also remembers supporting Berryman's breaks, only to have the last pass not arrive when a try seemed inevitable.

'They were the best tries I've never scored', he jokes.

'Normy just carved them up. A couple of times he beat four or five tacklers on his own, but then sold the big dummy and got taken to ground when we were all lining up outside of him!'

A try might not have materialised, but Reihana will never forget the thrill he felt performing the haka at Murrayfield.

'It was magic. Everybody was so pumped. I just knew that we were going to play well.'

'A lot of us felt that we had a lot to prove in that game', Daryl Gibson says.

'Because the All Blacks hadn't gone so well that year, we all knew that there was a lot at stake personally, as well as for the team, playing on such a big stage. That showed, both in the way the team played, but also in how many of the guys went on from that game to bigger things.'

Gibson was one of them. He was among six members of the victorious Maori side who returned to Edinburgh 12 months later as members of the All Black side that beat Scotland 30–18 in a hard-fought Rugby World Cup quarter-final.

Ironically, Gibson's substitution during the New Zealand Maori team's win remains one of Matt's biggest coaching mistakes.

> *Daryl was having a stormer against the Scots, and then I took him off and sent Leon MacDonald on. I still don't know why I did that. He played his way into the All Blacks for the next year that day, and I did him a great disservice by replacing him. When a guy is playing well like he was, you leave him out there. You don't tinker with something if it isn't broken! Looking back, I suspect my action was predetermined. That we'd always planned to send Leon out there for Daryl at some stage. If that was the case, we got it badly wrong on both counts. Not only did we pull a player off that we should have left on the field, but Leon ended up getting injured quite badly.*

Shortly after taking the field, MacDonald went down in a heap. His injury was part of a bizarre finish to the game, which saw the Maori medical team working overtime as MacDonald, Flavell (medial ligament strain) and Ron Cribb (broken thumb) all required attention. Of the trio, MacDonald's damage was by far the most significant.

'By the time I got out to him, he was in quite considerable pain, but, being the brave guy that he is, he refused a stretcher and limped off the field', Stewart recalls.

'That was typical of Leon, but it turned out that he was pretty crook. He'd ruptured his spleen, so he ended up in the local hospital and couldn't head home with the rest of the team once the tour was over.'

The then 20-year-old was forced to convalesce in Scotland for a couple of additional weeks before he was deemed fit enough for the flight home.

As for the Scots, they licked their wounds and learned from the experience, putting up a brave fight against the All Blacks, in what was Telfer's last match as coach, a year later during the World Cup. Featuring 14 of the same players who'd lost to the New Zealand Maori side, the Scots out-scored the All Blacks 15–5 in the second half of that match, losing the tournament quarter-final 18–30.

'The Maori team proved to me when they were at Murrayfield that they were as good as any international side – and they proved it again seven years later when they beat the Lions', Telfer says.

'I always found them to be lovely people off the field … but not so friendly on it!'

The Scots were also so impressed with Berryman's performance that they tried to lure him across to play for their newly created third professional team, Borders, in 2002.

> The Scots were generous in their praise of us after the match, and I'm sure that it was genuine, but we could also see that the outcome had rocked them a bit. They were hurting, and so were pretty quiet. I think both sides probably realised that the score had flattered them a little bit. Our guys had got a bit excited, and weren't quite as clinical as we might have been. That was probably just as well for the Scots, but it also gave me something to work with as we looked ahead to our third game on tour.

Prior to the third game, however, was the post-Test feast; a tradition that had been built up in Maori teams and that was looked forward to by the players. Although there was food on offer during the official after-match function at Murrayfield, few of the Maori players indulged, preferring, instead, to save the room in their stomachs for the team meal that was to follow.

> It must have been quite disconcerting for our hosts to have a formal dinner and not have the visiting players eat much at all. If only they had known what was to come.
>
> Under the direction of Mike Stewart's strictly balanced diet regime, which the players referred to as 'cow food', the real kai had been organised for the hakari [feast]. The hakari consisted of one pig, 20 boxes of watercress, three bags of pumpkin and kumara, eight bags of riwai [potatoes], heaps of paraoa parai [fried bread] and dough boys [boiled dumplings] ... we had the whole works!
>
> The players reckoned it was the biggest boil up in Europe. They were certainly in seventh heaven, having previously sung at the after-match for their supper, although we got some strange looks from our hosts.
>
> One of the Scottish waiters had wondered openly what the steroids were that the Maori team was on. When the boil up arrived in the wharekai [restaurant] we were at, it certainly hit him in the nose! I also heard one of his female colleagues comment later that she'd never seen grown men devour so much food before!

Having another match to play after the Test, against the Glasgow Caledonians at Perthshire, represented a difficult challenge for the tourists, but one that Matt responded to in an unorthodox way.

> There were four days between the Test and the final game. The challenge was to keep the guys from going off tour, from loosening up in that time and losing their focus. We still had a job to do, and could have undone all the previous good work from the year if we'd dropped that last game. To get around that, I called everyone into the team room a couple of nights before the game and related a story to the players based around my army experience.
>
> I told them that the situation we were in was a bit like being in the military, when you go out on patrol into enemy territory. At the start, everyone is hyped up and on edge. It is only towards the end of the patrol, once you are heading home again that people start to relax. I told them that was the most dangerous time, the time when mistakes were often made, the time when a patrol often took its casualties. I then told them

> that wasn't going to happen to us, that we weren't going to slip up. To make sure it didn't happen, we were going tight!

As open-mouthed hotel staff watched on, mattresses from the player's beds were transferred onto the floor of the team room.

'Matt commanded that all of the chairs and everything else went from the room, and the mattresses went in there, instead. That room became our marae', Cashmore says.

'I don't think the hotel staff could believe it, but the boys all loved it. They couldn't get in there soon enough!'

'It was a clever way to keep everybody focused on the job at hand', Gibson says.

'While we liked to think that we were as professional as the All Blacks were, our environment off the field was never that intense. We didn't carry the pressure of public expectation that the All Blacks did, especially in Scotland, playing against a provincial team. That game could easily have been a danger one for us, but Matt made sure that everyone knew what was expected of them.'

'It just seemed so natural in that team', Reihana says.

'The Scots must have thought we were crazy, but most of the guys spent almost all of their time in the team room once it was set up like a marae with our mattresses everywhere. Boys were just kicking back, relaxing, watching videos or enjoying each other's company. It was certainly a very different way to prepare for a match, but probably an appropriate one, given the family-type atmosphere that had developed within the team.'

> The key thing it did was bring everyone back to earth after the hype of beating Scotland, and the feeling that the mission had already been accomplished. By the time kick off came around, the players were all fizzing again, and we ended up smashing them!

Although the Glasgow side scored more points against the tourists than had been conceded in the first two matches combined, they were still held try-less, losing 53–15, while the New Zealand Maori side added another six tries to their tally for the tour – taking the haul from the tour's three matches to 19.

> It was a pleasing way to finish, playing the attacking style of rugby that we'd endeavoured to maintain from the start. It was also good, from my

point of view, to have had All Black selector Gordon Hunter along with us throughout the tour. Because he was with us, he was able to see for himself how professional the players had been in terms of their attitude to the job we had, as well as seeing how well they had played. The benefits of that probably showed the following year, when six of the players who came away with us went on to make it into the All Blacks Rugby World Cup squad.

Matt might have returned home a happy man wearing his coaching hat, but there was another outcome from the tour that wasn't quite so successful. Aside from coaching the side to victory, another of the tasks Matt had been set for the tour had been given to him by his uncle Sonny. Sonny wanted Matt to check out their Scottish roots from the Cadman side of his family and return home with some Cadman tartan.

When news of Matt's quest spread, a number of the players also took it upon themselves to investigate their Scottish ancestry. This resulted in a good portion of the squad returning to New Zealand with additional baggage in the form of their clan's kilt, while a dozen of the players posed for a photo in the Scottish media wearing the kilts of their ancestors – which prompted the local press to dub them the 'McMaoris'!

Sadly, Matt was not among them.

Sometimes it can be dangerous to do too much digging. You might not like what you find! After a fair bit of running around from our local Scottish liaison man, who was well connected in terms of those sort of things, we were able to establish that the Cadman side of my family tree was actually English, not Scottish! That wasn't greeted as good news when I got home. Most of the family are in denial and still reckon I got it wrong!

11

The 1988 New Zealand Maori World Tour

'Planes, trains and slaves'

The New Zealand Maori side's three-match expedition to Scotland in 1998 was a novelty to most involved, but not to tour manager Mattie Blackburn.

Blackburn had been the Maori coach a decade earlier in 1988, when a 27-man squad had made an exotic 11-match voyage of discovery through France, Italy, Spain and Argentina.

The squad chosen for that tour was a powerful one, with 13 of the tourists either past, present or future All Blacks. The strength showed in the New Zealand Maori team's results, with nine of the 11 matches won, while another was drawn.

It was, Blackburn says, a remarkable journey, quite unlike any other undertaken by a New Zealand representative team in the modern era of the game.

'The thing I remember most about that tour is the tremendous camaraderie we had amongst our group', Blackburn says.

'The spirit was excellent; we played some great rugby, enjoyed ourselves and forged friendships that will last a lifetime. We also showcased Maori and New Zealand rugby to different parts of the world, from the regions that players would normally get to tour to.'

The tight bond between the players was perhaps enhanced by Blackburn's open selection policy.

'We never had a First XV on that trip', he says proudly.

'All the players knew that if they missed out on one game, they'd play in the next. Everybody was in the number one team!'

In many ways, the tour represented an oasis in the middle of what had been a desert of major fixtures for the New Zealand Maori team.

Prior to the invitation, which was issued by the French Rugby Federation, New Zealand Maori had not featured in a plum game since its 1982 tour of Wales.

Once the tour concluded, the side didn't play on a major stage again until it met the British & Irish Lions in 1993.

'The schedule was a tough one – with 11 games in just five weeks, spread across four countries – but it was a lifeline for the Maori team', Blackburn says.

'The French met all our costs for the bulk of the trip, and got us to call in on their fellow Latin nations, Italy, Spain and Argentina while we were on the road.'

Interestingly, no New Zealand national men's side has played in Spain since the Maori visit in 1988 to help further that country's development in the game, even though the Spanish have since participated at the 1999 Rugby World Cup.

In a situation that was to reoccur 11 years later in Fiji, when Blackburn was team manager, the venture was dogged from the outset by a row over player payments. This occurred because the New Zealand Rugby Union refused to pay the accepted International Rugby Board daily allowance rates to the Maori players, because the side wasn't the country's first-choice team.

'It was left to our manager, Keith Pearson, to sort out, because he was the Maori representative on the [NZRU] Council at that time', Blackburn recalls.

'The Rugby Union got a bit of stick for its stance on that issue, especially in the press, but we were just happy to be going on the tour.'

If the wrangling with the NZRU over money had impacted on the side before it departed, further financial issues were waiting during its first stop, in Italy, for a game against an Italian Barbarians side loaded with overseas internationals.

Although the New Zealand Maori side overpowered the Barbarians comfortably, running out 57–9 winners against an opposition that included Springbok first-five-eighths Naas Botha and All Black winger Craig Green, amongst others, the game nearly didn't take place.

'We got hit with a US$1,500 laundry bill at our accommodation in L'Aquila, and our local liaison man just happened to go missing in action around that time', Blackburn recalls.

'Keith was just going to pay the bill, but the rest of us all felt that the money he was going to use to buy the Italians off could be better spent on the team. The bill wasn't our responsibility – it was the host union's – so I got together with some of the senior players, along with my assistant coach Bill Bush [who was fluent in Italian], and we decided that we weren't going to pay it.'

Predictably, this stance created a fuss with the locals, who at first insisted that the team must pay the bill, until the stakes were upped when the New Zealand Maori side threatened to refuse to play the game against the Barbarians unless the financial arrangements were sorted out.

'It was funny how quickly the Italians suddenly found some money, and the bill was paid, once they realised that we were serious and that the game was in jeopardy', Blackburn says.

'I was very fortunate on that tour to have senior people like our tour skipper Buck Shelford, and my assistant coach Billy, who knew what they were about in terms of dealing with some of the peripheral issues that we had.'

Shelford, who was All Black captain at the time, earned notoriety during the New Zealand Maori team's 10–10 draw with a Pyrenees' Selection in France, after taking his players to the side of the field while an interpreter was summoned to communicate with the local referee, who allegedly spoke no English.

The incident, when reported back in New Zealand, caused a huge uproar, although Blackburn insists that the story grew legs of its own.

'They did meet on the sideline, but that was only because the players were having difficulty understanding the referee, and we wanted our liaison guy to talk to him', Blackburn says.

'There was certainly nothing untoward going on, as was later reported in the press. There was definitely no suggestion at any stage of the team walking off the field, as was also rather mischievously reported later on!'

'The referee caused that problem', Eric Rush, who played in the game, recalls.

'He wouldn't speak to Buck during the game, but we knew he could speak English, and Buck could speak French, so he didn't really have an excuse for trying to ignore us.'

Allegations of referee bias were also sparked during the match that the New Zealand Maori side lost, 25–31 to a Languedoc Selection in Narbonne.

'We didn't play that well, but the refereeing that day was shocking', Rush says.

'It was so bad, even the local French players said they were embarrassed about it when they spoke to us afterwards!'

The difficulties the touring team encountered with the local match officials followed on from their brutal introduction to the six-game French leg of the tour at the Mediterranean sea port of Toulon.

Although the New Zealand Maori side achieved a victory, 22–9, which was something the All Blacks could not do when they visited the city two years later, the game was marred by the ejection of three players, including New Zealand Maori prop Arthur McLean.

'The French flankers, Alain Carminati and Eric Champ, were really going after us in that game', Rush recalls

'Buck kept saying to us: "Play rugby and we'll beat these guys", but then our prop, Chris Kapene, got kicked in the head and was knocked out cold. And the ball had been on our side of the ruck when it happened. While they were carrying Chris off, the rest of us got together in a huddle and Buck laid down the law. He said: "From this penalty, we are going to kick it out, we're going to have the lineout, and there's going to be a fight!" He also left us with no illusions that we all had to support our mates. In other words, no one was to stay out of it!'

As it happened, the lineout didn't even take place before the 'action' started, with Zinzan Brooke launching a pre-emptive strike by whacking the chief French perpetrator of the trouble, Carminati.

'Zinny belted him good and proper, and then it was all on, everyone was in', Rush remembers.

'Even little Frano Botica, our first-five, was in there getting a hiding! I guess that just shows how scared he was of Buck that he'd rather have taken his chances with the French!'

Once normality was restored following the big 'stink', the three players were sent from the field, and New Zealand Maori went on to take out the match. However, it was not to be the worst of the fighting that marred the tour.

That came against the Argentinian club champions Tucuman, who were later banned from playing against international touring teams as a result of the violence that consistently blighted their matches.

'Before we played them, they told us they'd beaten Australia, England and everybody else in Argentina, so we knew we were in for a big game', Rush says.

'When we ran out of the tunnel prior to the game, the place was pretty quiet and didn't seem too hostile so we all thought: "This isn't too bad, what is all the fuss about?" We soon found out why they had their reputation!'

When the Tucuman team took the field, Rush says, the crowd went 'nuts', highlighting to the tourists the reason why the ground was ringed by tree-high fencing and a moat around the arena, which prevented the patrons from attempting to invade the field.

'Once the crowd starting going off, Buck pulled us all together and said we had to stand up and be counted', Rush says.

'From that point on, we were probably on a count-down to the trouble that occurred, because we knew that we couldn't afford to take a backward step.'

The locals didn't disappoint.

Rush recalls that the dirty tactics employed by the Tucuman players started from the opening whistle, resulting in ongoing brawls that eventually saw All Black prop Steve McDowell and one of his Argentine counterparts ordered off.

'I was so engrossed in the game, I didn't even see Steve get sent off', Blackburn says.

'It was a pretty rugged game. It was only once he sat down beside me, and I asked him what he was doing, that I discovered he'd been sent from the field.'

McDowell might have departed, but it didn't stop the trouble, with Rush suggesting that the locals had badly misread their opposition.

'I don't think those guys [the Argentines] quite appreciated beforehand that we could handle ourselves', Rush says.

'We were winning the fights and the game. That probably stirred them up even more! To give them their dues though, once the crowd started throwing bottles at us over the fence when the game was stopped, the

Tucuman guys settled down very quickly and surrounded us, forming a defensive shield while calling on the crowd to stop.'

Even the Tucuman players could not prevent one member of the crowd from venting his anger directly on a Maori player, after the referee chose to bring the game to an end 10 minutes early, with the New Zealand Maori leading 12–3.

As he walked from the field, Otago prop Steve Hotton was attacked by a patron who was vigorously wielding an umbrella.

'The attack came from behind him, so Steve couldn't see who it was', Rush says.

'He just turned around, threw a punch and decked the guy! It turned out that it was quite an old fella.'

Counties fullback Lindsay Raki, who proved himself one of the real characters of the tour, was one of the last players to leave the field at Tucuman. Raki didn't endear himself to the locals when he gave them the time-honoured two-fingered salute as he departed.

'Here we were, absolutely shitting ourselves, with the crowd going wild, and he was giving them the fingers', Rush says.

'Mind you, his actions caught on. The local police chief told us we'd have a full police escort back to our hotel, but as we pulled past the hotel where all of the Tucuman fans were congregating after the match, just about the whole team was over that side of the bus giving the locals the 'bird'. The old police chief just about had a heart attack!'

While the tour had featured no official Test, the match against the French Barbarians at Mont-de-Marsan always shaped as the tour's toughest rugby assignment, although Blackburn kept to his word and rotated the side selection. Even skipper Shelford ended up sitting out that match because of injury.

Shelford's non-appearance robbed the game of a match-up between the present and former All Black captains, with the Barbarians being led by 1987 Rugby World Cup-winning New Zealand skipper David Kirk, who was by then UK-based as a Rhodes Scholar.

In Shelford's absence, Zinzan Brooke did a sterling job, scoring two of the New Zealand Maori team's tries during its comprehensive 31–14 win.

Brooke was one of the stars of the whole tour, along with Otago winger John Timu, who Blackburn admits had been the last player selected for the trip.

'When we were sorting out the team, we were agreed on every player bar one, and it came down to Timu and North Harbour winger Richard Kapa. We eventually called it a night at 3.00 am, and decided to reconvene the next morning, but I was pretty sure that one of my co-selectors, Chas Ferris, would opt for Kapa – given that he was also from North Harbour.'

Instead, Ferris, who coached the New Zealand Maori team against the Lions in 1993, went for Timu. The selection proved to be an inspired one; within 12 months, Timu had been whistled up by the All Blacks as a replacement on their tour of Wales and Ireland.

'It was an awesome tour to be involved in', Rush says.

'We had a great group together and we went to so many different places. We also had a great guitar school in the team, led by Bruce Hemara. Just about every second player in the team could play. It was on that trip that I learnt how to handle myself in that area.'

The tour also introduced another aspect to the team environment – a slave culture!

'Raki and Botica started it all', Blackburn recalls.

'They were always having a go at each other. There was plenty of banter. Then, one day, they had a kicking competition at training, which Botica won. The prize was inheriting a 'slave' for the day. That meant that Raki had to do everything that Botica told him to do, making his bed, cleaning his boots and other menial chores like that.'

The 'slave' also became the team's official supplier of bananas.

'We were on the way to our next game and stopped at a café for lunch', Blackburn says.

'Botica decided that he wanted a banana, but the café didn't stock them so he summoned his 'slave' and told him to go and get some. It turned out that the nearest supply of bananas was at a shop about a kilometre away, so off Raki went. He got one back on his 'master', though, by returning with a whole box of bananas, which Botica had paid for. It kept the team in bananas for the next three days!'

Rush also remembers Raki's performance as a slave with the bananas.

'He kept saying: "Nothing's too good for my master!"'

Not that Rush had much to laugh about, as he too found himself a slave for a day, after losing a ten-pin bowling shoot-out with 1987 All Black winger Paul Simonsson.

'I had one pin to hit with my last ball, but started showing off too early and put my ball in the gutter', Rush recalls remorsefully.

'Boy did he make me pay. He caned me! I had to carry him everywhere piggy back, take all of his bags, because we moved hotels. Then I had to tidy his bed and read his book to him that night.'

It was one of just two disappointments Rush had on a trip that was, in every other respect, the experience of a lifetime.

'We'd been having a try-scoring competition right through the tour', Rush says.

'And I was leading it, along with Auckland halfback Brett Iti, until we got to Rosario in Argentina for our second-to-last game of the tour. We won 88–12 and Brett got six tries. That well and truly blew me away!'

12

On the back burner: 1999–2000

'New stars for a new century!'

Matt Te Pou might have been the assistant coach of the Chiefs for 1998 but, by then, his name was synonymous with Maori rugby, even amongst the players.

So much so that it was through his association with Matt in the Chiefs that promising Waikato first-five-eighths Glen Jackson came to appreciate his Maori background.

'I was fairly oblivious to my heritage to start with, but my consciousness of the Maori team grew as a result of having Matt as my Super 12 coach. Then my late grandmother Elaine gave me my whakapapa', Jackson recalls.

'She was dying of cancer at the time, but pointed out to me that I was a member of the Tuhoe tribe. Naturally, I made sure that Matt knew about that. My grandparents were over the moon when I then got selected for the team the following year!'

Having heard so many of the tales that his Waikato and Chiefs teammates had brought back with them from the New Zealand Maori tour of Scotland the previous year, Jackson was delighted to be able to check things out for himself.

His first selection was for the New Zealand Maori side that visited Fiji in 1999.

'The stories the boys told of that trip, and other times with the team, certainly increased the desire to become a part of it', Jackson says.

'But so, too, did the knowledge that it [selection] meant so much to my grandmother. Fortunately, I made it before the cancer eventually claimed her life, because she was really proud of that achievement.'

The New Zealand Maori team's two-match tour of Fiji was undertaken in the shadow of the fourth Rugby World Cup, which was to be played in Europe three months later.

Not only were the Fijians, under the direction of former All Black prop Brad Johnstone, on a countdown to the tournament, so too were the All Blacks, which created its share of difficulties for the New Zealand Maori side.

> *The biggest problem we had was the scheduling, in terms of the fact that the New Zealand A side was playing the Australian Barbarians just before we went away. That created an issue over player usage – in terms of the pecking order for selection.*
>
> *We were already without our All Blacks, who were in the middle of the Tri-Nations, and there were suggestions that we would be denied access to the New Zealand A players as well.*
>
> *That naturally created a bit of friction. Had we allowed it to be the case, we would have been left fielding what would virtually have amounted to a C team, and that wouldn't have honoured the jersey at all!*

The situation was not entirely dissimilar to what would occur in the first year after Matt stepped down as New Zealand Maori coach, when the side was again relegated behind the A side (now known as the Junior All Blacks) in the selection priorities for 2006. But while Matt's successor Donny Stevenson was understandably relatively powerless to prevent such a demotion seven years on, in his first year in the job, Matt had been around the block a few times when he was faced with the problem. As a result, he was able to change All Black coach John Hart's mind with regard to the release of the A players to the New Zealand Maori team.

> *The Rugby World Cup was the main focus of New Zealand rugby for the year. We understood that. Because of the tournament, we had to take a back seat to some extent, and we were happy enough to do that, but we still felt that there was no reason why the A players couldn't be available to strengthen our side. Their programme was finished by the time we went away to Fiji.*
>
> *Fortunately, John accepted our argument – the dialogue we had with him was always fairly good – so we were able to incorporate the A squad players into our side after they'd finished their two-match series with the Australian Barbarians.*

The outcome of Matt's negotiations saw the New Zealand Maori side's nine A team representatives – Bruce Reihana, Glen Osborne, Caleb Ralph, Norman Berryman, Rhys Duggan, Troy Flavell, Paul Thomson, Norm Hewitt and Slade McFarland – bus to Auckland from Whangarei following the A side's 40–17 win over the Barbarians, in order to depart with the rest of the Maori side for Fiji.

It was a sensible outcome. It created a few logistical issues for us in terms of our preparation, in that we had to start getting ready for our first game of the tour without having the whole team together, but we were prepared to accept that difficulty in order to be able to field the strongest possible side.

We tried to avoid playing the A guys in our first game over there, although it was inevitable in some cases – both of the A team's hookers were in our party, for example. As it turned out, all of those players contributed hugely to the success of the tour, with three of them ending up making it into the All Blacks' World Cup squad.

The selection debate was one of two issues that dogged the New Zealand Maori side during its Fiji tour. The second controversy was sparked by the relative paucity of the payments that were being made to the Maori players by the New Zealand Rugby Union while the team was assembled. Whereas the New Zealand A players had been earning $1,500 per seven days while carrying out their duties as part of that national team the week before, the Maori players were being offered a token $60 a day in expenses.

The players were only being given amateur rates, and they dug their toes in. I could understand where they were coming from, especially when compared with what some of the same guys had been earning the week before with New Zealand A.

As an officer of the union, and the team coach, however, it was clear what my role was; my job was to prepare the team to win our two games. While I had sympathy with the stance the players were taking, it was not for me to decide what they should or shouldn't be paid.

'The crux of the matter was that, as professional players, we felt that we were being treated unfairly', Bruce Reihana recalls.

'It did seem a bit silly, that you could be earning an amount playing for one national team, and then be earning a mere pittance a week later playing for another. For us, the whole issue was as much about the principle as anything else. The boys resented the fact that the Rugby Union, by its action, was effectively trying to treat the Maori team as second class.'

Slade McFarland recalls that the players presented a united front.

Well, almost so.

'Norm [Hewitt], as captain for that tour, was our spokesman, but we were all behind him', McFarland says.

'Well, at least we thought we all were. The boys had agreed in a team meeting not to accept the Rugby Union's original offer. It was only later that we found out one player in the team had! That news didn't go down well. As a result, a few of the boys made it their business to touch that guy up for selling his brothers out, the next time their provinces played his!'

While the issue was left to the New Zealand Rugby Union's Maori board member, Tom Mulligan, to resolve (and was later settled to the satisfaction of all parties), the squabble over money left a big impression with the players.

'The senior players led the opposition to what was going on, but it was important that we all stood our ground', Jackson says.

'In a way, it was no different to other issues that have happened since between players and the officials, especially when it comes to money. If you let them, the administrators will run all over you. All we were arguing was that we should be treated properly.'

If the national governing body had aroused the team's ire, their humour wasn't improved when they arrived in Lautoka for their lead-up match against the Fiji Warriors (Fiji's Second XV) to find that they needed to clear the field of glass and nails before they could train.

'It certainly had the feel of being second-class citizens about it', Mike Stewart says, 'especially given everything else that had been going on in the background. By the time we had been up and down the number two field at Lautoka, we'd picked up about two buckets full of stuff!'

Prior to the assembly of the full squad, Matt had formed a Maori Invitation XV consisting of the non-New Zealand A players, to play a shake down match against a Harlequins XV at Hamilton. The game was played as the curtain raiser to Waikato's successful Ranfurly Shield defence against Wairarapa-Bush, which had also featured a number of Maori tourists.

The Maori Invitation XV had won 76–5, but it quickly became clear that the Fiji Warriors would not prove such an easy pushover.

On the back burner: 1999–2000

After leading 20–0 at halftime on a wet field that closely resembled a bog, New Zealand Maori was held scoreless in the second period as the Fiji Warriors scored two unconverted tries to close to a 10–20 final score.

The money thing was a distraction that we could have done without, but the Fiji Warriors did us a favour before the Test by the way they came at us. Their performance certainly underlined to the players the severity of the challenge that was ahead of us playing Fiji, especially as the Fijians were all effectively playing for places at the World Cup.

I decided to use the players' anger over the allowances that they were being offered to my advantage by telling Norm that it was absolutely imperative that we beat Fiji if they were to prove their point.

The players responded in emphatic fashion.

Despite the concession of 10 early points in front of an excited crowd of 14,000 Fijians (who'd taken time off on a Tuesday afternoon in order to attend the match), the New Zealand Maori team quickly recovered its poise to run out eventual 57–20 winners.

Making light of the soggy conditions, the side ended up out-scoring their hosts by seven tries to three. Hewitt, who by then had been publicly tagged by the media back in New Zealand as the ring leader in the player revolt, made a major individual statement by grabbing three of the visitor's tries. Jackson, showing few nerves in what was his international debut, played like he had the ball on a string all afternoon, with his goal kicking relentless as he collected 22 points.

Jacko arrived as a player of top quality that day. He'd always suggested that he had the potential to be an international player, but he really stepped up against the Fijians.

We were under the hammer early, with Waisale Serevi on fire for them and showing the genius that made him such a great sevens player, but Jacko was probably even more dominant for us once the game developed and we got ourselves on the front foot. He controlled the game tactically with his boot, kept the ball in front of our forwards and literally shut them out of the contest.

Such was the level of his accuracy, his cross-kick for Norm's third try was as good as you will ever get. It literally landed right in the bread basket. All Norm had to do was catch it and fall over the goal-line for the try.

> Jacko could have, and probably should have, been an All Black at some stage in his career. It was a pity for the New Zealand game when he was lost to English club rugby, because there was still a lot that he could have contributed back here. The game in this country can't afford to keep losing players like him, who are potential internationals, but also contribute hugely at the next level down from that.

'It was a bit of a dream debut', Jackson, who is now based with London club Saracens, recalls.

'A few things went the right way for me early on, and it just sort of went from there. I remember with that cross kick, Norm reached out and grabbed the ball with just one hand to score ... it was that sort of day.'

Not that the Fijians surrendered without a fight.

'There was quite a bit of tension early on', Jackson reports.

'A lot of their players had played in New Zealand, so we knew them pretty well. Scooter, their captain [Waikato hooker Greg Smith], was a team-mate for some of us back home, but that didn't stop him and Ratty [New Zealand Maori halfback Rhys Duggan] having a huge scrap after Scooter had deliberately dropped his knees onto Ratty's back during a tackle. A lot of us had a good laugh later about how Ratty had changed direction on the field to go after Scooter. I think he came off the best out of the brawl too.'

The altercation between the two Waikato provincial team-mates continued a stand off between the teams that had started when Fiji's New Zealand-based back, Nicky Little, had challenged the haka by replying in Maori.

> Because a lot of the people that run the game in New Zealand never get up to the islands, they don't probably appreciate how difficult it can be playing there. The All Blacks haven't been to Fiji since 1984, and that's a huge shame because it is a great experience for the players. It also provides a much tougher level of competition than you get playing the island teams in New Zealand. You only have to look at the results, like our close game in Fiji two years ago [2005], which was followed by their 91–0 hiding from the All Blacks in Auckland a week later, to see that.

'Everyone was pretty hyped up. It was a huge game, as every game against New Zealand opposition is, for us', Johnstone says.

'The New Zealand Maori team is held in high regard in Fiji, and that particular side was an awesome one ... they were all Super 12 players that most of our people had only previously seen before on television.'

Because of its close association with the Pacific Islands teams, having been the first overseas international side to visit Fiji on a tour in 1938 and a consistent visitor since, Johnstone says the New Zealand Maori side is admired and appreciated by Fijians.

'There's only one All Black team, and Fijians are probably as fanatical in their support of the All Blacks as New Zealanders are, but there's huge respect and warmth in their attitude towards the New Zealand Maori too', Johnstone says.

'The Maori team has done a lot for rugby in Fiji, in terms of the regular contact over the years, and Fijians appreciate both that fact, and the style of rugby that the team plays. When the Maori side is up, there's not a team in the world that can hold them back. They can be a bit of an enigma, though, and in that way are a bit similar to the Fijians themselves.'

Ironically, it was in the forward battle that the New Zealand Maori team ultimately crushed the will and resistance of Johnstone's side, which was unusual, given the attacking flair both sides possessed.

'The conditions, which were wet, dictated the way the game was played, and they were just too skilled for us up front where it mattered. They pretty much blew us away', Johnstone says.

'But that, in a way, was a good awakening for some of our forwards ahead of the World Cup, in terms of the manner in which we were shown up. Everyone here in Fiji thinks it's marvellous to be able to run around with the ball in their hand, but when it comes to shunting in a scrum, or showing their commitment in the bottom of a ruck or maul, it's often a different situation. I've never read in a newspaper here how wonderful a prop is at scrumming, or how marvellous a lock is at ripping the ball out of a maul, yet those are both important fundamentals of the game.'

The set piece was an area of the Fijian game that the tourists had targeted.

'We got up there to find that [Counties Manukau flanker] Api Naevo was talking it up in the local newspaper about how they would handle us up front', New Zealand Maori assistant coach Jim Love says.

'Naturally, I made sure that the players were aware of Api's comments. We made it our business to ram those confident words back down his throat!'

The Fijian forwards might have been comprehensively dismantled by New Zealand Maori, but Johnstone says the match provided major long-term benefits.

The Fijians went on to beat Canada and Namibia at the 1999 World Cup, and would almost certainly have beaten France in a major upset as well, were it not for a controversial refereeing call by New Zealand official Paddy O'Brien during a game the Fijians eventually lost 19–28.

That game had huge repercussions for the tournament, and New Zealand rugby as a whole, given that France later beat the All Blacks in a match that probably wouldn't have occurred had the Fijians not been denied.

Fiji later bowed out of that tournament short of the quarter-finals when it lost a repechage match 21–44 at Twickenham. However, the physical nature of that contest took its toll on the victors too, with England subsequently losing to South Africa in its World Cup quarter-final four days later.

'The World Cup had been our focus for the whole year, and the Maori game was the toughest one we played before it', Johnstone says.

'So it proved to be valuable that we were shown up so badly by their forwards. It certainly told my forwards that they had to work a lot harder, which they did. As a result, we were doing 50 scrums a training session after that, which would have been unheard of beforehand. The Maoris showed my guys in a fairly dramatic manner that you've got to be able to win the ball before you can use it!'

As part of his own trip to the World Cup to watch his son Matthew play for Tonga, Matt was at Twickenham in London when the All Blacks beat England 30–16 in a titanic contest that sparked controversy in New Zealand afterwards; not because of the manner of the All Black performance, but more because the pre-match New Zealand national anthem had been sung in Maori.

While I was obviously in England, and so missed most of it, I later learned that there had been a huge debate back in New Zealand as to the merits of the national anthem being sung in Maori. That's one of the funny things about change. People can resist things at the time, but later on it can become second nature. A year later, no one had any problem with the anthem being sung in a Maori verse then the English one. Now we're all singing it!

The linguistic debate with regard to the anthem quickly became a memory.

In rugby terms, however, the world changed totally for New Zealanders at the same venue, 22 days after the England pool match, when the All Blacks were upended 31–43 in the semi-finals by France.

The shock defeat led to the resignation of Hart as the national coach following the tournament, with Wayne Smith taking over the coaching reins for 2000.

For the New Zealand Maori side, the year following the World Cup proved to be the quietest of Matt's decade-long tenure as coach.

There was just one match on the schedule, but it proved to be a close-run thing as World Cup quarter-finalists Scotland headed to the southern hemisphere, with revenge for the defeat against the New Zealand Maori in 1998 on their agenda.

Despite their beating England 19–13 to deny the auld enemy a first-ever Six Nations Grand Slam in the final outing before heading to New Zealand, the Scots arrived in the country to find their tour prospects scoffed at by the local public and media.

The TAB was so confident that the Test series would be a mismatch, they added further fuel to the public debate by announcing that they would not be taking head-to-head betting on a contest they regarded as a forgone conclusion.

It was a complacent attitude that, returning New Zealand Maori second-five-eighths Mark Mayerhofler says, filtered through to the Maori camp and nearly got the side into big trouble.

'Outwardly, we respected the Scots, but I suppose deep down most of us expected that we'd win pretty easily', Mayerhofler recalls.

'It was probably a fairly easy mistake to make. We had a strong side, while Scotland had been whacked [16–42] by a scratch side that had been thrown together only a couple of days before, when they played an invitation team in Northland the week prior to us playing them.'

Mayerhofler returned to the New Zealand Maori side for the 2000 season, having been absent since the game against Samoa three seasons previously. A hamstring injury had prevented him from making the tour to Scotland at the end of 1998.

'The team was quite different, in terms of some of the faces, from what it had been when I was last there, but off the field it was still the same', Mayerhofler remembers.

'We only got together in New Plymouth a few days before the Scotland game and there was no training kit provided for us. That made the boys wonder whether the Rugby Union was starting to run out of money!'

The issue of the lack of a team kit proved a bonus for Mayerhofler's employer, Canterbury International, because it meant that the side trained initially in Canterbury gear supplied by the local Taranaki Rugby Union, as opposed to the kit of the New Zealand Rugby Union's new official supplier, adidas.

'We trained in the Taranaki NPC jerseys one day, and a photo of us wearing them turned up in the local paper, the *New Plymouth Daily News*, the next day', Mayerhofler says.

'I was like: Sweet! My bosses at Canterbury are going to be stoked. I should claim all of the credit for it and ask for a pay rise!'

Another distraction in the lead up to the match was provided by Matt's decision to try out Reihana at first-five-eighths, the position where he had begun his club career in Te Awamutu.

We felt that 'Bruiser' [Reihana] had all the skills needed to play there, so we thought it was worth a look.

When I contacted Wayne [All Black coach Wayne Smith] and ran it by him, he was happy for us to try it, but emphasised that it was our decision. He did not want to be seen to be interfering with how we ran our team, which was fair enough.

As it was, we started with Jacko at 10 and kept Bruiser on the bench, but it was always our intention to give him a run at first-five at some stage, which we did in the second half. Our backs hadn't been functioning as well as we'd hoped, up until that point, so we felt that injecting Bruiser into the game as the Scots tired a bit might help break it open for us.

For his part, Reihana was happy to return to the position where he had begun his career, before being remodelled into a wing and fullback by his Waikato provincial coach John Boe.

'I'd played there enough to be comfortable in making the change, but it turned out not be the best game to try it again', Reihana says.

'The conditions were quite difficult. The ball was wet and greasy, and the Scots really got stuck into us. In the end, the game was a bit of a lottery, and we were lucky to get out of it.'

Although both teams scored two tries, the game didn't turn out to be the open spectacle the home side had hoped for and they had to dodge two major bullets before prevailing 18–15.

With the scores locked at 15–15, Scotland's first-five-eighths Duncan Hodge missed with a relatively handy penalty attempt. Then, after New Zealand Maori fullback Adrian Cashmore had put his side ahead with a 30-metre goal, Hodge fluffed a dropped goal attempt from close range that would have forced a draw.

'We were probably guilty of being a little naive in the tactical approach we took to that game', New Zealand Maori centre Daryl Gibson says.

'The conditions pretty much demanded a more conservative approach, and that is certainly the way the Scots played it. Tactically, they played it like you would a Test match, but we were still trying to chuck the ball around and score a few thrills, even though the greasiness of it made that next to impossible.'

McFarland believes the expectations that engulfed the side prior to that match contributed to how it unfolded, and the expansive tactics the New Zealand Maori side attempted to employ.

'Everyone expected us to win, and win well. It was just not a situation that we were used to', McFarland says.

'Maybe, subconsciously, we all relaxed too much and thought we could just go out there and play like supermen. I'm not sure. They way we played it, we certainly seemed to think that we could gain the edge without doing all the hard work first – and the game is never like that. In a way, we were almost battling ourselves as much as we were them. Scotland certainly put up a huge fight. I don't think I was ever as relieved after a game in the Maori jersey as I was that night!'

While the home side was struggling to adjust its mind-set to dealing with the expectation of an expected victory, the goal-kickers from both sides were also battling to successfully pilot the new adidas ball that the New Zealand Rugby Union had introduced that season.

Later described rather memorably as a 'pig' by record All Black point-scorer Andrew Mehrtens, the ball had received plenty of attention at training, where Cashmore had put in the hours in order to get comfortable kicking it.

The fullback's diligence paid off.

'I had been doing quite a bit of practice with it because it was different to the balls we had been playing with previously', he says.

'The saying goes that it's a poor technician who blames his tools, but I had a little bit of sympathy for the Scottish kickers with the chances they missed to have at least tied the game. I was just happy, when it was my turn, that I hit my kick well and it went over. If you didn't hit that ball in the sweet spot, you tended to lose control almost totally over its trajectory, which made every kick a real challenge.'

The three-point winning margin represented the closest match of Matt's era as head coach to that point. The players were not to know at the time, but it was also the last of the 21 first-class matches in succession that the New Zealand Maori side would win prior to suffering its first-ever reverse during Matt's time in charge.

Not that the unbeaten record, which had received much pre-game publicity, came to mind when Cashmore was lining up what turned out to be the winning goal.

'I knew the potential importance of the kick, in terms of winning the game, but I didn't think much beyond that', Cashmore says.

'You don't really have time to. Besides, if you are goal-kicking for long enough, sooner or later you will end up taking kicks that decide matches. It's something you practise for, and why you learn to treat each kick the same, regardless of the match situation.'

So was he confident, given his relative unfamiliarity with the ball?

'I was actually', he says. 'I'd been hitting them quite well in training, and had already got a couple over before that kick came up, so I knew I had a fair chance of getting it.'

Up in the grandstand, as the final whistle blew at the 'Bull ring', Matt knew his side had been lucky.

We got away with one, no doubt about it. While we bombed some tries early on, and always looked more threatening in the backs than they did, we didn't adapt to the conditions as well as they did. We also didn't show them the level of respect we should have.

The Scots were a far better side than they had been when we'd played them in Edinburgh two years earlier. We should have clicked on a lot sooner than we did that they were going to fire a few shots at us because they felt they owed us one!

A classic match, it might not have been, but it is still an occasion that former Taranaki prop Greg Feek will not forget in a hurry.

Although he returned to his old stomping ground again two years later with the New Zealand Maori side, the former All Blacks' first appearance at New Plymouth's 'Bull ring' in a national jersey still represented a major moment for his career, rating alongside winning the Ranfurly Shield with Taranaki in 1996.

'It wasn't the greatest game, but a win is a win. It was nice to achieve it in front of so many friends who were in the crowd', Feek says.

'It was also nice to keep the winning run that the team had going, because it was getting a lot of publicity by then, and almost building up a momentum of its own. To have lost it against a side that we felt we were better than would have been terribly disappointing.'

Thanks to Cashmore's goal, the record remained intact. So, too, did the New Zealand Maori team's reputation as an opponent to be feared.

The team didn't appreciate it at the time, but the Scots weren't the only ones watching closely as Cashmore's winning goal sailed between the uprights.

Across the Tasman, the brains trust of the world-champion Wallabies were also taking an interest in the New Zealand Maori side and its formidable record, as they shaped their strategy to prepare for the following year's much anticipated visit of the British & Irish Lions.

The time had come for the New Zealand Maori team to take on the best team in the world!

13

Taking on the world: 2001

'The ultimate Test'

The Australian Rugby Union's decision to invite the New Zealand Maori side to play a match against the Wallabies as a lead-in to Australia's eagerly anticipated series against the British & Irish Lions, rekindled a relationship between the two teams that had lapsed for 43 years, since 1958.

In the time between 1931 and 1958, the New Zealand Maori side had played Australia on nine occasions for three wins, four losses and two draws. The seven games played between New South Wales and the New Zealand Maori side in the period between 1920 and 1928 had also retrospectively been granted full Test status by the Australian governing body, because the New South Wales side had effectively represented the Australian side during those years.

> We saw their invitation as a huge privilege, but one we had earned over a number of years leading up to 2001 due to the compilation of our unbeaten record. It hadn't come about by accident. The Australians were looking for a worthy level of competition to get them ready for the Lions.
>
> If we hadn't been performing, they wouldn't have been looking at us! There's no doubt that the invitation to go and play in Australia, against a side that was the current Rugby World Cup holder at that time, recognised the standing we had achieved for our side.
>
> While we hadn't talked about it much with the players in the earlier years, and had had to be fairly careful, because we didn't want to be seen to be not showing proper respect to the opponents we had been playing, games like the one against the Wallabies were what we had been striving to achieve.

> *Although the New Zealand Maori team had a history with Australia, the relationship went back quite a few years, and they hadn't been the top of the hit parade back then. By 2001 they were, and had the Webb Ellis trophy [the Rugby World Cup] to prove it!*

Matt was not the only one excited by the challenge.

When news of the invitation reached the ears of the players, long-serving stars like Crusaders midfielder Daryl Gibson also interpreted it as a reward for the side's sustained period of continued achievement.

'Obviously, the Australians had their reasons for wanting to play us, they were looking for strong opposition to test them before the Lions series', Gibson says.

'But that didn't distract from the fact that they were recognising all that the Maori team had achieved. We'd earned the shot at them. Putting our unbeaten record on the line gave the game an added edge.'

The maintenance of the winning record aside, Matt was also more aware than he let on to his players at the time, about the importance of his side putting up a credible performance in its biggest test to date.

> *It was all very well being invited to perform on the big stage, but we'd pretty quickly have ended up back where we'd come from, playing against the lesser teams, if we didn't prove that we were worthy of the honour. The credibility aspect was something I was keenly aware of, although I didn't feel that it was fair to burden the players with it. To do that would have been to admit to potential doubts, and I believed, as the players did, that we had a great chance of beating Australia if we played at the level to which we were capable.*

Matt was not the only coach aware of the significance of the challenge ahead of the New Zealand Maori side. All Black coach Wayne Smith, who'd had the Bledisloe Cup agonisingly pulled from his grasp in injury time when the Wallabies had kicked a penalty goal to beat his side in Wellington the previous year, lent his support to the Maori team's efforts by releasing eligible All Black players to the team.

> *Wayne went out of his way to support us, which was a big boost and was much appreciated. While he had an All Black campaign to plan for, and had his players in camp at the same time, that decision made Taine Randell, Norm Maxwell and Troy Flavell available to us, and they all had a big impact on the game.*

The mere fact that the All Black guys had been released probably indicated the extra pressure that was associated with this game to everybody involved.

For us to be competitive with the Wallabies, and maybe even win, we had to go up a notch from where we had been – and the players all knew that. It showed in the intensity of our trainings in the lead up to the game, which were a lot more full-on than usual.

I took great pleasure on the eve of the game in Sydney when Taine likened our preparation to any Test build up that he'd been involved with. That said to me we'd done everything in our preparation that we could have, in order to have the guys as ready as they could be.

'Having all of the All Black guys around, when the rest of that team was in camp somewhere else, definitely raised the stakes a bit', Glen Jackson recalls.

'I roomed with Carlos Spencer. I'd never really met him before, but got to know him quite well in the lead up. It was good having him there, because that game was easily the biggest of my career to that point, and probably would have been even more nerve wracking for me than it was anyway, had I not had the reassurance of having an experienced guy like Los to talk to.'

Randell says one of the most remarkable aspects of the New Zealand Maori team's heroic performance against the Wallabies was how quickly the team was brought together.

'The build up was very limited. The team only assembled the week before the game, but it showed what could be achieved in aligning people very quickly towards the one goal', Randell says.

'People always talk about team spirit and all working together, but inevitably there are different agendas that bubble away to certain degrees beneath the surface among any group of people. It was probably that way within the Maori team, too, but, if it was, it was certainly never obvious. It never appeared to be an issue at all.'

We brought the players in for a planning day in groups, and worked out the tactics we would use, a few days before assembling properly as a whole squad.

Originally, we were only going to be able to bring in the players who weren't involved in the Super 12 semi-finals, but that was the one year

> that all of the New Zealand teams missed out – so we got everyone in. That cleared the situation so that all of the senior players could have an input.
>
> By the time we assembled, a few days later, everybody had a fair idea how we were going to play, and could spend the week leading up to the game working on carrying out our plan, prior to heading across to Sydney two nights before the actual game. By the time we flew across the Tasman on the Thursday night, I was confident we were ready to play!

If Matt boarded the team bus for the trip from their King's Cross accommodation to Moore Park and the Sydney Football Stadium quietly confident about what lay ahead, a surprise was waiting for the whole team in terms of the level of support that greeted them on their arrival at the match venue.

'Looking out the window of the bus, the scene was amazing', Jackson says.

'There was just a sea of black. There were Maoris everywhere doing hakas, cheering for us and geeing us, and themselves, up. It seemed as if half of New Zealand was in Sydney for the game!'

One particular fan captured the attention of the whole side by honouring them with a haka as they alighted from their bus.

'All the boys got off and watched him until he'd finished before moving on into the stadium itself', Jackson says.

'It was amazing and really got the blood pumping.'

> The thing about that game, and that weekend, was that it was a window of opportunity for Maori rugby. Like the Lions game four years later, the All Blacks weren't playing at that time. We had the stage to ourselves, and the country's full attention. And that showed. The players could certainly feel all of the media interest, and the support they had – both in Sydney and back home – and it wasn't just a Maori thing.
>
> The groundswell of support behind us was a national phenomenon, and it was the first time, in the eight years since I'd been with the team, that we'd really experienced a situation like that. It happened again for the Lions, which served to reaffirm, not just how important the New Zealand Maori team is to Maoridom, but how important it is to the country as a whole.

The visiting players weren't the only ones to notice that they appeared to have the majority backing of the spectators.

Arriving on the Australian bus, Wallaby first-five-eighths Stephen Larkham recalls he experienced something new in his career in Australia, when the team was greeted by as many boos as there were cheers from the crowd, as they made their way through the throng to the changing rooms.

'I'll be honest and admit that the Maori game wasn't one that I'd been especially looking forward to', Larkham says, 'because I knew that it would be tough and extremely physical. What made the game even more difficult for us was that we suddenly found ourselves in the position where we almost felt that we were the away side. The crowd really turned out for them, and some of them were incredibly hostile, even more so than you would usually get for an All Black Test. Here we were, in the middle of Sydney, and it really did feel like we were playing an away game!'

Nor did the lack of understanding locally, as to the concept of the New Zealand Maori team, assist in lessening the expectations on the world champions.

'Because it was the Maori side, and not the All Blacks, people over here, who weren't really into their rugby, probably had the expectation that they wouldn't be as good. The reality proved to be far from the case. They pushed us as hard as the All Blacks did that year, and were probably harder to play against because they were more unpredictable. We didn't really know what to expect from them because we'd never played against them before. I remember thinking afterwards: Gee, the All Blacks are lucky that they don't have to play against these guys!'

Wallaby front rowers, prop Glenn Panoho and hooker Jeremy Paul, could have been forgiven for thinking along the same lines as their first-five-eighths, especially as they both boast strong Maori pedigree.

Paul's heritage was set to be turned against him as part of a plan hatched by the New Zealand Maori veteran and All Black hooker, Norm Hewitt.

'We were well aware of the fact that Paul was Maori, and so the boys decided they should upset him early and get him on the back foot', physiotherapist Mike Stewart says.

'As a result, Norm had sorted it so that Rigger [New Zealand Maori lock Mark Cooksley] would punch through the scrum at the first engagement to hit Paul and add to his uncertainty. The only problem was that Norm was paranoid that Rigger would mistime the punch and end up hitting him instead!'

The tentativeness of the Australians' initial approach didn't go unnoticed among other senior Maori players.

'I'm not sure if they really knew what they were up against', Slade McFarland says.

'The atmosphere inside the stadium seemed to be a pro-Maori one, and that appeared to shake them a bit. It certainly felt like we were playing in New Zealand, which obviously gave us all a huge lift. But, for a few calls that went against us, and these things happen – especially when you are not expected to win – we could have taken them. We certainly gave them a real fright!'

While Australia did prevail 41–29, to end the New Zealand Maori team's seven-year, 21-game winning sequence in the first-class arena, the match was a thriller, containing several key turning points.

Perhaps the most critical was a 14-point turnaround toward the tail-end of the first half, after a heavy hit by New Zealand Maori centre Caleb Ralph on Larkham.

The Wallabies had been swinging onto the attack, when Ralph crunched the Australian first-five-eighths around the shoulders, jolting the ball free on impact.

It was then quickly scooped up by Flavell who galloped to the end of the field to score beneath the Australian goal-posts, raising his arm in a triumphant salute to the crowd as he did so.

'It was a cheap shot', Larkham says.

'He blindsided me. I didn't see him coming and ended up winded as a result. I guess the hurt was greater for them than it was for me, though, because it cost them a try at a pretty crucial stage of the game.'

While he had expected to be punished personally for the offence, Ralph was dismayed when South African referee Mark Lawrence cancelled out the try Flavell had just scored.

'It wasn't malicious. It was really a matter of bad timing, and was a split-second thing, in terms of where I caught Larkham', Ralph says.

'As soon as the referee turned around after Flav had scored, and started talking to the touch judge, I knew they'd be coming for me. I didn't think they'd call back the try, though. The referee told me it was a late tackle and gave me 10 minutes in the sin-bin, but I was really gutted when they ruled out the try. As soon as I went off, they then scored a seven-pointer. It was a 14-point turnaround.'

> *I can't say that the referee was wrong in his ruling, but it had a huge impact on the game. Had our try stood, they wouldn't have subsequently got theirs, and who knows how the game might have developed. It was bad enough losing that try, but we later had another one not given, which, if the television replay referee had been going then, would have given it to us. As it was, we had the Australians under the hammer for much of the rest of the game, in the second half, especially. They'd wanted a hard test before they played the Lions. They certainly got it!*

One area of the game where the Australians were especially exposed was at their lineout, where the New Zealand Maori side's tall jumpers, Cooksley and Maxwell, repeatedly made their presence felt to harass their opponents and disrupt their flow of possession.

'We had some big guys in our forwards and knew that we could put them under pressure there, although it probably worked out even better than we initially thought', forwards coach Jim Love says.

'A lot of the ball they did win from that phase was scrappy, which probably sent them back to the drawing board in that area before they played the Lions.'

It was a lesson the Australians took plenty from, with Justin Harrison, who hadn't faced the New Zealand Maori side, providing a critical lineout win against the throw in the decisive third Lions' Test, to become virtually an overnight star.

'We had a great deal of confidence in our ability to carry out the plans we'd set up, and that showed through in the game', Gibson says.

'One of the strategies was to really get after George Gregan, and put pressure on him. It would be fair to say that he ended up having a fairly tough night!'

He wasn't alone.

'While the New Zealand Maori team played a style of game that was a lot like the way the Pacific Island teams played, in terms of their physicality, they were far better drilled than the Pacific sides, and a lot fitter – which you would expect of a New Zealand side', Larkham says.

'We knew they'd try to intimidate us, and had prepared for that, but the other aspect of their performance that night which stood out for me was the way they wouldn't go away. Normally, the Island teams will come at you hard but then blow out when you get on top. The Maori side wasn't like that. Even when we got on top of them for significant periods of time during the game, they kept coming back at us. At no stage did we ever feel comfortable. It was a battle right to the end.'

Although the Australians finished with a five try to two count, New Zealand Maori also had Flavell's effort disallowed, while Norm Hewitt was driven over the line, and television replays confirmed that he had scored, but referee Lawrence was forced to rule that he was unsighted.

The two tries New Zealand Maori did score both came from Spencer, who was operating from the unfamiliar, for him, position of fullback.

There was no pressure from the All Black selectors in that decision. It was my call. Los was recovering from an injury, so we decided to take a bit of the pressure off him by trying him further out in the backline, where we felt he could attack from anywhere on the field, back his skills and create mayhem. And it worked.

He had them on alert that whole night, and showed that he'd quickly adapted to running the lines, and to the timing that was required at fullback, by hitting a ball at speed to pierce the gap perfectly off a set move that we tried from a scrum. Roger Randle had come in off his wing and held up their defensive line perfectly, which allowed Los to scream through the gap to score one of his tries.

Although beaten, the New Zealand Maori players headed back across the Tasman with their heads high.

'It was played like a Test match, and the boys were still buzzing about the experience for a fair while afterwards', Bruce Reihana, who'd made his All Black Test debut on the previous year's tour of France, says.

'The thing about the game was, even though we'd lost, the boys all knew that they'd done the Maori team's heritage, and the jersey, proud. That was reflected by the way our performance was received back in New Zealand.'

It was not just the fans at home who had been impressed. The host union liked what they had seen, too.

So much so that an invitation quickly came through following the match for the New Zealand Maori side to play Australia again the next year, this time after a build up with matches against state sides Queensland and New South Wales.

'The level of achievement from that night was probably best summed up by their coach, Rod Macqueen, when he said that the game had provided them with the best possible preparation they could have had for playing the Lions', Gibson, who was in his last year with the side, says.

'That was probably the biggest compliment we could have had. The other thing about the game was that it had given all New Zealanders, not just Maori, great pride. That was special, in terms of Maori being seen in a good light, because we are represented in the bottom third of a lot of the social statistics, and so often get portrayed in the media in a negative light. Sport is an area where Maori consistently overachieve and the good thing about our success in the Maori team, even including that game against Australia where we lost, was that it made people back home feel good about themselves. On that Sunday morning after we had played Australia, there would have been a lot of people who were able to wake up back in New Zealand feeling good about the fact that they were Maori.'

Gibson, who played his way back into the All Blacks for the 2002 season before embarking on a British career at the end of that year, says the first Australian game highlighted how the New Zealand Maori team's playing style had evolved.

'The way we played had changed. It had to in order to adapt to the way the game had changed as professionalism developed', Gibson says.

'But one thing that didn't change was the philosophy the team employed, even on the biggest stage like that night against the Wallabies. The plan was still to have a go, back our skills and have fun. Those are all qualities that can sometimes be diluted to an extent in today's professional environment.'

As he reflected on the evening's events among his players, friends and many supporters back at the team hotel, Matt accepted that the loss represented the end of an era, but not of a journey.

> *It was the end of our unbeaten record. That was obviously disappointing, although, in its own way, it did take a bit of pressure off us going forward. The other thing we had to recognise was that it had taken the world champions to finally bowl us!*
>
> *I was proud of the way the team had played on the night. The Australians knew that they had been in a wonderful contest, and they showed their*

> *respect for us, both by going on to beat the Lions in the series that we had helped them to prepare for, but also by the fact that they invited us to come back!*

As far as the New Zealand Maori side went for 2001, however, the show wasn't yet over. After a short break, the squad gathered again, this time minus its All Black representatives, to play a lead-up match against the invitation Bay of Plenty Wasps club before tackling the touring Argentine Pumas.

The Wasps match, which New Zealand Maori won comfortably at Rotorua, should have represented the official first-class debuts of Rico Gear and Blair Urlich, but the match was denied that status after Wasps coach Gordon Tietjens used more than the allowed number of replacement players.

Tietjens' actions left Love, in particular, fuming.

'It was downright disrespectful. He [Tietjens] took us for granted, and that should never happen to a national team', Love says.

'A couple of young lads made their debuts in the New Zealand Maori jersey that night, only you won't find it in the record books because the Wasps used too many players. They, and the Maori jersey, didn't deserve that!'

> *It was disappointing, because it made the game a bit of a farce in the end. There were players coming and going left, right and centre. As a lead-in to the Test against Argentina, we got what we needed out of the night, in terms of a run together, but it was tough on Rico and Blair. Fortunately, they both got to make their 'official' first-class debuts for us down the track.*

Gear, who had started with the New Zealand Maori Colts three years previously, had been included in the squad that went to Australia but wasn't required to don his playing kit for the game. Even so, the occasion made a big impression.

'Just being involved in the build up was another stepping stone for me, which was then built on when I got to play against the Wasps, even though it didn't count for the official records', he says.

Tietjens' actions aside, some members of the New Zealand Maori team were having other battles with the NZRU's official boot supplier, adidas.

It was an issue that the team physiotherapist inadvertently found himself caught in the middle of.

'With adidas having come on board as the New Zealand union's main sponsor in 1999, from that time on, all of the players were required to wear adidas boots', Stewart says.

'The problem was the adidas boot template is taken from an English foot. Because of that, the Polynesian guys sometimes struggle wearing them, because the boots are quite tight and don't allow for bigger feet.'

Players came up with ingenious ways of getting around the issue of being contractually required to wear the adidas equipment. This included blacking out the original logos of the boots they preferred to wear, and then painting three white stripes on them, so that they looked for all intents and purposes like adidas boots.

'The thing was that this was an issue the Rugby Union pursued quite rigorously. They had boffins back at the union head office studying the tapes of games to check that all of the guys were wearing the right boots, as required by their contracts. A couple of our players didn't have the adidas boots on during the game in Sydney and got in strife because of that', Stewart says.

'They were informed that they were in breach of their contracts. As a result, the players were told that they would have their boots checked by an official from the union in the tunnel before they ran onto the field for the game against Argentina. If they had the wrong boots on, they wouldn't be allowed to play.'

The saga caused a particular issue with Hewitt, with Stewart estimating that he presented the former All Black hooker with 10 different pairs of adidas boots, before Hewitt finally settled on a set that he felt were comfortable enough.

'Once he decided that he had a pair he thought he could use, I had to take them down to a local cobbler and have them worked on and expanded, so that they would fit more comfortably for him', Stewart says.

'He played in them against Argentina and had the cheek to tell me afterwards that he "quite liked them"! I could have flattened him!'

Counties Manukau loose forward Kristian Ormsby, who made his New Zealand Maori debut against Argentina, was less fortunate.

Not only was he later sent off for stomping three minutes from the end after appearing on the field as a replacement, he was also fined by the Rugby Union for being in breach of his contract on the boot issue. The fine came after the water-based paint Ormsby had used to insert the three white adidas 'stripes' washed off, revealing to the union's eagle-eyed 'boot police' that he was wearing a rival brand's product.

You've always got to defend your players as strongly as you can when they get in judicial trouble, and that was the case for Kristian, as it would be for any other player in our side. I do remember thinking, though, after being shown the video footage of his stomp on the Argentine player: 'Gee, we're going to have our work cut out here!'. Needless to say, he got a suspension.

The sentence was perhaps the only downside to an otherwise successful night for New Zealand Maori as the Argentinian side was put to the sword 43–24.

The Pumas had been allowed just three nights recovery from a 19–67 Test loss to the All Blacks in Christchurch the previous weekend.

Even so, the tourists put up a good show, scoring two tries and displaying plenty of spirit before they were eventually over-run by the greater flair and finesse that the New Zealand Maori side possessed.

While the backs contributed five of the home side's six tries, with wingers Randle and Reihana getting two each, the platform was laid by a solid effort from a relatively inexperienced forward pack.

'We saw it as a major challenge. They had some very big men who loved the tight stuff', prop Greg Feek recalls.

'We scrummed pretty well that night. I wouldn't say we dominated them, but we certainly gained parity, and that was all we needed with the quality of the backs that we had.'

With the All Blacks having returned to the Test arena following the Sydney match, the Argentinian result also highlighted the extent of the depth that was prevalent in Maori rugby, which proved to be important, given that All Black availability would become a major issue in the run-up to the 2003 Rugby World Cup.

The Argentinians fired a few shots at us, but we had a class side. With the All Blacks out of the picture, we were able to introduce a few younger players, who served us pretty well over the next few seasons.

Not only did the Argentinian match represent the start of another winning run, it also saw the New Zealand Maori side unveil a new haka, Timatanga, designed to distinguish the side from the traditional Ka Mate routine that had previously been performed by both the All Blacks and the New Zealand Maori side.

Not that Timatanga's introduction was a totally smooth one, with the board of the New Zealand Rugby Union initially trying to block the switch, before reluctantly accepting the team's desire to confirm its own identity.

It [the introduction of Timatanga] was led by the players, and once again showed us that they were taking ownership of the team. Even though the faces were gradually changing over time, the sense of belonging, in terms of the team, was still strong. I saw that as a very good sign. Just because we'd lost our unbeaten run, it didn't mean that we were going to stop being successful. If anything, a new challenge had been created, to build even further on the momentum we had gained.

It was a challenge that was to be complicated further as the landscape changed again in New Zealand rugby. By the time the New Zealand Maori team got together the following year, a new chief would be calling the shots in New Zealand rugby because the All Blacks would have a new coach!

14

Boks, barbed wire and rugby

'The 1981 Springboks recalled'

Performing the haka is a moving moment for Maori people on any occasion.

Seldom has there been a more emotive performance of the famous ritual, however, than in the McLean Park dressing room immediately prior to the New Zealand Maori team's match against the 1981 touring South African side.

Jim Love, later Matt's assistant through a large period of his term as New Zealand Maori coach, but No 8 against the South Africans, remembers the occasion as one of the most pivotal in the modern era of Maori rugby.

'With everything that had been going on during that tour, it was a major triumph for the game that a contest between a New Zealand Maori team and the Springboks actually went ahead', he says.

'Not only was that game important for the tour, it was of huge significance for the Maori team because the playing of it placed us back on the world stage. It gave us an opportunity to take on the best and prove that we could compete with them.'

The hardest bit, Love recalls, was not the game itself, but the waiting beforehand.

'Because of all of the anti-tour protests that had been going on around the country, which had already led to the Waikato game being abandoned because they [the protestors] had got out onto the playing field, we left for the ground straight after breakfast', Love says.

'The Boks arrived shortly after us, which meant you had this sort of phoney war going on – them on one side of the ground in one changing room, us on the other. And both sets of players were careful to avoid each other beforehand, in the six or so hours of waiting time that we had before kick-off.'

The tourists were less put out by the pre-match wait. By that stage of the tour, their tenth match counting the abandoned game in Hamilton, the players were getting well used to waiting around for hours on end.

'It was something we had to put up with, but it was worth it just to get the opportunity to play against the New Zealand teams', Springbok halfback and captain against the New Zealand Maori team, Divan Serfontein says.

'Looking back now, I suppose you could say that it was ironic – we were the ones being protested against, yet we were a multi-racial side with a coloured player, Errol Tobias, in our lineup, and we were playing against a racially selected side! Not that we felt aggrieved about that. We were hugely respectful of the Maori team for their massive tradition, and in terms of the way they played the game. From our perspective, that match was the fourth Test of our tour. We were just pleased to have been afforded the opportunity to play against them, especially given the circumstances surrounding the whole tour.'

'We didn't speak at all about the politics of the tour', Love, who played for New Zealand Maori between 1976 and 1985, says.

'The Springboks are one of the game's icons and are always a strong side. We were just desperate to beat them!'

Love remembers the players filled in the time before the match by singing songs and chatting quietly among themselves, although the emotion of the occasion caught up with them all immediately prior to taking the field, when the team performed its impromptu haka.

'I'm not sure how it came about, it came out of nowhere, really, but it was the most moving moment of my career', Love says.

'What it said was that we were all there for each other, and were ready to go out and do the job that we had to do, which was to not let them beat us.'

Ironically, Love, who was played at No 8 although he was more regularly known as a lock, was the last player selected for the New Zealand Maori side, according to 1981 selector Mattie Blackburn, who would later coach the side in his own right before acting as manager for Matt.

New Zealand Maori had beaten Counties 12–8 in a lead-up match before the team to face South Africa was finally confirmed.

'The debate raged around the size of the South African forwards, and how we were going to counter that strength', Blackburn remembers.

'We wanted to field a big pack with big loose forwards to counter their size. As a regular at lock, Jim added height, which gave us a better balance to our trio, because we had a relatively short openside flanker in the form of Frank Shelford. All the players were practically in their pyjamas by the time we finally got around to naming that team!'

On the evening before the match itself, a meeting was called at the Maori team's hotel, where all the players were asked by coach Percy Erceg what their contribution was going to be the next day.

'The general theme of that meeting was that we weren't going to take any nonsense from the South Africans', Love says.

'When it came to my turn to speak, I said that I was going to deck one of them!'

Love was as good as his word. When his Springbok counterpart Johan Marais rather unwisely chose to push him away from the ball, the response of the giant Marlborough man was immediate and decisive, and Marais was floored by a clear-cut punch.

'One of the South African players was dishing out a bit of racial abuse, but while it was a physical game, generally it was reasonably clean', Love says.

'My opposite number copped one, but that's what tended to happen a bit in those days, when you could take the law into your own hands a bit more. He certainly didn't try to shove me again!'

The game itself was a thriller, with New Zealand Maori dominating the first half to push out to a 9–0 lead thanks to two penalty goals by halfback Richard Dunn and a dropped goal from future All Black second-five-eighths Steve Pokere.

The advantage became 12–0 after the halftime break, when Dunn placed his third penalty of the afternoon, before the Springboks upped the tempo of their play and began to claw their way back.

'We decided at halftime that things weren't working as well in the backline as we'd like them to, so Divan had a talk to both myself and Errol and arranged for us to switch positions', Springbok starting centre Colin Beck says.

'I'd played my whole university career in Cape Town as a flyhalf [first-five-eighths], and had been originally selected as a flyhalf for the tour, so I was quite comfortable with the move.'

Serfontein says the decision to move Tobias out to centre, and bring Beck in closer to the action was brought about by the need to change the momentum of the game.

'They were stifling up our backline, so we just needed to try something a bit different to change the pattern of the game', Serfontein says.

Beck was to become the day's key figure, but only after the Springboks had closed to 12–9 on the back of a Beck penalty goal, as well as a converted try by winger Gerrie Germishuys. The try came after Beck had spied New Zealand Maori winger Mike Clamp out of position, and had placed a kick in behind him for Germishuys to run on to for the score.

Germishuys then appeared to have won the game for his side when he crossed the New Zealand Maori line again with just a couple of minutes remaining, only to have the try ruled out, when Taranaki referee Brian Duffy decided that he had knocked the ball on.

'We all thought that Gerrie had scored', Serfontein says. 'Most of the guys were so adamant about that fact they were talking more about the try we should have had, than the final kick that determined the outcome, back in the dressing room after the game.'

A series of scrums near the New Zealand Maori goal-line followed the non-try. For the tourists, trailing by three points, it was decision time.

'It was a case of either going for another try to attempt to win the game, or taking the dropped goal opportunity if it presented itself, to try and draw it', Beck says.

'Ultimately, that decision came down to me as the flyhalf, and was something I had to live with. I decided on the dropped kick. It was the safer option. Also, that New Zealand Maori team was so talented and such a strong team, for us to draw the game was almost like a win.'

The decision made, Beck's fateful kick wafted towards the posts. It went very high above the uprights, but appeared to drift wide.

At least that is what the New Zealand Maori players and the Hawke's Bay crowd thought until, to their astonishment, referee Duffy ran back to halfway to re-start play, indicating that he believed the kick had gone over.

'It missed', Love says.

'I was standing in front of the goal posts and had a very good view of it. It didn't miss by a little bit either, it was quite obvious. At least it was to us. We were beginning to form up for the 22 metre drop out, and so were some of the South Africans, until the referee started going back to halfway! I still, to this day, haven't been able to find anyone who saw him signal the goal, other than South Africans of course, who say that the kick actually went over!'

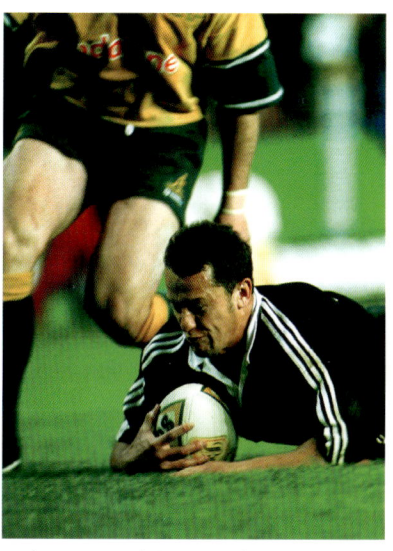

Carlos Spencer slides across for one of his two tries against Australia at the Sydney Football Stadium in 2001. © PHOTOSPORT

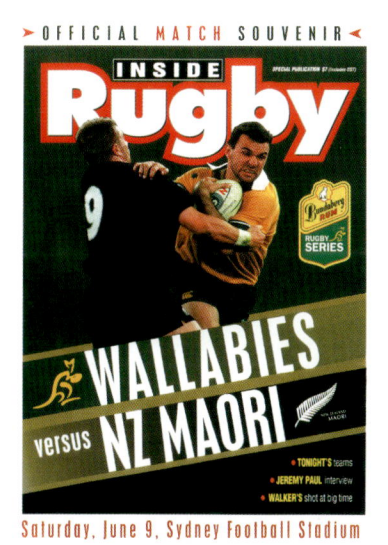

Australia–New Zealand Maori match programme, 2001.

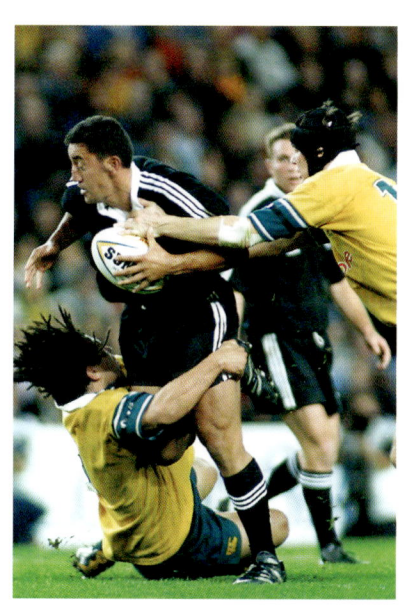

The Wallabies are at full stretch containing Daryl Gibson at the Sydney Football Stadium. © PHOTOSPORT

Caleb Ralph gives Argentina's Gonzalo Quesada the slip at Rotorua in 2001. © PHOTOSPORT

'He's behind you!' Springbok winger Carel du Plessis has New Zealand Maori flanker Frank Shelford bearing down on him as fellow South African Colin Beck watches on in action from the 1981 clash at Napier's McLean Park. © Peter Bush

New Zealand Maori–South Africa match programme, 1981. © Peter Bush

'Barbed Wire Bro's!' A portion of the crowd who packed into Napier's McLean Park to watch the New Zealand Maori side tackle the 1981 Springboks. © Peter Bush

New Zealand Maori halfback Richard Dunn and Jim Love (8) in action against the 1981 Springboks. © Peter Bush

The New Zealand Maori and Springbok players mixed together freely and enjoyed each other's company after the match. © Peter Bush

The moving ovation given to Maori and All Black great George Nepia by the crowd at Swansea during the New Zealand Maori team's 1982 tour of Wales and Spain is a memory that will stay with long-time lensman Peter Bush for ever. © Peter Bush

'Nice one, Bruiser!' Bruce Reihana is across for a try, and the New Zealand Maori side is on its way back during the cliffhanger against the Wallabies at Perth's Subiaco Oval in 2002.
© PHOTOSPORT

Matt's long-time assistant and close friend, Jim Love. © PHOTOSPORT

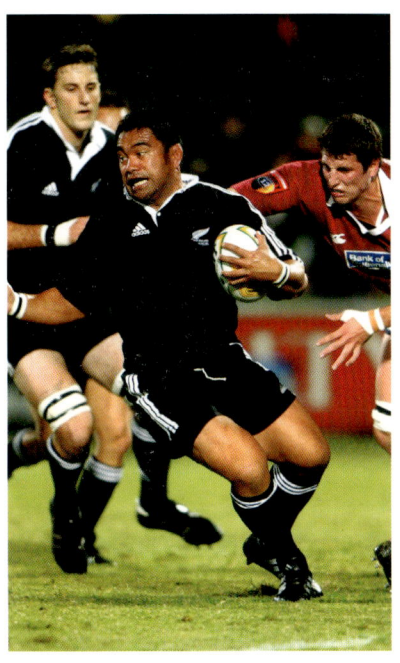

Slade McFarland struggles to get away from the Queensland defence during the New Zealand Maori team's shock loss to the Reds at Brisbane in 2002. © PHOTOSPORT

Taine Randell was a reluctant leader of the New Zealand Maori side against England in 2003. © Pro Sport Photos

Glen Jackson says his Waikato and New Zealand Maori captain Deon Muir was 'a bit of a softy', but the Wallabies might find that hard to believe as the visitors' leader charges at them menacingly in 2002. © PHOTOSPORT

Mark Mayerhofler is caught in a 'Barbarian sandwich' during his final career outing for the New Zealand Maori team in 2002. It was a night where Matt says that Taine Randell (right) should have been playing for his team, rather than against it. © PHOTOSPORT

Bruce Reihana beats Tana Umaga (obscured) to the ball for one of three tries during his farewell to the New Zealand Maori jersey in the 2002 loss to the New Zealand Barbarians at North Harbour Stadium. © PHOTOSPORT

Glen Jackson spies a gap, but these were generally few and far between in the English defence as the soon-to-be Rugby World Cup winners kept the New Zealand Maori tryless at New Plymouth in 2003. © PHOTOSPORT

Slade McFarland (centre) and Greg Feek prepare to engage the England front row during a torrid night at the office in 2003. © PHOTOSPORT

Christian Cullen offered great value to the New Zealand Maori side in 2003. © Pro Sport Photos

Naturally, Beck and Serfontein see it differently, without either actually being prepared to say that the kick went over for certain!

'I didn't really see it', Serfontein says. 'It did go very high. I was certainly happy to see the goal awarded though! For us to get a draw against a very strong team like the Maori was a huge morale booster for the whole tour. It showed too, because the Test team went on to beat the All Blacks in the second Test down in Wellington, which was the next game.'

Beck was the Springbok with the best view of the kick.

Showing some neat footwork that would do any politician proud, let alone a promising South African rugby player, Beck won't say categorically that his kick was successful, but nor will he confess that it missed.

'If you look at the television replays, which I have done many times, the ball went very high so you can't really tell one way or the other', he laughs.

'So we have to believe the referee's decision, and he said that it went over. We certainly accepted that at the time and I'm not going to challenge him now!'

So it finished a 12–12 draw.

Not a win, but still an outcome about which the New Zealand Maori team could be extremely proud, especially in light of the Springboks' crushing 24–12 second Test win over the All Blacks just four days later.

'We were obviously disappointed not to have won, but it was still an historic result for Maori rugby', Love says.

'They hadn't beaten us, and that was our goal. Deep down we really knew that we'd won by not being beaten. The morale victory was ours. Besides, everyone knows really that their last kick missed. It's only the record book that says different!'

Blackburn, who'd fended off criticism from his neighbour as to his involvement in the match against the Springboks, echoes Love's sentiments.

'We'd done so much hard work to win it. To get denied on a referee's call that was plainly wrong was a tremendous shame', he says.

'But it didn't dampen what was an historic and proud day for Maori rugby. I'd seen the New Zealand Maori side lose to the Springboks in 1965, and I was proud to be able to say that the side I'd helped to select got a bit closer!'

After avoiding each other in the lead-up to the game, the two teams mixed freely at a social function back at the New Zealand Maori team's hotel after the match, enjoying each others' company.

The function highlighted the spirit of respect between the two teams.

'After the sourness of the Waikato game, which I'd been at, the Maori game at Napier, was one of the saviours of the whole tour', veteran news and sports photographer Peter Bush says.

'I'd been to a supporter's function the night before the match, where the beer was flowing freely and there was plenty of good humour. That theme followed into the game itself, where it became clear from the early stages that the crowd was in good spirits and there was going to be no trouble. While the barbed wire was still there, surrounding the playing field, the atmosphere totally lacked the menace and high-voltage tension that had been present at all of the other games.'

The nature of the occasion was summed up, Bush says, by the way players from both teams joined together after the final whistle, leaving the arena in groups side-by-side.

'I later won a high-profile photographic award for a shot I got of New Zealand Maori captain Billy Bush and Springbok Errol Tobias walking off the field arm-in-arm as they traded their playing jerseys', Bush says.

'I know it's a tired old cliché, but that was one day during a bloody-minded tour where rugby truly was the winner.'

Bush adds that the Springboks voted with their feet, in terms of acknowledging the warm hospitality they had received in the Hawke's Bay, by opting to remain in Napier to train until the day before the second Test in Wellington.

The New Zealand Maori team's achievement in holding the might of the Springboks to a draw was recognised a year later, when the side was invited to tour Wales.

Twenty-six players took part in the nine-match tour, which encompassed seven matches in Wales, including a Test against a Welsh XV, as well as two matches in Spain.

For Love, the trip represented his second overseas tour with the New Zealand Maori side; having been part of the 1979 outfit that won six and drew another during a seven-match journey through Australia and the Pacific Islands.

The 1979 New Zealand Maori side drew 18–18 with a Queensland side stacked with Wallabies at Ballymore, before beating Samoa (26–3), Tonga (26–9) and Fiji (19–13) in the tour Tests.

Future Counties Manukau NPC coach Mac McCallion captained the side.

'It was a hard tour, but a hugely enjoyable one', Love says of his first overseas touring experience with the New Zealand Maori side.

'Queensland had a bit of help from the local referee when we played them. We were up 18–15 on fulltime, and he kept the game going until Paul MacLean was able to kick the levelling penalty goal for them, but, other than that, we were successful.'

Nor was the New Zealand Maori team environment, at that stage anyway, all that different from the culture-based environment developed by Matt during the professional era.

'The philosophy, in terms of the culture, hasn't changed that much, although it did get lost for a little while there', Love says.

'It was there on our 1979 tour, although it was driven by our coach [former All Black and New Zealand Maori representative] Waka Nathan and the senior players, as opposed to being co-ordinated on a more formal basis by a kaumatua, as it is now.'

In McCallion, an ex-Vietnam veteran like Matt, the 1979 side, too, benefited from the impact of army-style discipline.

'Mac was a hard task master. Our trainings on that trip were quite ruthless, but that paid dividends', Love says.

'We tended to be more disciplined than our opponents, and that experience had a huge influence on my own career as a coach. Maintaining good discipline in adverse circumstances was something both Matt and I pushed with the Maori team.'

Love says that discipline, within the sporting environment, helps to provide focus.

'Discipline is everything with young Maori', he says.

'The talent is usually there, but the discipline needs to be there as well to ensure that the talent is channelled in the right direction. You have to provide a good balance between work time and play time to get the best out of the players.'

It was a balance that Love believes was perhaps lost on the 1982 tour of Wales, where the touring side won just five of its matches, losing three, with another one drawn. Two of the wins were 60-point score-lines achieved against modest Spanish opposition in Barcelona and Madrid at the tour's end.

'We got conned a bit', Love says. 'By that, I mean that we ended up spending a lot of time socialising at rugby clubs. Guys were often out quite late. We were doing television appearances and other public relations-type activities all the time. The team even went to a combined Harry Secombe-Kiri Te Kanawa concert! There is a time and place for those types of things in moderation, but we got the balance wrong on that tour. At times, it did make some of us wonder whether we were over there to be rugby players or celebrities!'

Prior to their departure from home, the New Zealand Maori side had been undefeated in 22 matches, dating back to the 19–22 loss to the British & Irish Lions in 1977.

New Zealand Maori had led 19–6 at one point in that particular game, although Love had unfortunately missed out on the occasion, having broken his collar bone while playing for his Waitohi club.

The record remained intact for just two further matches; a 17–10 win over Cardiff at the famous Cardiff Arms Park, followed by a 10–10 scrape against Maesteg.

Unfortunately, the tour went downhill from the next game against Swansea, where New Zealand Maori surrendered a 12–3 halftime advantage to lose 12–15. Wins over Monmouthshire (18–9) and Aberavon (34–6) were split by a 9–16 loss to the powerful Llanelli side, before the New Zealand Maori team lost 19–25 to a full-strength Welsh side back in Cardiff, having struggled in the second half as they tried to chase the game in wet conditions after trailing 7–16 at the halfway point.

'The talent was definitely there in that team, but we fell into the trap of trying to keep everybody happy', Love says.

'As a consequence, the guys appeared flat and lethargic at certain times. As a team, we played that way.'

While he shared Love's disappointment at the tour's overall outcome, Blackburn, who helped select the side, maintains the expedition was still a worthwhile one.

Blackburn had followed the tour from a close distance, leading the first-ever Williments Travel touring party, which consisted of 26 keen rugby fans.

'The boys gave the Welsh a huge hurry up in the Test, which finished at two tries each', Blackburn says.

'It's true they'd earlier lost a couple of games that they probably should have won, but they were a credit to themselves and the Maori jersey on that tour. Percy Erceg, who was their coach, did a very good job with that side.'

Bush, who also led a tour group, concurs with Blackburn that the esteem in which the Welsh held Maori rugby, as a result of that tour, should not be underestimated.

'It was a very happy tour, and the Maori players were literally adored by the locals in the valleys of Wales', Bush says.

'Everything the players did, from mixing with the Welsh people to the rugby they played, earned huge respect from the rugby-loving populous over there.'

The respect was encapsulated, Bush says, by the reception that the Welsh accorded former Maori and All Black great George Nepia, who accompanied the tour and was introduced to the Welsh crowd before one of the matches.

'It was one of the great all-time moments in rugby history and will live in my memory forever', Bush says.

'When George was introduced to them, the local crowd went nuts, and they stood to a man to honour him. There could be no higher show of respect to both George as a person, and the Maori style of game that he represented, than that.'

15

The wild west: 2002

'Wallabies versus New Zealand Maori, episode II'

As massive as the task of playing the world champions for the first time on their home patch had been, the challenge laid out for the New Zealand Maori side 12 months on was even greater.

Not only were they to take on the conquerors of the British & Irish Lions again, this time they would be facing the reigning Rugby World Cup champions and Tri-Nations title holders without the services of any current All Blacks.

It was a daunting prospect, and one made more imposing by the loss of the surprise element that had accompanied New Zealand Maori when the team had landed in Sydney the year before.

If anything, thanks to the memory of that pulsating 29–41 defeat, the Australians were now on alert, and treating the contest as everything but a gentle warm up to the more important engagements down the track.

> *We always knew that playing Australia without having access to the All Black guys, who were assembled with John Mitchell for the two home Tests against Ireland, was going to be a huge test of our overall depth. What we perhaps underestimated a bit was how we were now perceived in Australia, as a result of what had happened in the game the year before. Whereas, before that game, we were largely an unknown quantity to the Australians, now it was almost like we were the All Blacks. The public and media attention in the build up was fairly major. Once we got to Perth to prepare for the game against the Wallabies, it was made clear to us that the locals certainly saw it as a Test match.*

Which was a huge compliment to the New Zealand Maori, if a little bit flattering to the status of some of the players who had been included in the visiting side's 26-man party.

As Mitchell had selected eight players with Maori eligibility in his squad to play domestic Tests against Italy and Ireland (twice) during the time in which the New Zealand Maori side was away, Matt was forced to look further down the national player rankings he kept of eligible Maori players, in order to fill in the gaps.

Among those promoted to the All Black squad were Caleb Ralph, Daryl Gibson, Taine Randell and Norm Maxwell, who'd all featured prominently in the previous year's clash between New Zealand Maori and the Wallabies.

> We had no problems with that. Playing for the All Blacks was the ultimate. The selection of those players showed that we had done our job, in terms of pushing their careers forward, especially in the cases of Gibbo and Ralphy. They'd both been out of the All Blacks for a while, but had fought their way back to be selected again. What the loss of the All Black guys did mean for us, though, was that we had to use our lead-in games against Queensland and New South Wales wisely.
>
> Our whole focus for the tour was built around the Test. Even though Queensland and New South Wales were going to represent hard matches in their own right, we had to use all of the players we'd selected in those two matches and give each one of them a decent opportunity to put their hand up for selection in the team to play against Australia. It had to be that way because we couldn't base the core of the team for the Test around the All Black players, as we'd been able to do the year before.

Such was the relative inexperience of the touring team, compared with the 2001 side, three of the players included – second rowers Reece Robinson, Steve Jackson and Bryce Williams – hadn't even featured in the just completed Super 12. They had essentially been selected straight out of club rugby.

Of the match day 22 who finally fronted up to the Australians in Perth, just eight remained of the group that had performed so heroically at the Sydney Football Stadium 12 months earlier.

Not that all of the new faces belonged to novices.

In one case, that of experienced midfielder Mark Mayerhofler, the tour of Australia represented a return to New Zealand Maori colours after a two-year absence, having watched on enviously the previous season as the side had tackled the Wallabies.

'I would have loved to have been involved in that game', Mayerhofler, who, at the time, had just returned to New Zealand following a stint at French club Grenoble, says.

'So when I heard that the team was going to Australia again, I made it my goal to make that tour.'

A useful Super 12 with the Blues helped Mayerhofler achieve selection for the tour, but he then found that a few things had changed since his previous assembly in 2000, when he joined up with the team prior to its departure.

'Off the field, the cultural aspect was probably even stronger than it had been before', Mayerhofler says, 'but the biggest thing was the new haka – Timatanga. Because there were so many new players to the team from the previous year, the guys had all been split up into groups with a senior player as a leader, whose job it was to teach everyone the new haka.'

One of the 'teachers' was Bruce Reihana, who relished the role as a cultural leader after being 'schooled up' on the routine by team kaumatua, Whetu Tipiwai.

'Among the other leaders were guys like Deon [Muir] and Slade [McFarland], who'd both given a huge amount to Maori rugby and were held in high regard as a result', Reihana says.

'To be given a leadership role alongside of them was something I regarded as a huge honour. It meant a lot.'

Reihana would later show how he'd developed his on-field leadership skills during the Test, but the team's readiness for that assignment seemed a long way off after New Zealand Maori was surprisingly beaten by a below-strength Queensland side 28–25 in the opening game of its tour.

'The team environment had always been fairly relaxed, but it was almost too relaxed before that game', Mayerhofler recalls.

'We went out for our traditional team coffee on the morning of the game, after that, on the way back to the hotel in the bus, the boys got the driver to stop and we all piled out and did the new haka on the side of the road. It was a great feeling at the time, but it almost felt afterwards like some of the boys had put more focus into getting the haka right than they had the match that followed it.'

The pre-match 'performance' did not go unnoticed by locals either, with Mayerhofler recalling the team getting some strange looks from passers-by as they went through the routine.

'It was really disappointing to lose that game in Brisbane', Reihana says.

'Maybe it was because they didn't have all of their Wallaby players, but we took them too lightly. It was almost as if we all thought it was just going to happen for us – it didn't!'

Mike Stewart points to a couple of pre-match incidents that, with hindsight, were indicative of the collective attitude within the team before that defeat.

'It was almost like, with the buzz of getting back together again, and the excitement of the game against Australia, that the guys slipped into holiday mode', Stewart says.

'Everything was just a bit too casual. We had one player who got to the ground having forgotten his playing jersey! Another had forgotten his boots, which resulted in our local liaison man having to race back to the hotel to get them. Collectively, as a group, the guys just weren't switched on mentally. That showed out on the field.'

> *There's no doubt that complacency was an issue, and that was a concern because it wasn't a problem we usually had. Watching from the sideline, you could see it manifest itself in the number of mistakes that we made in their attacking red zone, inside the Queensland 22-metre line. Once we got down there, we just couldn't seem to hold onto the ball. Instead of taking the chance to really nail them while we had the field position, generally we were just handing them back the ball. Do that often enough and the opposition will hurt you, which Queensland did.*

While the surprise loss to a state side hardly bode well for the more demanding assignments ahead, Matt wasn't too despondent. Any concerns he might have had were also quickly erased by the manner in which the players themselves reacted to the set back.

> *I made it clear to the players after the game that the quality of their performance against Queensland hadn't been acceptable. I also reminded them that we'd only been given the opportunity to come back to Australia because of the quality of our performance against the Wallabies the previous year. As a result, that was a badge of honour that we had to uphold. I didn't go on too much, though. Only the players could sort it out on the field so, having spelt out a few home truths, I left it to the senior group to see how they responded. From their actions on the training field,*

it was pretty clear that some of them were even more annoyed about what had happened than I was!

'We knew that we'd let our standards drop in a big way, so the game against New South Wales couldn't come soon enough', Slade McFarland says.

'The Waratahs game became an issue of our credibility. It was imperative that we put everything right by playing well and getting a good result before we faced up to the Aussies.'

Rico Gear remembers the intensity within the camp increasing significantly in the four days that elapsed between the two state games.

'There had been a lot of excitement when we'd first joined up together, but that gave way to a harder edge before the New South Wales game', Gear says.

'The senior guys really put it on the rest of us for about the only time I can ever remember during my time in the team. It was probably the only time they'd ever needed too. The general theme of the preparation was that we hadn't lived up to the heritage and tradition of the jersey, so we had to put that right. The fact that, after we played New South Wales, there was only a week until the Test, brought everyone together real tightly too.'

While Bob Dwyer's men were coming off a season where they had made it to the Super 12 semi-finals for the first time, the Waratahs were eventually over-run by a revenge-fuelled New Zealand Maori side.

Both the 43–18 final score-line, and the seven tries that the visitors scored, which included three in an almost totally one-sided final 15 minutes, represented huge confidence boosters ahead of their trip across the Nullabor Plains to Perth for the date with the Wallabies.

I was fairly confident before that game that we'd get a result, having watched on as the senior players had stepped up and really put it on the rest of the guys. Even so, I hadn't expected us to go out there and blow them away towards the end of that game like we did. The Waratahs were a good side, and they were a confident one, too, having done so well in the Super 12.

What the performance said to me was how much the guys were desperate to put right the damage they felt they had done by their non-performance against Queensland. That, again, showed how much the team, and the jersey, meant to them, which was significant looking at the bigger picture because we had so many guys on that trip who were relatively new to the team.

For a lot of those players, though, the New Zealand Maori team was their All Blacks, and it was times like that New South Wales game that their pride really showed through.

For Reihana who, like a number of his team-mates, was experiencing his first-ever success at the Sydney Football Stadium after years of heartbreak, the Waratahs performance provided redemption.

'The guys all knew that we had to step it up', he says.

'We all knew that we were a lot better than what we had showed against Queensland. We used the game against New South Wales to lay down a marker. That performance brought the confidence and the belief flooding back into the side, which was important given that we didn't have as much experience within the group as we'd had in some of my earlier seasons. By the time we got on the plane to head across to Perth after that match, we all felt we were ready to really give it to the Wallabies.'

While the players departed Sydney in a far more comfortable frame of mind, so too did the team management, literally!

Having all been upgraded to business class by Qantas for the five-hour flight across Australia, the nine members of the management team were sitting comfortably in their seats, supping on complimentary wine, as the playing staff finally boarded and shuffled passed them to their 'cattle class' seats.

'Just by the looks on their faces, especially some of the senior players, as they all filed passed, you could tell that we were going to pay for that big time at some stage further down the track', Stewart recalls.

'There's an unwritten rule that the management doesn't ever set itself apart from the players, in terms of the creature comforts, and we'd done that by all accepting the invitation to take the upgrade. We knew that, by moving to business class, they'd get us when the time came. They didn't miss, either!'

The player's retribution to their wayward leaders – as administered by the team's 'back seat', or senior player grouping – was to force the entire management team to try and sit together on one seat during the team's court session following the Wallaby match.

'As they seemed to like each other's company so much, and were happy to set themselves apart from the players, we figured it was appropriate', McFarland says.

'It was quite hard case when the sentence was delivered but, to be fair to them all, they gave it a bit of a go.'

Understandably, it wasn't an especially comfortable feeling for the individuals involved, but it at least offered them an insight on how their Wallaby counterparts had felt earlier in the evening as the New Zealand Maori side had roared back at their charges during the frantic final moments of the Test.

Adding to the Australian side's discomfort, was finding themselves again confronted by a crowd that appeared to be as much pro-Kiwi, as it was for the home side.

'The guys who had been involved the previous year had talked about how we'd had the crowd then, and the support we received in Perth in the lead-up to the game pretty much told us that it was going to be the same again', Mayerhofler recalls.

'At the mayoral reception they held for both teams in the middle of downtown Perth the day before the game, we got more cheers from the locals than the Wallabies did. I now play with the former Australian fullback Matt Burke at Newcastle [England], and any time we mention that match, he still moans about how it felt to them like it was a home game for us!'

Gear remembers running into a number of people that he hadn't seen for years.

'It seemed like just about every second person in town that week was Maori', Gear says.

'At the reception in the city, most of the crowd were cheering us and booing the Wallabies, which must have been pretty tough for them, given that they were the home team. It didn't worry us, though. If anything, we encouraged everyone and stirred things up further by doing an impromptu haka for the crowd during the reception. The boys all kept their shirts on, but it was still pretty well received!'

Nor was the pre-game banter just restricted to geeing up supporters.

One particular story to emerge from the preparations tells of how a member of the management team, who boasted a background in covert operations, had allegedly dispatched a spy to view Wallaby trainings and then report back on what he had seen.

While espionage between sporting teams is not so unusual, the suggestion that the spy concerned was a deaf Indian armed with a tape recorder who went totally unnoticed by the Australians, caused much mirth amongst the Maori players even though, as is usually the case, the story proved to be totally without foundation.

Of more serious concern for Matt and team manager Peter Potaka than the alleged 'international spy ring' was the situation regarding Southland lock Steve Jackson. The well travelled 29-year-old, who'd been a stalwart provincial servant but had been forced to wait until relatively late in his career to achieve higher honours, found himself faced with the dilemma of having his wife back in New Zealand due to give birth to their first child.

> *There was really no decision to make as far as Steve's situation went in the end. We are into balance and are family oriented as a team, so we felt that it was important that we released Steve to return home for what was a special time for his family. He offered to pay his own airfares home and back, which took any economic questions out of the picture. As it was, he shot home, was present at the birth, and was then back 48 hours later, in plenty of time to play his part supporting the boys, even though he didn't actually get to take the field himself.*

Although training in Perth had gone well, and the team was lifted by the amount of support it had received, Matt was still wary of the potential backlash his players might face from the Australians as a result of their tough encounter the previous year. He was also only too aware that, with just five of the same players from the XV that had started the first Australian game, his side was light on experience when it came to operating under the blow torch at the highest level.

> *We weren't going to be able to catch them off guard, in terms of what to expect from us, like we had the previous year. It was also clear, by the vigorous manner in which they started, that the new Australian coach Eddie Jones had instructed his players to get out there and take us out early.*

> *They came at us in the opening minutes like they really felt they had something to prove, and scored a try almost before we had touched the ball. It was also clear that they had studied us very closely in our first two matches because they seemed to have answers for every move that we were trying. They second-guessed everything we did, so that we hit a solid gold wall every time. I take the responsibility for that. We'd showed our hand in the lead-up matches against the states, which was something we shouldn't have done.*

As well as dealing with the fired up Wallabies, some of the New Zealand Maori players also struggled to keep their own emotions in check during the early moments of the evening.

'As we were in the huddle before the game even began, I looked across at one of the other front rowers and I could see a few tears running down his cheeks', McFarland says.

'The game hadn't even started and the emotion of the moment was clearly preying on some of our players. That probably explains why it took our guys so long to get into that game and to really start believing that we could win it. It was a pity our belief didn't come just that little bit earlier, because the whole game turned around pretty dramatically once the guys started to really play!'

'I think the guys believed in themselves as a result of getting so close to the Australians the year before, but their fast start definitely rocked us, and it took a while before we were really able to regroup', Mayerhofler says.

'Looking back, it was probably a mark of respect the way the Australians came after us at the beginning like they did. They obviously didn't want to take any chances. As it was, once the passes started sticking for us, we nearly reeled them in.'

'Even when they got away to their lead, no heads dropped', Reihana says.

'We knew that we could come back, but we had to change things. It was clear they had prepared well for the way we had been playing. That left us with no alternative but to take the chance and mix it up.'

Reihana's thoughts corresponded exactly with how Matt was thinking as he prepared to address his troops in the dressing room at halftime, with the Subiaco Oval scoreboard showing New Zealand Maori trailing 6–13.

> *I had already reached the conclusion that we would have to vary our game, but then Bruiser [Reihana] spelled out for me exactly what I had been thinking when, as I reached the shed, he intercepted me before my team talk and said: 'Matt, we're going to have to back our skill set'. I had time to reflect later on how that action showed Bruiser's development as a senior player. In the moment itself, it confirmed for me that the senior players were already thinking as I was. We were going to have to throw out our play book and just have a crack at them off the cuff, so that was the sermon I delivered.*

While, initially, the Australians appeared quite comfortable with the change in tactics, and blew their lead out to 27–6 with two tries in the first 10 minutes after halftime, as the second half progressed, the cracks in the Wallabies' defensive armour began to be exposed.

With the New Zealand Maori side throwing the ball all over the park, Reihana started the fight back when he crossed for a try in the sixty-fifth minute of play.

Inside of two minutes after that score, Reihana was try-bound again. Three minutes after that, New Zealand Maori fullback Willie Walker crossed-kicked cleverly for Gear to win the race for the ball and his side's third try in just over five minutes. Suddenly, the scoreboard had closed to 23–27, and what had previously seemed implausible, that New Zealand Maori might win, suddenly became a possibility.

> *The Aussies weren't happy. By the time we scored our third try, you could see from the sideline that our comeback had thrown them right out of their comfort zone. They had probably expected at halftime that they would be able to coast to the final whistle, but instead, here they were, with their backs to the wall as our guys threw everything they had at them.*

Out on the field, Gear confirms that the side was 'running on adrenalin'.

'The guys were all giving it everything', he says.

'At various stages, you looked at different players and they seemed as though they were absolutely spent, but then we'd score and the same guys would lift again. Our collective lack of experience might have ultimately told on us, in terms of the slow start that we made to that game, but you couldn't have asked any more of any of the guys that played. To get so close to them in the end, was pleasing in terms of showing our spirit, but it was also disappointing in that we all felt the game had been within our grasp. Everyone was really bummed when the referee blew it up to finish the game.'

The final whistle came only after an extraordinary flurry of activity, where New Zealand Maori retained the ball through 20 phases and over three minutes of play, trying desperately to find a way through the Australian defences one last decisive time.

'We were all trying so hard', Reihana says.

'By then, I think, we all probably believed that we were going to do it. When he blew the whistle for the end, it was pretty gutting. You just had to see the looks of relief on the Australians' faces to see how worried they had been. We were so close to beating them!'

> *They were panicking at the end. Little George [Australian captain George Gregan] had spat the dummy big time. I was down on the sideline for the finish and we could hear him screaming at the South African referee, Andy Turner, to end the game. That was probably the best indication as to where their mind set was by the time it finished. Just one more clean break, that's all we needed, but it wasn't to be. Even so, I was incredibly proud of my team, probably more than I had been the year before, when we'd also lost.*
>
> *They hung tough throughout that game, both when the heat was on in the first half, and then in the second, where we had to chase the game and we put it on the players to go out there and back themselves. When we were down at halftime, things could easily have gone the other way, the players could have lost their belief and we could have ended up being spanked, especially when they hit us with those two tries straight after the break. In those circumstances, a collapse might have even been understandable, given that we didn't have the experience across the board, in terms of the seasoned All Black players, that we'd had the previous year.*
>
> *To rally like the guys did spoke volumes of their character. It also said a great deal about the influence of the senior players we did have and the leadership qualities among them. One who had stood up was Jono Gibbes. He showed us that night that he was our next captain in waiting.*

The final whistle in Perth would probably have been a fitting finale for on the New Zealand Maori team's programme for the year.

However, there was still one match remaining to be played, although it was not to prove the team's finest hour.

While the scheduling of a match between the New Zealand Maori and the festival New Zealand Barbarians club revived a tradition of matches between the two entities, the timing of this particular contest, as an add on to the main focus of the programme, was unfortunate.

The game was only added to the fixtures schedule by the New Zealand Rugby Union to do its duty for the North Harbour Rugby Union, which had been promised hosting rights to a major fixture but had then been omitted from the Test match allocation for the year.

With New Zealand Maori not having had the opportunity to play at home prior to departing for Australia, the match was not one the side could afford to turn down, although Matt now acknowledges that he underestimated how difficult it would be to prepare for.

> It was an opportunity to showcase the team in front of New Zealanders, but it did prove hard for the players to get up for the occasion after the hype of the previous weekend in Perth. It would be like having the All Blacks play the Bledisloe Cup decider against Australia one week, then having them back up against Italy the next.

> The game was played the night before the second All Blacks–Ireland Test in Auckland, so it lost a lot of its focus through that being on. There were also a number of disruptions to our build up, with the primary one being in terms of our travel arrangements getting back from Australia. Even allowing for all of those mitigating factors, it was still disappointing to lose the way we did. Like a couple of weeks before in Queensland, we had chances to take the game, but simply weren't good enough on the night to make the most of them.

The players were given an inkling as to the difficulties in store for them when their return to New Zealand the day after the Perth Test was disrupted by fog in Melbourne. This closed the airport and left them stuck on the wrong side of the Tasman Sea for an additional day.

> What made that situation worse was that there was always the hope that we might get out of Melbourne that night. As a result, instead of getting out of the airport and going and doing something else, we sat around for most of that Sunday evening before they finally cancelled the flight and bundled us off to a hotel. The players were still on a high after the previous evening's game and the court session afterwards where they'd sewn the management up. I did notice a few of them sneaking in a few shots of alcohol. In that instance, I was happy to turn a blind eye. It's not as if I was dealing with kids. I knew they would all act responsibly, and they did.

'The two worst aspects of that wait, was that we couldn't go anywhere or do anything in case our flight suddenly got called', Stewart says, 'but also when we did end up having to go off to a hotel, none of us had any gear other than what we'd travelled in, because it was all still loaded on the plane!'

The travel frustrations came on top of a difficult situation that Matt found himself in with Crusaders hooker Corey Flynn, who'd performed superbly for the side after coming on as a replacement in the final 20 minutes against Australia.

The 20-year-old had enjoyed his debut experience with the Maori side so much he wanted to stay with the team and return to New Zealand for the Barbarians game, even though he had been selected for the New Zealand Under-21 side. It had previously been agreed that Flynn would head from Perth to South Africa following the Test to link up with that team for the Under-21 World Cup.

> It had been all organised beforehand that Corey would come with us initially, but then leave us after the Australian game and continue on to the Colts tournament, where he ended up playing in their last four games.
>
> The trouble was that Corey became a little reluctant and expressed a desire to stay with us. That was pleasing to hear in one way from a team perspective, in terms of the fact that it showed he had enjoyed himself and was comfortable in our environment. However, there was also the issue of the commitment we'd made to the Under-21s to release him to them. There was never any question of us going back on that. In the end, I asked Greg Feek, who was also from Canterbury, to become involved. Greg spoke to Corey and helped smooth things over so that the original arrangements would be stuck to.

'That tour was really the start of us beginning to see how good Corey was going to be as a player', Feek says.

'Within a couple of years of that, he'd progressed on to be an All Black [in 2003] and then captain of New Zealand Maori the year after that. But he'd been one of the youngsters with us at the Crusaders earlier in 2002, although he'd still had a few games and done pretty well. After we had a chat about it, he was okay to move on and join the Under-21s, although he said that he would have liked to have stayed with us. What the whole thing showed was that we do ask quite a lot of these young guys sometimes, in terms of the number of different team commitments we get them to make.'

The Flynn issue might have been resolved, but Matt was livid when, after acting in good faith with the Under-21s by honouring their commitment, he felt that favour wasn't returned by the All Black coach, John Mitchell.

On returning to New Zealand, Matt was dismayed to learn that Taine Randell and Kees Meeuws, who'd both previously appeared for New

Zealand Maori, would this time be lining up against the side for the Barbarians.

> There was no communication from him [Mitchell]. It was not a situation I was happy about. As far as we were concerned, there was no issue. We, as a national team, had precedence over the Barbarians in terms of selection. If he [Mitchell] had wanted those two players for the All Blacks, that is one thing. But the Barbarians were not the All Blacks, even if he was using the game as a bit of a trial. Both Taine and Kees should have been playing for us.

Matt wasn't the only one who felt that way.

'We didn't get a choice', Randell says.

'I did ask John if I could play for the New Zealand Maori, or alternatively play club rugby back in Dunedin the following day, but was told that I would be playing for the Barbarians. It was a game I didn't want to play, though. It felt exactly the same as it would have felt if I'd ever been asked to play against Otago. It just didn't feel right. There was nothing I could do, though. I don't mind admitting that I felt like it was almost a punishment. I seemed to be on the outer with him at the time, and I did feel like I was being deliberately made to play against the New Zealand Maori because he knew that I didn't want to.'

As it was, Randell finished up on the winning side, although he felt little joy in the Barbarians 37–22 victory.

The fact that a scratch side, which had only been assembled a couple of days beforehand, could beat a New Zealand Maori side that had been on tour in Australia for two weeks served to highlight how difficult it had been for the Maori players to motivate themselves.

> The guys just weren't up for it, as much as they tried. Los [Carlos Spencer] probably best illustrated the difficulty we had. He had a bit of a nightmare that night and, the harder he tried, the worse it seemed to get. At times I reckon he was trying to beat them by himself. It was almost like we were still back in Perth, where I'd told the players to throw the rule book out the window at halftime!

Spencer wasn't alone in feeling flat.

Mayerhofler, in his final game for New Zealand Maori, recalls the evening being a major anticlimax after what had been an enjoyable tour.

'I sort of had a feeling beforehand that it could be a bit of a struggle', he says.

'Unfortunately, it turned out that way. There just wasn't the atmosphere there, in either the team, or the crowd to be honest. The crowd, which wasn't the biggest anyway, seemed unsure as to which side they should be supporting. In the end, it turned out to be one of those games where just about everyone at the stadium couldn't get it over and done with quickly enough!'

Reihana, who also ended up making his last appearance in the New Zealand Maori jersey that night at North Harbour Stadium, concurs.

'It was very difficult to come back down again after all the hype of Perth', he says, 'and that showed throughout the Barbarians game. The boys tried – the commitment was certainly there – but the edge was lacking. The top two inches still counts for a lot, and we just didn't have the mental spark, and also made a lot more mistakes in the game than they did.'

While Reihana signed off from his New Zealand Maori career by scoring three tries against the Barbarians, it still isn't an evening he looks back on with any fondness.

'In the context of that year, it was a disappointing finish. We were a much better team than we showed against the Barbarians.'

> *I felt really sorry for Bruiser, given that turned out to be his final game, with him leaving for a new career with Northampton at the end of that season. He gave so much to our team during his time, and even fired some shots against the Barbarians, although he didn't have much support.*
>
> *For a player for whom the Maori jersey meant so much, it was sad that he went out on a performance like that. We let the jersey down, and I blame myself as much as I do the players. While I firmly believe that it is absolutely vital that the New Zealand Maori team continues to be seen playing in New Zealand, it shouldn't be as an after-thought. That was one game that we quite clearly shouldn't have accepted.*

16

Canadian capers: 2003–2004

'A Churchillian conquest!'

A familiar opponent, with an even more familiar face, kicked off the New Zealand Maori programme for 2003, as the side made its first appearance for the year against a Tongan outfit coached by Matt's assistant from 1998 to 2001, Jim Love.

Love had taken leave from his position with the Maori team just prior to the commencement of the previous year's programme in order to take on the role of preparing Tonga for the 2003 Rugby World Cup.

Not that the pair's friendship, and Matt's support for Love's decision to coach the Tongan side, prevented a fair bit of banter between the two prior to the match at North Harbour Stadium.

> *We'd communicated a fair bit in the lead up, and there were quite a few cheeky comments thrown in there. They were in the situation of obviously having the World Cup to look forward to, while we had England and a tour of Canada to come, so there was plenty on the line for everyone involved in that game.*
>
> *While I'd been happy for Jim to take on the Tongan role when it came up, I didn't see that as the end of his role in Maori rugby, and with the Maori team. I also knew that, Jim being Jim, the Tongans would be as physical as always when we played them, and that they probably wouldn't drop off towards the end of the game like they had usually done in the past.*

Love didn't disappoint his friend on either count, although he admits to finding it difficult being in the opposite dressing shed to the New Zealand Maori side.

'I probably underestimated that side of the role', Love says.

'It was a good game for us to have, because I knew Matt would field a strong side – stronger than some of the teams we would face at the World Cup later in the year, but the whole preparation on the day really brought it home to me what I had left behind. Normally, I'm into psyching my guys up to go out and smash the opposition, but I found that hard with the Maori game – given that I knew them all so well. In many ways, I felt like an alien that day, because the Maori team was still part of me. I found the whole experience quite sad.'

Not that Love's charges disappointed Matt, in terms of the intensity and physicality they brought to the game.

While a strong second half propelled New Zealand Maori to a comfortable 47–12 win, the score had been just 19–12 at halftime, after Tonga twice punished the home side for inaccurate play by snapping up two intercept tries.

> *I felt for Jim afterwards. You could certainly see his handiwork in the way the Tongan forwards performed. That was the third time I'd coached against Tonga during my stint as New Zealand Maori coach, and Jim's mob was easily the most well-drilled, in terms of their set piece work, of the Tongan teams that I came up against. The Tongans were always physically strong guys, but this time they were well organised in the lineouts and scrums, as well as hitting us hard at the breakdowns.*

'I wasn't too disappointed with how we'd played, because the rub of the green had gone against us a couple of times, and it wasn't the top side that we could field either', Love says.

'There were still a few of the overseas-based players to come back at that point. It was the meeting up with all of the Maori guys at the after-match function that brought it home to me what I was missing out on. While the opportunity to take Tonga to the World Cup had been an attractive one, and I thought that it would help develop me as a coach, I only had to look around that room after the game to see what I was up against. Seeing all of the class players in the Maori side underlined how much work I had ahead of me with Tonga!'

While hindsight is a great thing, if he had his time again, Love admits he would have skipped the Tongan opportunity in order to retain his place in the New Zealand Maori pecking order.

'Even when I talked it over with Matt and agreed to take up the Tongan opportunity, I made that move with one eye on the head coaching position with the New Zealand Maori team', Love says.

'That was my long-term goal, and I made the move with New Zealand Rugby Union support, although I unfortunately found out later that that wasn't worth very much. Once I was gone, it seemed to me that I was pretty quickly forgotten!'

> Coaching against a guy I knew so well, and had worked so closely with, gave me an insight into how the players now found it in the professional era, especially for the guys in provincial teams who were then drafted into other Super rugby sides, and wound up having to play against their mates. The situation with Jim and myself around that game was really no different to that – I was just in the fortunate position that I had a little bit more class among my backs!

Among the class backs to whom Matt refers from that day was one Christian Cullen, whose selection for New Zealand Maori had caused a major uproar, given that there had been no public knowledge of his Maori heritage prior to his missing the All Black cut after seven years in that side.

Although Matt agrees that the process by which the former star All Black fullback's eligibility was examined and confirmed was not explained at the time as well as it might have been, he stands by the integrity of the selection and Cullen's eligibility.

> We were very clear, in terms of doing our homework on that selection, as we did on all of the players we ever selected – and Christian certainly wasn't the first European-looking Maori to play for New Zealand Maori.

> The thing that was probably central to the issue was the surprise element to his selection, because we'd never really been in the position to look at him before. He'd always been a shoe-in for the All Blacks and was, therefore, never available.

> When it became apparent to us that Christian could be available, I detailed our team manager Peter Potaka and kaumatua Whetu Tipiwai to examine his whakapapa. They did that and came back with the thumbs up, so we knew that Christian's genealogy stood up to the test before he was named. We have had our failures, in terms of guys we were interested

> in not proving to be Maori once we examined their family history. The Mauger boys, Aaron and Nathan, for example, fit into that category. So too does Daniel Carter; Keith Lowen as well. They were all players that we examined at one stage or another, but got the big thumbs down.

Part of the problem, Matt believes, in terms of the eligibility situation, goes back to the core issue of what determines whether one is Maori.

> In Cully's case, we knew there would be critics of his selection, and we acknowledged that his Maori 'percentage' wasn't big, but the facts were that he did have the bloodlines in his family which made him a Maori. It did go back a few generations in his particular case, but that was irrelevant. It doesn't matter whether you've got 1 percent Maori blood in you or 99 percent, either you've got Maori lineage or you haven't.
>
> We had guys that were of Pacific Islands origin that we looked at, but if there was no Maori heritage there, then a line was ruled through their name.
>
> One player I especially remember was Tafai Ioasa, who went on to captain the New Zealand Sevens team. Tafai had played in a Hawke's Bay regional Maori tournament and we were interested in him as a result, but we still checked his family history. It turned out that his family lineage was all from the Pacific Islands so he has never played for the New Zealand Maori team.
>
> There was also one quite high-profile player around that time, who went on to be an All Black, who had been adopted and had a Maori parent. We were interested in him so we looked at his genealogy. As a whangai, he is viewed within the Maori community as a Maori, but our eligibility tests are based around bloodlines and genealogy. And, in that regard, we couldn't consider him as a Maori, so he was never selected for the team.

Almost as quickly as the Cullen saga had died down, Matt was presented with another dilemma.

Fifteen minutes into the outing against Tonga, the new New Zealand Maori captain, Jono Gibbes, went down with an injury that turned out to be a dislocated knee. It ruled him out of the rest of that year's programme.

> To lose Jono was a huge blow. As he proved three seasons later against the Lions, he had this capacity to lift the guys around him. He had made a big impression with us in Australia the year before, in his first tour, and

so had become the obvious replacement when Deon Muir decided, at the end of 2002, to try his luck in Japan.

What bowled us when we lost Jono was that we didn't have the depth of leadership within the side that we'd had in times like when EB [Errol Brain] had been captain, where we had provincial captains all over the place. Because of that, I had no real option but to make Taine Randell captain for the game against England that followed. I knew by then that he was headed to England to play for Saracens, and so wasn't going to be about to take the team to Canada, but we needed someone who could step in and pick up the leadership reins without causing any disruption. With all of his previous experience with Otago, the Highlanders and the All Blacks, Taine could obviously do that.

So, as he'd started his New Zealand Maori career, eight seasons previously, Randell finished it; captaining the side.

'While it is always an honour to lead a side in an international, and I really enjoyed being in the Maori environment again, having to take on the captaincy for the game against England wasn't ideal', Randell says.

'I was never going to turn it down, but realistically I probably wasn't up for the job mentally. Things had almost sorted themselves out at that point, in terms of my taking up a contract with Saracens, and I had hoped to be able to play for the Maoris without having any other outside pressures. Because it was going to be my last time with the team, and any national New Zealand team for that matter, my main desire was just to make sure that I enjoyed it.'

Once I spoke with Taine, there was never an issue with him taking over. I admired him for that. I knew he was quite happy being one of the boys on that tour, that he'd wanted to be in the background, but the team needed him and he stepped up.

This is more than can be said for the Taranaki weather!

After training in dry conditions during the lead up to the match against a side that would be the world champions by year's end, the heavens opened on the day of the game with England, and the rain didn't stop bucketing down.

'It had been fine all week, so to wake up that morning and see that it was heaving down, well, to say it was disappointing would be an understatement', New Zealand Maori first-five-eighths Glen Jackson says.

'Everything that we'd practised, and our total match plan revolved around running their big men around. Unfortunately, the conditions that we ended up having to play in made that strategy next to impossible to carry out.'

> *It was almost a total replay of the weather we'd had when we'd last been in New Plymouth three years earlier for the Scotland game. If we'd had the same players as then, because you learn from your experiences as a team, we might have played it a bit differently. But we only had four guys – Glen Jackson, Matua Parkinson, Paul Tito and Greg Feek – back from that game. To be fair to the players, they tried gamely to stretch England wide like we'd planned to before it rained, but the task was just too great in the wet. Inevitably, we had a high turnover rate, and the ball was difficult enough to secure against their big forward pack anyway, without us giving it straight back to them.*

Even allowing for the treacherous conditions, and the fact that the home side struggled to match the massive English pack in the set piece exchanges, the New Zealand Maori side battled gamely and remained in contention for much of the contest.

England led just 10–6 at halftime and 16–9 until well into the second half, before halfback Andy Gomarsall's try, five minutes from time, finally killed off the Maori challenge to clinch a 23–9 success.

'To be fair to them, they played to the conditions pretty well, and used them to their best advantage', Jackson says.

'They copped a fair bit of treatment in the papers afterwards for the manner in which they'd played but that was just ignorance on behalf of the press guys concerned. The English knew that our backs, especially our outsides, posed a threat, so they played a territory game and did a fairly good job of limiting our attacking opportunities.'

Despite the possession restrictions that were placed on them by the performance of the English forwards, the New Zealand Maori side still managed more clean line breaks than did their opponents.

They also nearly scored a critical try from one of them, when Rico Gear chased through after a fly hack from deep inside the Maori half, only to be run down from behind by England winger Dan Luger as the ball sat invitingly in the England in-goal area.

'My legs hit the wall', Gear recalls. 'It was a long chase on a mucky ground, but he [Luger] got their first.'

The near miss, Gear says, only added to his team's frustration on the night.

'Had I been able to score then, it might have got us started', he says.

'As it was, they didn't really do that much to beat us. All they had was a good forward pack, but they played the tight game a lot better than we did. Although our guys hung in there, the conditions just didn't suit the way we wanted to play, which was annoying. I'd love to have got them on a dry ground!'

Although England only fielded two of the forwards – props Trevor Woodman and Phil Vickery – from the side that would topple Australia in the Rugby World Cup final, five months later, Slade McFarland confirms they were a well-schooled opponent.

'They were big, well disciplined, and quite probably more used to playing in conditions like that than we were', he says.

'As much as we tried to disrupt them, they knew what they were about. Their performance basically showed what was to come later on in the year at the World Cup.'

Not only did England showcase its forward might in suppressing the New Zealand Maori, another impressive aspect of the display put on by Clive Woodward's side was the blitz defensive system it employed to shut down its opponent's infrequent attacking raids.

The system, which was all the rage in the English premiership, hadn't previously been seen to any great degree in New Zealand, and proved as effective five days later against the All Blacks in Wellington, as it had against New Zealand Maori.

Having won in New Plymouth on the Monday night, England rounded out its trip by recording just its second victory over the All Blacks in Tests in New Zealand, 15–13 the following Saturday, before then scoring a first-ever victory over the Wallabies in Australia on their way home.

> *While the conditions helped, in terms of slowing our ball distribution down a little bit, we still had chances out in the backs, but their blitz defence got in our faces and just shut us down. When there was contact, their forwards would then arrive at the breakdowns in numbers very quickly, so our go-forward via that method was virtually impossible.*

It is a tribute to the England defence that the game was the only one in Matt's decade-long tenure as New Zealand Maori coach where his side failed to score a try.

> While we were always close enough on the score-board, and possibly could have stolen it if the breaks had gone our way, that would have been unjust. They played Test rugby and put us under a level of sustained pressure that we simply weren't used to. While we knew that their game was based around a strong and mobile pack, and had planned to counter that, when combined with their overall defensive screen, it was just too difficult for us to break down. A lot of the players might have been different come the World Cup final later in the year but the methodology wasn't. They showed us that night how they planned to win the World Cup!

The England strategy was based to a fair degree on brute strength up front, but they also showed against the New Zealand Maori that they were prepared to use their 'smarts'.

> Troy Flavell had a big game for us, and was our main lineout man, but they worked that out pretty quickly and moved to make it hard for us in that phase. By squeezing the gap at the front of the lineout when it was our turn to throw, we were forced to go long all the time, which was a risky business in those conditions. It wasn't necessarily Slade's fault, it was a big ask of him to have to always go to the back, but their big men, Simon Shaw and Steve Borthwick, in the middle of the lineout, picked off a fair few of our throws.

The injury to Gibbes, and Randell's departure to England necessitated changes in personnel to the squad prior to its departure for Canada just over a month after the initial phase of the programme had concluded.

They were not the only complications.

Due to previous convictions, three of the original selections – flanker Matua Parkinson, inside back Riki Flutey and second rower Reece Robinson – were unable to make the tour as they'd been denied entry visas by the Canadian government.

> It was a difficult situation for us because it was something that we had no control over. The Rugby Union worked things through with the Canadian High Commission based in Canberra, but it was no go. Because of the player's prior convictions, there was nothing we could do about it as that was Canadian law. Riki had struck trouble in Argentina a year or so before, where he'd ended up in jail after an altercation with some locals, so we knew we might be in trouble getting a clearance for him. One of the others had a conviction for driving while

> *intoxicated, but the Canadian authorities wouldn't even give us a waver for that.*
>
> *We were straight with the players, and the news media, as to what the situation was right through the whole process. What we did find a bit disappointing after we got to Canada though, was that the local rugby officials were quite fired up about our having to leave the guys behind. Apparently, the non-entry clause gets waived quite a bit for gridiron players, and for participants in more high-profile sports over there.*

There was an amusing post-script to the saga at the team session following the 65–27 win over Canada at Calgary in the first game of the tour.

'Matt had basically dedicated the game to the three guys that couldn't come on the tour, and had used that to try and help motivate everyone beforehand', McFarland says.

'He even went to the extent of having their photos in the changing room so that they were still 'with us' in spirit. When he told us that we were 'playing for them', I was trying not to laugh and had to duck my head so that he wouldn't see me!'

Not that McFarland, who headed up the 'back seat' on the trip, was prepared to let the incident rest afterwards when the players convened in a more light-hearted atmosphere.

'I re-enacted what Matt had said to us in front of the team, only I changed it around a little bit', McFarland says.

'I said: "now, we're playing today for these three criminals!" At that, the whole team just cracked up.'

> *That was the thing about those guys. They played for each other as if they were brothers, but they could be quite ruthless about each other, too, when it came to taking the mickey. I've got to admit, when Slade started imitating me at the court session and was going on about the criminals, I just had to laugh. It was pretty funny.*

The humour further added to the comfort the touring party had felt virtually from the moment it touched down in Canada, to be greeted by an official welcome from the country's native Indian community.

> *The difference in terms of where we had come from, hit us basically as soon as we stepped off the plane. It set the scene for the whole tour. The welcome was done along traditional lines, with their chief speaking to*

us, before our kaumatua Whetu responded. What really blew me away, though, was when I was chatting to the Indian chief later. He told me that his family was Maori. It turned out that he was married to a Maori lady from Waikato and her kids were in the Indian welcome group.

If the arrival ceremony had proved something out of the ordinary for the team's most seasoned tourists, it was positively from another world for the team's rookie, Wairarapa-Bush flanker Germaine Anaha. The only current player from the second and third divisions to be selected for the side, Anaha had needed to get a passport and a credit card, as he'd never before been out of New Zealand.

'I'd played for the New Zealand Divisional XV against Samoa and Tonga earlier in the year and had run into [New Zealand Maori selector] Willie Hetaraka, who'd told me that there had been a few injuries, and that I should be prepared', Anaha says.

'Willie had been my coach in the Maori Colts, but, while it was nice to hear that, I didn't really think anything would come of it. On the day I did get selected, I was driving to Palmerston North with my wife and had the mobile phone switched off when they were trying to reach me. It was only later on, when I heard it mentioned on TV that I realised I was in the team.'

A tree cutter by trade, Anaha was given the week off by his boss prior to the team's assembly in Auckland, so that he could make all the arrangements he needed to ahead of his trip.

The only player he knew in the side was Robinson, who he met up with at Palmerston North airport as they flew to Auckland for the assembly, even though Robinson was ultimately unable to tour.

'I didn't know what to expect, so I got all dressed up and was in my Wairarapa-Bush 'number 1s' [team suit] when Reece turned up at the airport in his casuals', Anaha recalls.

'After seeing that, I was kind of hoping that the rest of the players would all be in their '1s' when we got to Auckland, but they were casually dressed as well. I'd spent a fair bit of time beforehand polishing my shoes, too!'

Anaha's presentation wasn't the only thing that impressed the coaching staff.

He might have been an unknown to the rest of the team, but they warmed to him pretty quickly. He got stuck in at training and quickly earned their respect. We'd been watching Germaine for a while. I'd watched him play

> *NPC for Wairarapa-Bush against Horowhenua-Kapiti the year before, and we'd kept an eye on him with the Divisional XV as well.*
>
> *His selection wasn't totally from left field. While he only received his opportunity because the other players were forced out, the thing about Germaine was that he reminded us of the backgrounds we'd come from. The majority of all Maori players start out in rural communities like he did. I think all the guys could identify with his infectious talk and his raw enthusiasm.*

'I'd only ever seen most of the players before on TV, but I was quickly made to feel right at home', Anaha says.

'I was pretty nervous around some of the guys to start with, but fortunately we had a few training runs before we left and I was able to get stuck in. If anything, I was probably a bit too keen to earn their respect for a start. Fish [Paul Tito] and Flav [Troy Flavell] took me aside on the quiet and told me that I didn't have to be everywhere. "Just pick your opponents and make sure that you are effective with each one" was the general theme of their message. It was advice I took on board and will never forget.'

Unfortunately, the Wairarapa-Bush man injured his back shortly after halftime in the match at Calgary and was forced to leave the field. The injury handed Waikato flanker Wayne McEntee starts in the last two matches of the trip. Anaha finally made it back onto the field as a replacement shortly before the end of the second Test against Canada.

'Wayne had been my understudy in the Divisional XV, but he really took his chance and played well', Anaha says.

'It was still an amazing experience to be part of that tour, even if I didn't end up getting as much game time as I'd initially hoped for. When the boys hung up the pictures of the players who hadn't been able to go at the 'courty' after the first game, it was almost like something out of that television show *Crime Watch*. "Have you seen these men?"'

Anaha was not the only player who relished what was a totally new experience. Cullen, the veteran of 58 All Black Tests, also thrived.

'He got right into it', Jackson says. 'After all of the rugby he'd played, Cully seemed to really appreciate the point of difference that the Maori environment had. I got the feeling afterwards that he wished that he'd been able to play for the team a little bit more.'

> *The Canadians loved Cully. After he scored a try in the second game against the All Stars at Ottawa, he was mobbed by the locals as he left the*

> field. None of the crowds at the three games we played on that trip were huge, but those that are into their rugby over there are wildly enthusiastic about the game. A lot of them had travelled large distances, from all over the country, just to attend the matches. It was obvious to us that they appreciated what a great player Cully had been for the All Blacks and were rapt with the opportunity to see him play in the flesh.

Cullen wasn't the only star name in the touring party. Seven of the players had previously been All Blacks while another, Gear, was playing with such dash that he was to achieve the honour the following year.

'The locals probably saw us as much as the New Zealand team, as they did the Maori side', Gear says.

'But while they were enthusiastic, the atmosphere around the games was also quite relaxed, and that suited the boys.'

Cullen appreciated the change as, once again, did Norm Berryman, who'd arrived back in New Zealand after a stint playing overseas in time to resume his position in the team following a two-season absence.

'Normy was all over the place on that trip. He kept us entertained', Gear says.

'Matt always allowed guys to be themselves, and Norm thrived on that. Some guys can be like mice in other teams, but Matt always gave everyone a bit of space. It was one of the best things about the team, and one of the reasons why everyone always put up their hands to be a part of it.'

After beating Canada impressively first up, the New Zealand Maori side's second match took them out into the country to a small ground on the edge of the city of Ottawa.

> For a while, we didn't think there would be much of a crowd, but as we were warming up, people started arriving from everywhere. It was a very rural setting, but we ended up playing in front of a good-sized crowd who created a great atmosphere. The players really enjoyed it.

Naturally, it helped that they were winning, with the New Zealand Maori side running in eight tries during a 52–11 victory over the local combination, which was drawn from Canadian players not included in the national side.

Although the Canadian national side proved a lot more competitive in its second crack at the tourists, the North Americans still struggled to combat the speed at which the New Zealand Maori side played the game and its superior support play.

The visitors scored five tries in the final outing of the tour, winning 30–9 at Toronto. In all, they'd scored 23 tries in their three matches.

The Canadian players are big, strong and fit. They're good athletes. Where they lack a little bit is in having a true natural instinct for the game. That only comes with experience, and I guess is a result of the gridiron background that a lot of their players have. They're just not instinctive as rugby players.

For all that, the Canadians benefited from their exposure to the New Zealand-style of play that they gained from New Zealand Maori team's visit. At the Rugby World Cup three months later, they were able to tie the All Blacks down for long periods in a pool match, before eventually succumbing to the tournament heavyweight's superior firepower, 68–6.

Although the Canadians couldn't live with the visitors, one particularly cheeky member of the touring party met his match in the team's high-rise Toronto hotel on the eve of the final game of the tour.

The players were sharing rooms in the hotel, but had only one door swipe-card between them, so our resourceful man came up with the ingenious idea of hiding his behind a fire alarm that was on the wall in the hallway near his room door. This made things easy for the player, and his room-mate, to come and go as they pleased.

The only trouble was, in stowing the swipe card in its hiding place at one point, the player accidentally tripped the alarm system, which resulted in the whole hotel having to be rapidly emptied out while the local fire brigade conducted a thorough check of the premises.

The timing of the 'fire' proved especially inconvenient for a huge Indian wedding party that had gathered on a lower floor for the ceremony.

'There were over 600 rooms in the hotel, and they all had to be evacuated', Stewart recalls, 'so everyone was left to mill around outside at 11 o'clock at night. Some of the hotel guests were in their pyjamas. It would be fair to say that quite a few of them weren't especially impressed!'

Not that the team gave up the cause of the disturbance, although Matt says the incident did serve to 'quieten down' the player's off-field behaviour – for a short while at least!

The fire alarm incident aside, as a public relations exercise, Matt believes that the visit was a major success. He judges this, not just on the Canadians' reaction to their visitors, but also on the fact that the New Zealand Maori side was so quickly invited back, to participate in the inaugural Churchill Cup tournament the following year.

> *The team got to mix a lot with the opposition, and also with the Canadian public. That was a good experience for all of our players. We were always very conscious of our role, both as ambassadors of Maori and New Zealand rugby, but also as marketers for our country.*

Some of the 'ambassadors' did go missing in action on occasion.

'There were quite a few girls running around in bikinis while we were over there, given that it was their summer', Stewart remembers.

'This wasn't lost on the players. It would be fair to say that the 'Dirty Dirties' [non-playing members of the squad] did go walkabout a bit at various times.'

Cowboy hats, as modelled by the locals, had also become a popular addition to the players' attire by the tour's end. For those who missed out on securing theirs on the 2003 visit, the return trip to North America for the Churchill Cup tournament offered another opportunity.

> *We knew virtually straight after the 2003 tour that the invitation to return was coming. What the Canadians had told us was that the style of play we employed was a big attraction, in terms of having proved popular with Canadian rugby followers. They also felt that, with the high profile the New Zealand Maori team now had in Canada as a result of our first visit, it would further help promote both the tournament and the game in general if we were involved.*

While the Churchill Cup has been positioned as a North American event, it is directed from London, with the (England) Rugby Football Union having a major role in the tournament organisation.

The relationship between the North Americans and their English 'overlords' is one that is not without friction. This is something the New Zealand Maori side discovered after finding out that they were the overwhelming favourites with the locals to win the tournament, having made the final against England A.

'Having England involved definitely added a bit of extra intensity to that second trip to Canada', Jackson says.

'As well as having them to play, there was also a trophy at stake. We were pretty keen to be the first team to get our name on it.'

Running parallel to the Churchill Cup tournament for the men was a tournament for the women, which saw the New Zealand Black Ferns women's side accompany the New Zealand Maori side on their tour.

'We travelled separately, but there was a lot of mixing between the two sides during the tournaments', Stewart recalls.

'Some of the guys were quite surprised how professional their set up was, and how strict their diet was on tour. For their part, the feedback we received was that the girls were amazed at the types of food we were allowing our players to eat!'

> Having the Black Ferns over there playing at the same time as the curtain-raiser to our matches worked out really well. There is a strong Maori participation rate within the national women's side. As a result, the similarities between the two team's cultures were fairly easy to see. What made the whole venture even more successful was that we both ended up coming home as winners, although they certainly had it a lot easier in their final against England [which the Black Ferns won 38–0] than we did in ours!

One of the most notable aspects of the 26-man squad Matt selected for the tour was that it included the return of two grand servants from earlier in his time as head coach.

Fullback Adrian Cashmore was back in the mix after having returned home from a stint in Japan, while Caleb Ralph was also available again. After attending the World Cup, Ralph had found himself surplus to the requirements of the new All Black coach Graham Henry, when the former Welsh and Lions coach succeeded John Mitchell.

'The tour came straight after the Super 12, which had seemed to come up pretty quickly after the late finish we'd had to the year before, because of the World Cup', Ralph says.

'As a result, I was hanging out for a break from rugby after the Super 12 finished, but Matt talked me round into going on the tour. I was glad he did, too. Once I was there, it was just like old times being back with all of the boys. It was a great tour.'

The acquisition of Ralph added another senior figure to the team hierarchy, and one who had the credibility to keep his fellow players on the right track.

'It was exciting being able to go to Canada. All of the boys were up for it after the stories that had come back from the year before, and I shared their enthusiasm. It was my first time going there', Ralph says.

'But it was still important that we performed. I made sure that all the players, a lot of whom were quite young fellas, realised that. We owed it to all the guys who had gone before us in the Maori team, and who had been forced to play all of the low key games, to make sure that we performed. It was those guys, playing in those games, that had established the credibility of the Maori team which we were benefiting from.'

Like Ralph, Cashmore found his return to the New Zealand Maori environment invigorating.

After three seasons playing with the Toyota company team in Japan, the former All Black fullback had essentially returned to New Zealand to retire.

'Things didn't finish for me as well in Japan as I would have liked. I hadn't wanted to retire on a bad note, so I allowed my name to be put in the Super 12 draft, and ended up getting called up by the Chiefs towards the end of their run to a first ever semi-final', Cashmore says.

'It was refreshing to go into such a professional environment. Things just kept getting better for me after that. I went on the New Zealand Maori tour, then we won the Ranfurly Shield off Auckland with Bay of Plenty. I had been going to finish but it turned out to be one of the best years of my career!'

But while the New Zealand Maori team environment hadn't changed a great deal from that he had left in 2000, Cashmore did note a more hardened professional attitude among the players.

'That was mainly due to them all being so well versed in the requirements of professionalism through their Super 12 experience', he says.

'So after the games, it was all about recovery drinks and hot and cold treatments. There were no beers floating around the changing rooms like there used to be. Mind you, by then, there was just about no one left playing rugby in New Zealand who'd played as an amateur.'

What hadn't changed, Cashmore was pleased to see, was the appearance of the guitar in the hands of Tipiwai once the players had begun to relax in the dressing room after matches.

The time-honoured New Zealand Maori tradition of trying to 'jerk' team-mates also remained strongly in evidence.

This practice included the dishing out of retribution to team management when they had failed to properly fulfil their duties, as occurred after a communications mix up, which saw the team turn up for its game against the United States in Calgary without towels for the players' post-game showers.

'We managed to get our local liaison man to go off to a hotel to get some, but the damage had been done by then', Stewart says.

'It went to the 'back seat', and the management all ended up having to sit through the team session that night each wearing only a towel.'

Former New Zealand Maori player and All Black Stu Forster, who was on his first tour with the side as its technical advisor, along with another member of the management team also found themselves in the gun at various stages.

Forster's title caused great hilarity amongst the players because the Rugby Union's bulky analysis equipment, which the team lugged from place to place throughout the tour, returned to New Zealand in its box without having ever been opened!

'I remember everyone talking to Stu after one of the games and teasing him about wanting to review the game we'd played', one of the players says.

'But he said: "we look forward not back in this team boys! Let's move on to the next game". The thing was, he was our technical man, and he didn't know how to use the computer!'

'About as technical as he got was a pair of binoculars', another player adds, 'but he was not alone among our management, in terms of struggling with technology on that trip.'

Matt says that Forster made such progress in his area after that tour that the level of technical analysis he was able to provide the players during the Lions match was up with the standard on offer to the All Blacks.

Another member of the team's off-field hierarchy, who hailed from one of the country's rural provinces, struck 'technological trouble' during the Churchill Cup tour when he couldn't understand why his card wouldn't work in an ATM money machine.

It turned out that the individual in question, who was new to the use of money cards, had popped his into the machine and then verbally asked it for $50.00.

Naturally, he was confused when no response was forthcoming, until his wife informed him that the machine couldn't talk and that he had to punch in his personal identification number!

Unfortunately for the hapless team member concerned, his daughter proceeded to tell some of the players the story, which resulted in a lot of fun being had at his expense!

The players never missed an opportunity to cut someone down to size, no matter who it was and what role they had in the team. But, while it was

> *all good-natured fun, on the field, the boys showed their serious side. We played pretty well on that trip.*

After a one-sided romp against a British Columbia XV to dust off the cobwebs, the New Zealand Maori side's first tournament opponent was the United States. It was a knockout match, with the winner to progress through to meet England A, which had eliminated Canada 48–23.

> *We knew the Americans would be quite strong because they had beaten Canada the year before and we respected Canada as an opponent. They'd also gone within a whisker of beating Fiji at the World Cup. They played quite a similar style to Canada, in terms of being big guys who were extremely fit. You had to knock them over first time because, if you didn't and they got in behind you, they always had players coming up in support. It wasn't like playing the Island sides where the individualism of the players often takes over, and they try to do too much on their own.*

Although the Americans contributed richly to an expansive contest, and were well directed by the Wales-based and Australian-born first-five-eighths Mike Hercus, their efforts to police the hard running New Zealand players were no more successful than the Canadians had been the year before.

By fulltime, New Zealand Maori had scored 11 tries in advancing to the tournament final, with a 69–31 win.

'They were big guys, but they couldn't really handle it once the game opened up', Ralph says.

'While they were okay at the set pieces, once it got into general play, they got lost pretty quickly. By the end, we were just running through them.'

They might have ultimately been over-powered, but the Americans still made their mark. Their tally of 31 points against New Zealand Maori was bettered only twice during Matt's time as coach, during the losses to Australia in 2001 and the New Zealand Barbarians a year later.

> *They exposed us down the short side quite a bit, so we had to have a good look at that. We'd also dropped off a few too many tackles and knew that we couldn't afford a repeat of that if we were going to take England. They were still on a roll after the World Cup the year before. While we didn't openly talk about it, that result was in the back of just about everyone's mind. Off the field during that tournament, the English guys just seemed*

> *to have that swagger and that arrogance about them that wasn't there with the American and Canadian guys.*

Nor did the arrangements on match day, when the English tournament organisers delayed the kick off of the final by 30 minutes (without informing the New Zealand Maori team management), help relations between the two teams.

> *What that [the time change] meant was that we ended up doing our pre-match warm ups too soon. It threw our whole pre-match routine out of kilter, and meant that we basically just had to sit around for a bit waiting for the game to start. It may or may not have been a deliberate act on their part, but it certainly served to stir the guys up. The players were pretty wild!*

'I always felt that we were a lot better team than the English were, but we'd loosened up in the game against the Americans and it happened again in the final', says Ralph, who scored two of New Zealand Maori side's four tries against England A.

'We nearly paid for that when they forced a draw at fulltime, which meant that the match had to go into extra time. By the end of the 100 minutes we played, everyone was pretty stuffed.'

'It was a hot day and a hard track. But while the guys were pretty shattered at having to play the extra 20 minutes, it would have been worse for England. They lost', Jackson says.

> *It was a hard fought game, which was fitting for a final. It went to the wire and showcased the game in a great light, which was exactly what the tournament organisers had probably been hoping for. When England scored a late try to tie the game and force it into extra time, I figured the outcome had probably become a bit of a lottery. The momentum was with them, but I knew we had the experience to pull it back our way. It was a see-saw battle, though, until our old hands Jackson and Ralph conjured up a move to score the winning try. It was a great way to finish the tournament.*

Even though he hadn't played, the 26-19 Churchill Cup final victory was a great way for New Zealand Maori veteran Slade McFarland to sign off from the team, having been called onto the tour as a replacement.

Prop Deacon Manu had been injured just prior to the tournament and was unable to play in either game, which meant that McFarland came in to cover both prop, and his old position of hooker where Matt also had a few injury concerns.

'I'd been lying in bed at home one night when I got a text message from Feeky [New Zealand Maori prop Greg Feek] that said: "You are on your way boy!" I got a phone call from Matt shortly afterwards that confirmed I had to pack my bag. Just being over there, and being part of a successful operation, was a nice way to finish. It was great to get one last shot in that environment because it had been such a huge part of my life for a decade. Obviously, it was also an outstanding feeling to bow out with a win.'

Eight days short of a year later, as he was carried around Waikato Stadium on the shoulders of his Lion-taming props, Matt could identify with exactly how his long-serving hooker had felt.

Hearing the Lions roar: 1993

'Maori and Lions recalled'

Prior to 2005, the New Zealand Maori side had never beaten the British & Irish Lions in the seven previous attempts, going back to 1930. But they should have.

Among a handful of near misses, the performance of the 1993 side against the Home Unions' representatives showcased the best and worst of New Zealand Maori rugby prior to the commencement of the professional era.

After leading 20-0 at halftime and appearing in total charge, the New Zealand Maori side surrendered its momentum during the second period of a stirring contest at Wellington's old Athletic Park.

And, once it was gone, the home side never regained the initiative, as the touring side, inspired by its burly Scottish skipper Gavin Hastings, stormed home to win a thriller 24-20.

'It was a game that we never should have lost', former All Black and New Zealand Maori flanker Jamie Joseph says.

'The approach we had that day reflects the Maori way, and it is still the same today, although the team can tighten up when it has to, like it showed against the Lions in 2005. But back then, even though we had a big lead, we kept trying to attack, and kept playing freely even after they had started to claw their way back. With the big forward pack that we had, we probably would have been able to close the game down if we'd opted to play that way, but it just wasn't the Maori way. They had a greater fear of losing than we did, and that showed through in the different approaches to that game that the two teams took.'

Athletic Park proved to be a happy hunting ground for the Lions on that particular tour. Although they lost a fiercely competitive Test series with the All Blacks two matches to one, the Lions thumped the home side 20–7 in the second Test at the ground a few weeks after they had taken out New Zealand Maori.

But there were bumps in other places.

A week after losing to the Lions with New Zealand Maori, Joseph and New Zealand Maori skipper Arran Pene got their own back by helping their Otago side inflict a first tour defeat on the tourists, when their province came from five points behind at halftime to prevail 37–24. Halfback Stu Forster, another future New Zealand Maori representative who also joined Joseph on the coaching panel in 2006, was also a member of that victorious Otago side.

Doughty New Zealand Maori hooker Norm Hewitt also had the last laugh in his battle with the visitors, inspiring his province, Hawke's Bay, to a shock 29–17 win over the Lions just four days before they turned the Test series on its head by securing the second international back in Wellington.

Assistant coach to Donny Stevenson with the New Zealand Maori side in 2006, Joseph was one of six forwards in the New Zealand Maori front eight who either already had, or would before their careers were out, achieve All Black status among the pack that faced the 1993 British Lions.

This included an all international loose forward trio in the No 8 Pene, Joseph and then openside flanker Zinzan Brooke.

There were two more All Blacks in the backline including Eric Rush, who recalls the 1993 game marking the first time in a number of years that all of the top contenders had made themselves available to play for the New Zealand Maori.

'The fact that we'd had trouble getting a lot of the guys to play in the few years before that game probably reflected the itineraries that we'd had in those times', Rush says.

'A lot of the players found other commitments to keep them busy when we were just playing provincial sides, but there was a lot of competition to be in the side to play the Lions, even if that tour didn't have anywhere near the hype associated with it that the one 12 years later did.'

One player who left his mark on the day was Nelson Bays winger Allan Prince who upset more than just the tourists when he rather crudely gestured at Lions winger Rory Underwood after he'd been put in the clear to score a try.

'The boys weren't happy with him after that', Rush says, 'and he got told all about it as we headed back to our side of halfway to await their re-start!'

'Some of the forwards, especially, were pretty upset with him', Joseph says, 'because that sort of attitude is not what the Maori team is about at all. Having said that, it was his first game at that level whereas our forwards were all well used to it. Allan's gesture just highlighted the fact that he'd been a bit overwhelmed by the occasion.'

Showing his professionalism, Underwood opted not to return the 'compliment' in Prince's direction when the Englishman got on the scoresheet himself during the Lions' second-half resurgence.

With Prince scoring one try and Horowhenua first-five-eighths Steve Hirini another, it looked for a time as if there would be no stopping the home side.

There might not have been either, had they not been narrowly denied a third try just before the halftime break, when a last-ditch tackle near the goal-line prevented the New Zealand Maori side from completing a sweeping length-of-the-field attacking movement.

'Even when the Lions started coming back at us, I never really felt that we were going to lose, right up until the very end when Hastings scored that try to put them ahead', Joseph says.

'We had just relaxed that little bit too much and couldn't jump start again when we needed to, to be able to put them away.'

Nor was this the first time that the New Zealand Maori team had established seemingly a winning break against the Lions only to get overhauled before the finish.

The teams' most previous meeting to 1993, in 1977, had also witnessed the Lions come from an apparently hopeless position to win, after they'd overturned a 6–19 halftime deficit to beat Sid Going's New Zealand Maori side 22–19 at Auckland's Eden Park.

The 1966 clash between the two sides went down to the wire as well, before the Lions prevailed 16–14.

'Prior to the advent of professionalism, there just wasn't the same accountability on the players in the Maori team environment as compared to what the players faced back in their own provinces', Joseph says.

'That probably explains the attitude that the players took to the way that they played the games. Once you were selected in the team, you got to play. It wasn't like a provincial side, where you really had to front week after week to keep your place in the starting XV. With the Maori team, there were never that many games.'

Just by gaining selection in the New Zealand Maori side, Joseph continued a family tradition of involvement with the team. His father Jim had played for the side between 1968 and 1972.

In his first match, a low-key midweek contest against Wellington at Athletic Park in 1991, Joseph had the misfortune to appear in the first New Zealand Maori side to lose a match in New Zealand since the 1977 loss to the Lions.

Better results were to follow.

Joseph toured the Pacific Islands with the New Zealand Maori side the following year on a trip where the side won four of the five matches it played.

On a rugged tour, New Zealand Maori won the Tests against Tonga (33–10) and Fiji (35–34) as well as recording wins over a Cook Islands XV and a Samoan Development XV, but lost to a strong Tongan President's XV (15–22).

The make up of the touring party highlighted the general issues of availability that surrounded the top players at that time, with Joseph, Rush and Auckland prop Steve McDowell being the only All Blacks who participated in the trip.

18

Focusing on the future

'Maori rugby into the 21st century'

The New Zealand Maori team might be coming off the back of the most successful decade in its history, but the man widely acknowledged as the driving force behind that success is unconvinced that the future holds such promise.

Although New Zealand Maori continued along the winning path in Donny Stevenson's first year as head coach, capturing the 2006 Churchill Cup title in a decisive manner, it is how the team will be positioned in five years time and beyond that has Matt worried.

The fact that the New Zealand Maori side was not sighted in a playing capacity at home in 2006 alone, offers Matt cause for concern as to its future status.

> *It is absolutely vital that the New Zealand Maori team plays at least one match of substance a year at home. The people have to be able to see the team perform if they are going to continue to identify with it.*

> *The shame of 2006 was that we missed out on the opportunity to follow up on the massive nationwide support that the side received for the match against the British & Irish Lions the previous year. Had New Zealand Maori played Ireland during their visit, or had another game against Australia, it would have given the team the chance to build on the momentum the Lions game gave Maori rugby, while also ensuring that the next generation of Maori players had the chance to see their heroes play in the flesh. And that's important because young Maori do identify strongly with the team as their role model. It was something we,*

as a group, were always aware of, and something that the players never took for granted.

Bruce Reihana is one who was very taken with the role-model aspect of the side, having experienced difficulties of his own during his formative years.

'Kids have a lot of choices in society today, and a lot of young Maori make the wrong decisions', he says.

'That's why it is important that the New Zealand Maori team is seen by them playing in New Zealand. If, by seeing the players up close and meeting them, it helps inspire some of our young to set positive goals and chase them, then the team is making a hell of an important contribution to Maori society.'

While the mere fact that a representative side plays at the highest level offers encouragement to the next generation of potential players, there can be no doubt that the level of achievement maintained by New Zealand Maori during Matt's time as coach enhanced the team's value as a positive reflection on Maori society.

Yet the lack of a strong off-field strategic plan for the future threatens to undermine the prospects of continuing that success.

'You can't overstate how much of the New Zealand Maori team's success through the first decade of professionalism was due to Matt Te Pou', former assistant coach Jim Love says.

'The force of his personality, and his refusal to accept second-best down at Rugby Union HQ, was crucial. It meant that he had to fight a few fights, but the players always knew he was batting for them and the team. Because of that, they were prepared to put up with a few difficulties they otherwise might have had a few things to say about.'

Matt's skipper for the bulk of the critical 1996, 1997 and 1998 campaigns, where the foundations were laid for the team's ongoing success, Errol Brain, agrees.

'He's a very determined guy, as a few people who crossed him found out', Brain says.

'His demeanour might not change much, but he has this way of dispensing with the hot air and getting straight to the point. With Matt, you always knew where you stood. The players respected him for that. They also appreciated the level of his commitment to the team and the political odds that he was sometimes up against.'

Big Chief*s*! Matt is greeted by a North American Indian Chief as the New Zealand Maori team arrives in Canada for its ground-breaking 2003 tour. © PHOTOSPORT

Canadian tour programme.

New Zealand Maori technical adviser and former All Black Stu Forster with an important piece of 'technical' equipment, a rugby ball! Mike Stewart collection

Top of the Pops! The New Zealand Maori team entertains its Canadian hosts with song in 2003. © PHOTOSPORT

'Rocky Mountain Maori!' The boys take in the sights while on tour in Canada. © PHOTOSPORT

Rico Gear was all class for the New Zealand Maori against Canada in 2003. Less than a year later, he had graduated to the All Blacks. © PHOTOSPORT

Runaway Train! New Zealand Maori and All Black No 8 Ron Cribb on the burst against Canada. © PHOTOSPORT

One of the more perplexing questions that was posed to the Canadian defence in 2003: How do you stop a rampaging Norm Berryman? The home side never did find the answer! © PHOTOSPORT

'Red and Black!' A colourful local explains his philosophy on life to the players during the 2003 visit to Canada. © PHOTOSPORT

Star Spangled Maori! Captain Corey Flynn proves a handful for an American defender during the Churchill Cup tournament in 2004. © PHOTOSPORT

Matt and Ida are flanked by New Zealand Maori players, prop Joe McDonnell (left), Slade McFarland, and Wayne Ormond (right) at the 2004 New Zealand Maori Sports Awards where the side won Team of the Year. Matt Te Pou collection

Just like big brother! A year after Rico Gear had thrilled the North American crowds, his younger brother Hosea Gear starred at the 2004 Churchill Cup. © PHOTOSPORT

The New Zealand Maori team's influence as a positive role model for young people was an aspect of the environment that was never lost on either the players or the management. Here, Matt offers a few words of guidance to a Leadership Development Youth Group before departing on an activity in the Bay of Plenty. Matt Te Pou collection

Matt with the trophies after collecting the Coach of the Year award at the 2005 New Zealand Maori Sports Awards. © PHOTOSPORT

We had our fights, for sure, but some of those made us stronger. We had to prove that we were worth the respect that we got, and the opportunity to play the bigger games that we received, by performing consistently. When professional rugby arrived at the end of 1995, nobody was ready for it, so it was always going to take a while for the dust to settle.

Being further down the food chain than those with more pressing organisational needs, like the All Blacks and the Super 12 franchises, we had to accept that we would have to wait a little bit longer before a consolidated future strategy was put in place for us.

The problem is, 11 years on, we're still waiting. There is still no clear strategic direction for the New Zealand Maori team. The team is still being organised, in terms of the matches it is allocated, and the players it has available to it, on the same ad-hoc basis that was in place in 1995.

The most obvious example of this was provided in 2006 by the introduction of the International Rugby Board's Pacific Five Nations tournament. Having done the 'hard yards' against the Pacific Islands teams for much of their history, the New Zealand Maori side suddenly found itself excluded from its logical place at that table, instead, being usurped by the Junior All Blacks (previously New Zealand A).

Every time a new All Blacks coach comes into office, the goal posts seem to move!

The decision to put the Junior All Blacks into the Pacific Five Nations ahead of the New Zealand Maori, which was no doubt influenced by the preference of the All Black selectors, only replicated what John Hart had attempted in 1999, when he wanted to give the New Zealand A side selection preference over us.

John had the good grace to accept our argument at the time, and allow the A players to be released back to us. But, while the team going off to the Churchill Cup this year was better than having no programme at all, the Maori team should be playing in the Pacific competition. That's its natural fit.

In many ways, the situation that occurred this year reminded me of when the Chiefs first started, where political concerns overrode geographical logic, and North Harbour and Waikato were paired together. It took the New Zealand Rugby Union three years to change that. It won't surprise

> *me if, further down the track, the same thing happens in this situation, and the New Zealand Maori team ends up in the Pacific Five Nations.*
>
> *It should be remembered that the A team in its many forms has come and gone a couple of times already. Who says we'll even have the player base to support having an A side, which has a fairly limited history anyway, in the future, or whether the All Black coaches to come will want to operate that team.*

One of the consistent themes of the professional rugby era has been an increasingly singular focus by the game's administrators on the elite levels, which are represented predominantly by the All Blacks and the Super rugby franchises.

This has resulted in the likes of Sevens and Maori rugby being relegated to the background in terms of overall administrative planning at national union level.

While the increased emphasis is understandable to an extent, given that the elite levels provide the bulk of the revenue that drives the game, the lack of attention towards the longer-term needs of Maori rugby is surprising. It is also unwise, especially since the community has consistently provided 20 percent of the country's elite players in the 11 years since the Super rugby competition began, and is therefore a vitally important strategic area for the development of players.

> *Maori rugby in its truest form is heartland rugby, and amateur rugby. While, at the lowest levels, it remains strong, this is largely because it has been self-sustaining.*
>
> *The Rugby Union does fund the provincial Maori tournaments in the Northern, Central and Southern regions, but everything beneath those is run by volunteers who are involved because of their sense of community, and because of their love for the game. They're not complaining about that situation. They are happy to keep operating as they always have.*
>
> *The problem is that, as things stand at the moment, there is no clear bridge between Maori rugby at grass roots level and the elite level that the New Zealand Maori team represents. The development pathways that we once had through the national Maori trial and then the New Zealand Maori Colts team were both dismantled, but they weren't replaced with anything.*

> *The participation numbers of Maori players, both in the overall rugby playing population of New Zealand, and in the professional bracket alone, show that the Maori community is a fertile development area for players. That fact urgently needs to be addressed by the Rugby Union with the introduction of a proper strategic plan for the future that everyone has signed up to.*
>
> *While the New Zealand Maori Rugby Board [formerly Whakapumautanga] does its best, that body has no teeth. No strength. It can offer advice, but the New Zealand Rugby Union board has all the gold. They make the rules. They need to invest properly in the future of Maori rugby to make sure that we can sustain, and maybe even increase, the Maori people's contribution to New Zealand rugby in the future.*

One avenue that Matt believes should be looked at more closely is the New Zealand Maori team's value as a marketing tool for the country, both because of its heritage and the cultural education it offers.

> *I was told that they changed the name of the New Zealand A team to the Junior All Blacks last year, because having the word 'All Blacks' in the name made the team more marketable. Well, tell that to the people who turned up, or I should say who didn't, to watch them play in the Pacific Five Nations. None of the three New Zealand grounds they played at attracted big crowds.*
>
> *It was the same in Australia last year, where I was told that one of the crowds they played in front of would have been smaller than what we would get for an ordinary provincial fixture back here. Yet, while this is going on, we have the New Zealand Maori team, with a heritage that dates back to the 1888–89 New Zealand Natives team, so is in effect even older than the All Blacks. And we're not cashing in on that.*
>
> *If the Rugby Union put in place a proper strategic plan for the New Zealand Maori side, they could create opportunities where they could cash in on its mana and heritage, instead of appearing to simply tolerate the presence of the side, as seems to be the case now.*
>
> *Imagine, for example, how attractive a game would be between the New Zealand Maori side at full strength and the famous Barbarians club of England? Or the French Barbarians, France themselves or maybe even South Africa?*

> *In this age of national unions adding in extra games to the established international schedules in order to maximise revenues, there is great potential there. Not only could the games be moneymakers, they would also ease up the stresses on the top All Black players, by allowing a number of different players to carry some of the load. All it needs is for the powers that be to explore all of the opportunities that are out there to maintain and develop the New Zealand Maori team, instead of just slotting it in where the political dynamic suits, as is tending to happen now.*

Nor is Matt's idea of the New Zealand Maori team as an international 'attraction' that would make money a fanciful one. While the Australian Rugby Union twice hosted the side in 2001 and 2002, then Australian union chief executive John O'Neill had been keen on signing up the Wallabies to a five-year deal with the New Zealand Maori, only to have that prospect vetoed at this end. Interestingly, the prospect of regular trans-Tasman contact for the New Zealand Maori side was raised again in 2006, after the side beat the New South Wales Waratahs at the Sydney Cricket Ground, when Waratahs officials floated the idea of an annual fixture.

> *The need for a planned future is urgent because the team's success won't just continue to happen as of right. One thing that has become clear in recent years is that New Zealand rugby is now facing a lot of competition from Australia in the pursuit of players, both up in the Pacific Islands but also closer to home among young Maori.*

This was borne out by the presence of two players of Maori origin, Jeremy Paul and Glenn Panoho, in the Wallaby front row when the world champions played the New Zealand Maori team in 2001. Other players of Maori origin, like midfield back Morgan Turinui and first-five-eighths Manny Edmonds, whose uncle Huia played in the front row for the New Zealand Maori, have also offered great service to Australian rugby in recent years.

> *One of the critical issues we face is that of talent identification among young Maori players, especially those in the rural areas where the resources are not as plentiful as they are in the cities.*

> *Professionalism has accelerated the turnover of players and placed increased pressure on the younger ones coming through. Because of that, we have reverted to a development system that is heavily reliant on the players coming out of the High School first XVs. That's fine for them, but what about the players in the rural areas, where a lot of talented young*

Maori can be found? They are often being missed, and being picked off by other parties as a result.

How many Maoris are there from rural districts here who are now playing rugby league in Australia and, to a lesser extent, Great Britain? A great example of this is Kiwi league star Benji Marshall. Benji is a Whakatane lad, my home town, and still has family there. He was also originally a rugby player and played first XV in Whakatane, but then got picked up by Australian league, whisked across the Tasman, and now he's playing over there.

Benji is still playing for the Kiwis in internationals, which is great to see, but what say the Australian Rugby Union suddenly decides to target him and offer him the same sort of money they threw at Mark Gasnier and Matt Giteau? What then? We could easily have another top notch Maori player playing against us. And how would people feel if he ended up winning a World Cup off us?

The thing is there are plenty more potential Benji Marshalls playing in rural areas, but if we don't put the resources in place to identify them and nurture their talent, we may miss out. The talent is there, believe me. We've had a situation where a small rural area with just one shop produced four Super rugby players in Matua and Reuben Parkinson, Rua Tipoki and Willie Walker. They were fortunately all identified and ended up contributing to our game at the highest levels, although rugby only got Matua back after he'd done a stint in Aussie league.

A stocktake of the ethnic make up of rugby players in New Zealand in 2004 showed that 26,269 (or 20.3 percent) of the 129,000 people who were registered to play the game that year classified themselves as being of Maori descent.

If anything, the real figure was probably even higher, and remains so, given that many of the players who participate in Maori tournaments at club and tribal level aren't necessarily registered (and therefore counted) on the New Zealand Rugby Union's national data base.

It's not that the numbers of Maori playing rugby over the last few years have increased. If anything, our figures have probably only held their own. It's just that, with more people in mainstream society not playing the game for reasons of white flight or whatever, the overall Maori percentage, with regard to the whole picture, has become bigger.

Not that this is a reason for administrative complacency. Far from it.

At grass roots level, Maori rugby is carrying on largely as it has before.

The Maori club season in the predominantly Maori areas, like the Eastern Bay of Plenty and Hawke's Bay, tends to last for a couple of months after the provincial club competitions all finish.

There are a lot of traditional trophies that are played for, and the games are all organised along tribal lines. That can mean that some clubs, who play as separate entities in their own provincial competitions, then effectively combine for Maori rugby. Often what can also happen is that you will see members of the iwi who live in the cities coming back into the rural areas to play for their tribe in the games.

Maori tournaments are usually both sports and cultural festivals. Other sports than rugby are also played, netball for the girls, for example, but there will also be huge socials around the whole event. Not only have these events, which are held in all of the predominantly Maori regions of the North Island, not been diluted by the advent of professionalism, if anything it has helped increase their awareness, and their participation rates.

Often you will see bigger crowds at events like the famous 'Pa Wars' – which earned a public profile when Rua Tipoki got in to trouble at one of the tournaments a few years back – than you will at some provincial games. That's the power of the iwi or family.

It was something the East Coast Rugby Union quite cleverly tapped into a few years ago by promoting their tribal background through Ngati Porou. That served to unite the whole area, while also bringing back players who had left the region, which suddenly made the East Coast a major force to be reckoned with in the lower divisions. They went from being the easy beats to taking out the likes of Manawatu and Counties Manukau – which would have been thought virtually impossible just a decade before!

What the East Coast experience showed is the potential that lies within the Maori game at the grass roots level. The critical area, in terms of Maori player development, that needs to be looked at, is the status and usefulness of the provincial regional Maori tournaments. Like the New Zealand Maori team itself, these haven't altered at all in terms of their operation since 1995, yet the whole rugby world has virtually changed around them.

> *If we are to get full value out of these tournaments and help set up a proper development pathway, both for the New Zealand Maori team and New Zealand rugby in general, it's vital that we get the status and placement of the regional Maori tournaments sorted out.*

The suggestion Matt makes is to reposition the tournaments, from their current dates at the start of the year before club rugby kicks off, to a date once the Air New Zealand Cup provincial programme has concluded.

Although professional players involved in the Super rugby squads would not participate, Matt argues that it would provide a lot of advantages if the three regional teams, from the Northern, Central and Southern Maori areas, were put up against the Super rugby squads as warm-up matches before their competition the following year.

> *At the end of the three regional provincial tournaments, a representative side for that region is selected. If players had the incentive of knowing that, by making their regional side, they would get to play against the Super rugby sides the following year in warm-up matches before the Super 14 started, it would offer them a great incentive.*

> *It would also add credibility to the regional Maori tournaments by ensuring that a lot of the eligible players from the Air New Zealand Cup competition fronted. If they made their regional side, they would then have an additional opportunity to press their claims for Super rugby selection down the track.*

> *The involvement of all of these players would also naturally strengthen the Maori regional representative sides, bringing them back to where they used to be before professional rugby started, when most of the provincial guys played. This, in turn, would then make the regional Maori sides worthwhile opposition for the teams who were warming up for the Super 14. Naturally, this would all serve to add to the value of the regional provincial Maori tournaments, both as a development tool for the New Zealand Maori side and New Zealand rugby in general.*

Matt's concerns, both for the future of Maori rugby, and the state of the national game generally were behind his move, albeit unsuccessfully, to seek a place on the New Zealand Rugby Union board earlier in 2006.

Although he failed to unseat the current Maori board representative Paul Quinn, Matt remains passionate about the challenges facing the New Zealand game. He believes many of these challenges stem from successive administrators having 'taken their eyes' off the life blood of the game in this country – club rugby.

> *I am at fault, too. During my time as New Zealand Maori coach, I rarely looked beyond players at the top level. No one in the professional area of the game does. One of the biggest weaknesses we have in New Zealand rugby at present is that we are too All Blacks-oriented. Everything is done around, and for the benefit of, the All Blacks whereas, perhaps if we took care of the levels underneath, the flag ship of the game in this country would largely look after itself.*

The major worry, Matt says, is the ill-health of club rugby.

> *The game at club level is bleeding. We just don't have the playing depth in clubs now, especially relative to other countries. One of my sons is playing in Ireland. When I visited him recently, I was exposed to their club scene. While our elite players might be superior to a country like Ireland's, their clubs do seem to have a great deal more depth than we have.*
>
> *Irish clubs are able to field a multitude of teams throughout all of the grades. Compare that to the landscape here. In many of the smaller provinces, the clubs, especially in rural areas, are struggling just to field a premier team, let alone Senior Bs, Under-21s and beyond.*
>
> *The gap between club rugby and the top level of our game now is huge. Yet club rugby was the basis for 100 years of overachievement by New Zealand rugby players because it developed our players to better playing levels than other countries were able to achieve. Youngsters coming through regularly played alongside older heads, including established All Blacks and seasoned provincial players. Their presence helped the younger ones to learn the game. Having the 'name' players involved was also huge for the clubs, in terms of pulling along people to watch the games and support the clubs concerned.*

One of the problems experienced at club level in Matt's home province of Bay of Plenty, which he believes has been replicated elsewhere, is the centralisation of the best players around just a handful of clubs.

> *In the Bay, the top players are all focused around the clubs in Tauranga and [the nearby] Mount Maunganui. There used to be major battles between the Rotorua clubs, the Tauranga ones and our clubs over in the Eastern Bay of Plenty, but Rotorua and ourselves have dropped off now.*

The top players are all in one area, which has left the rest struggling. The three Eastern Bay of Plenty clubs left in the Baywide are all battling down at the bottom of the table. We've even had instances in 2006 of Premier clubs having to default games in the Baywide due to a lack of numbers. That is something that would previously have been unheard of!

Matt does not claim to have all the solutions to club rugby's problems. He also acknowledges that the recent introduction of the club liaison officer system by the New Zealand Rugby Union has offered major benefits.

There are some projects that are having a positive effect, but there is that much more that needs to be done. Most clubs are heavily reliant on gaming machine money for their operation, and that is drying up in some areas, so that is something that needs to be addressed.

There probably does need to be some action taken to provide a more direct source of funding to clubs so that the distribution on a national basis is fairer. At the moment, it can come down to what province you are in, whether you have adequate financial means or not.

Beyond the financial issue, it won't be a matter of having one blanket fix to sort out all ills. Different areas around the country have different challenges – city clubs versus country clubs, for example. We need to identify the individual issues that are facing clubs in the different areas on a more specific basis, and then see if we can help them overcome these issues.

In some cases, clubs may be forced to amalgamate. That won't be easy, but people will accept rationalisation if they can see some benefit in it. It won't always work though, and shouldn't be forced on organisations before all of the alternative courses of action have been explored.

What the game has to be careful not to do, is to have more situations like that which developed earlier this year, when the North Otago Rugby Union felt that it was left with no choice but to take the national body to the Commerce Commission.

All North Otago was arguing for was the right to survive. They've done very well down there in recent years and got a system going that is working well for them. Yet, instead of being encouraged and rewarded for the innovative way that they have overcome their challenges, the Rugby Union effectively tried to kick them back into touch.

To be forced into the extraordinary and rather public action that they were represented a cry for help. Instead of being heavy-handed, the game's administrators need to work with the people concerned to resolve these issues. Just because they are working from an office in Wellington does not mean that they have all the answers!

Statistics

Matt Te Pou coaching record 1990–2005

WHAKATANE MARIST 1990–1993

1990
Baywide championship first round
Beat Mount Maunganui	25–10
Drew with Te Teko	12–12
Lost to Ngongotaha	3–37
Beat Katikati	41–9
Lost to Paroa	13–20
Lost to Waikite	7–11
Beat Eastern Pirates	21–6
Beat Whakarewarewa	28–15
Lost to Opotiki United	15–21
Lost to Tauranga Sports	13–26

Second round
Lost to Whakarewarewa	12–17
Beat Opotiki United	28–7
Lost to Paroa	9–19
Lost to Ngongotaha	12–17
Beat Rotoiti	22–13

Grading Game (for 1991 season)
Beat Eastern Pirates	28–9

1991
Baywide championship first round
Beat Tauranga Sports	17–6
Beat Eastern Pirates	26–12
Beat United Pirates (Te Puke)	28–17
Beat Whakarewarewa	15–14
Beat Waikite	24–15
Lost to Ngongotaha	12–35
Lost to Kahukura	10–23
Beat Mount Maunganui	13–8
Beat Opotiki United	13–12
Lost to Te Teko	6–12

Second round
Beat Tauranga Sports	48–16
Lost to Opotiki United	9–13
Beat Kahukura	43–3
Beat Ngongotaha	24–3
Beat Rotoiti	54–3

Semi-final
Lost to Eastern Pirates	11–20

1992
Baywide championship first round
Beat United Pirates (Te Puke)	35–18
Beat Ngongotaha	27–6
Beat Tauranga Sports	24–14
Beat Te Teko	21–14
Beat Rangataua	23–10
Beat Rotoiti	44–6
Beat Opotiki United	20–9
Beat Mount Maunganui	24–16
Lost to Eastern Pirates	14–21
Lost to Waikite	3–11
Beat Rangiuru	34–4

Winner's first round

Second round
Beat Greerton Marist	29–11
Beat United Pirates (Te Puke)	30–3
Beat Tauranga Sports	51–22
Lost to Mount Maunganui	25–26

Beat Waikite	22–0
Beat Opotiki United	23–0

Semi-final

Beat Te Teko	36–7

Final

Beat Eastern Pirates	27–6

Baywide champions 1992

(Baywide statistics compiled by Brent Drabble.)

BAY OF PLENTY 1993–1994

1993

Beat North Harbour	36–21
Lost to Waikato	12–55
Beat King Country	32–24
Beat Thames Valley	76–17
Lost to New Zealand XV	5–93
Lost to Taranaki	22–35

NPC Second Division

Beat Wairarapa-Bush	72–3
Beat South Canterbury	53–15
Beat Southland	27–26
Lost to North Auckland	10–37
Beat Nelson Bays	43–18
Lost to Counties	11–30
Beat Manawatu	54–45
Beat Poverty Bay	48–15

Semi-final

Beat North Auckland	41–26

Final

Lost to Counties	10–38

1993 record

Won 10, Lost 6; Points For 552, Against 498

1994

Lost to Waikato	10–32
Lost to Auckland	33–39
Beat Fiji	36–26
Beat King Country	39–25
Lost to Counties	8–47
Lost to South Africa	12–33

NPC Second Division

Beat Nelson Bays	42–11
Beat Wairarapa-Bush	61–17
Lost to Southland	34–53
Lost to Northland	27–29
Beat Manawatu	45–35
Beat Horowhenua	43–19
Beat South Canterbury	35–25
Lost to Hawke's Bay	27–38

Semi-final

Lost to Hawke's Bay	18–65

1994 record

Won 7, Lost 8; Points For 470, Against 494

NORTHERN MAORI – PRINCE OF WALES CUP 1993–1994

1993

Beat Southern Maori	28–24

1994

Beat Southern Maori	36–32

NEW ZEALAND MAORI 1995–2005 (FIRST-CLASS MATCHES ONLY)

1995

Beat King Country	44–28
Beat Waikato	60–22

Statistics

1996
Beat Bay of Plenty	48–28
Beat Western Samoa	28–15
Beat Fiji	25–10
Beat Tonga Barbarians	26–19
Beat Tonga	29–20

1997
Beat Ireland A	41–10
Beat Argentina	39–17
Beat Western Samoa XV	40–8
Beat Western Samoa	34–20

1998
Beat Tonga	66–7
Beat England	62–14
Beat Edinburgh	69–3
Beat Scotland	24–8
Beat Glasgow	53–15

1999
Beat Fiji XV	20–10
Beat Fiji	57–20

2000
Beat Scotland	18–15

2001
Lost to Australia	29–41
Beat Argentina	43–24

2002
Lost to Queensland	25–28
Beat New South Wales	43–18
Lost to Australia	23–27
Lost to NZ Barbarians	22–37

2003
Beat Tonga	47–12
Lost to England	9–23
Beat Canada	65–27
Beat Canada All Stars	52–11
Beat Canada	30–9

2004
Beat United States	69–31
Beat England A	26–19

2005
Beat Fiji	27–25
Beat British & Irish Lions	19–13

(Record does not include six non-first-class matches against composite selections, all of which New Zealand Maori won.)

New Zealand Maori record in detail
(first-class matches only)

1995

New Zealand Maori 44, King Country 28
At Taupo, July 4

For New Zealand Maori: Tries by Norman Berryman (2), Arran Pene (2), Mutu Ngarimu and Jarrod Cunningham; 4 conversions and 2 penalty goals by Danny Love.

The New Zealand Maori team was: Jarrod Cunningham, Aaron Hamilton, George Konia, Norm Broughton, Norman Berryman (replaced by Paul Cooke), Danny Love, Shane Stone, Arran Pene (captain), Chris Mayerhofler, Mutu Ngarimu (replaced by Errol Brain), Jim Coe, Mark Cooksley, Graham Hurunui (replaced by Phil Coffin), Slade McFarland, Kevin Nepia.

New Zealand Maori 60, Waikato 22
At Hamilton, July 8

For New Zealand Maori: Tries by Norman Berryman (2), Paul Cooke (2), George Konia (2), Slade McFarland, Robin Brooke and Kevin Nepia; 6 conversions and a penalty goal by Danny Love.

The New Zealand Maori team was: Jarrod Cunningham, Paul Cooke, George Konia, Norm Broughton, Norman Berryman, Danny Love, Stu Forster, Arran Pene (captain), Chris Mayerhofler, Robin Brooke, Jim Coe, Grant Kelly (replaced by Errol Brain), Phil Coffin, Slade McFarland, Kevin Nepia.

1996

New Zealand Maori 48, Bay of Plenty 28
At Rotorua, June 11

For New Zealand Maori: Tries by Norman Berryman (3), Errol Brain, Glen Osborne, Dallas Seymour and Kevin Nepia; 5 conversions by Adrian Cashmore, penalty goal by Carlos Spencer.

The New Zealand Maori team was: Adrian Cashmore, Glen Osborne, Milton Going, Mark Mayerhofler, Norman Berryman, Carlos Spencer, Rhys Duggan, Errol Brain, Dallas Seymour, Taine Randell (captain), Jim Coe, Grant Kelly (replaced by Tiwini Hemi), Phil Coffin, Slade McFarland, Kevin Nepia.

New Zealand Maori 28, Western Samoa 15
At Auckland, June 14

For New Zealand Maori: Tries by Errol Brain (2), Tony Brown and Milton Going; conversion and 2 penalty goals by Brown.

The New Zealand Maori team was: Glen Osborne, Norm Berryman, Milton Going, Mark Mayerhofler, Daryl Gibson, Tony Brown, Rhys Duggan, Errol Brain, Dallas Seymour, Taine Randell (captain), Grant Kelly, Jim Coe, Phil Coffin, Slade McFarland, Kevin Nepia.

New Zealand Maori 25, Fiji 10
At Suva, November 1

For New Zealand Maori: Tries by Adrian Cashmore, Dion Matthews, Milton Going and Phil Coffin; conversion and a penalty goal by Tony Brown.

The New Zealand Maori team was: Adrian Cashmore (replaced by Jarrod Cunningham), Dion Matthews, Milton Going, Mark Mayerhofler, Eric Rush, Tony Brown, Stu Forster, Deon Muir, Dallas Seymour, Errol Brain (captain), Jim Coe (replaced by Dion Waller), Mark Cooksley, Phil Coffin, Slade McFarland, Kevin Nepia.

New Zealand Maori 26, Tonga Barbarians 19
At Nuku'alofa, November 5

For New Zealand Maori: Tries by Eric Rush and Dion Waller; 2 conversions and 4 penalty goals by Jarrod Cunningham.

The New Zealand Maori team was: Jarrod Cunningham, Eric Rush, Caleb Ralph, Mark Mayerhofler, Roger Randle, Murdoch Paewai (replaced by Tony Brown), Rhys Duggan, Errol Brain (captain), Mutu Ngarimu, Matthew Te Pou (replaced by Dallas Seymour), Mark Cooksley, Dion Waller, Lee Lidgard (replaced by Phil Coffin), Joe Edwards, Paul Thomson.

New Zealand Maori 29, Tonga 20
At Nuku'alofa, November 8

For New Zealand Maori: Try by Mark Mayerhofler and a penalty try; 2 conversions and 4 penalty goals by Jarrod Cunningham, dropped goal by Tony Brown.

The New Zealand Maori team was: Jarrod Cunningham, Eric Rush, Caleb Ralph, Mark Mayerhofler, Roger Randle, Tony Brown, Stu Forster, Deon Muir, Dallas Seymour, Errol Brain (captain), Jim Coe, Mark Cooksley, Phil Coffin, Slade McFarland, Kevin Nepia.

1997

New Zealand Maori 41, Ireland A 10
At Palmerston North, June 10

For New Zealand Maori: Tries by Jim Coe, Errol Brain, Michael Scott and a penalty try; 3 conversions and 5 penalty goals by Jarrod Cunningham.

The New Zealand Maori team was: Jarrod Cunningham, Daryl Gibson, Caleb Ralph, Milton Going, Norman Berryman, Steve Hirini, Michael Scott, Errol Brain (captain, replaced by Mutu Ngarimu), Craig Glendinning, Jim Coe (replaced by Chris Mayerhofler), Dion Waller, Norm Maxwell, Lee Lidgard, Norm Hewitt, Kevin Nepia.

New Zealand Maori 39, Argentina 17
At Napier, June 14

For New Zealand Maori: Tries by Rhys Duggan, Adrian Cashmore, Norm Hewitt, Milton Going and Eugene Martin; 4 conversions and 2 penalty goals by Cashmore.

The New Zealand Maori team was: Adrian Cashmore, Norm Berryman, Daryl Gibson, Milton Going, Mark Mayerhofler, Eugene Martin, Rhys Duggan, Errol Brain (captain), Craig Glendinning, Jim Coe (replaced by Mutu Ngarimu), Dion Waller, Mark Cooksley, Phil Coffin, Norm Hewitt, Paul Thomson (replaced by Lee Lidgard).

New Zealand Maori 40, Western Samoa XV 8
At Apia, June 18

For New Zealand Maori: Tries by Slade McFarland (2), Caleb Ralph, Eric Rush and Mark Mayerhofler; 3 conversions and 3 penalty goals by Jarrod Cunningham.

The New Zealand Maori team was: Jarrod Cunningham, Eric Rush, Caleb Ralph, Mark Mayerhofler, Norman Berryman, Steve Hirini, Michael Scott (replaced by Rhys Duggan), Martin Jones, Chris Mayerhofler, Mutu Ngarimu, Mark Cooksley, Norm Maxwell (replaced by Dion Waller), Lee Lidgard, Slade McFarland, Kevin Nepia.

New Zealand Maori 34, Western Samoa 20
At Apia, June 21

For New Zealand Maori: Tries by Rhys Duggan, Craig Glendinning and a penalty try; 2 conversions, 4 penalty goals and a dropped goal by Adrian Cashmore.

The New Zealand Maori team was: Adrian Cashmore, Norm Berryman (replaced by Daryl Gibson), Milton Going, Mark Mayerhofler, Eric Rush, Eugene Martin, Rhys Duggan (replaced by Craig McGrath), Errol Brain (captain), Craig Glendinning, Norm Maxwell, Dion Waller, Mark Cooksley, Lee Lidgard (replaced by Kevin Nepia), Norm Hewitt, Paul Thomson.

1998

New Zealand Maori 66, Tonga 7
At Whangarei, June 20

For New Zealand Maori: Tries by Roger Randle (2), James Kerr (2), Norm Berryman, Tony Marsh, Tony Brown, Troy Flavell and Daryl Gibson; 6 conversions and 3 penalty goals by Brown.

The New Zealand Maori team was: Eric Rush (replaced by Ray MacDonald), James Kerr, Norm Berryman, Tony Marsh, Roger Randle, Tony Brown, Craig McGrath, Errol Brain (captain, replaced by Deon Muir), Dallas Seymour, Adam Parker (replaced by Dion

Waller), Jim Coe, Troy Flavell, Orcades Crawford, Slade McFarland (replaced by Jason Hammond), Kevin Nepia (replaced by Lee Lidgard).

New Zealand Maori 62, England 14
At Rotorua, June 23

For New Zealand Maori: Tries by Norm Berryman (2), Adrian Cashmore, Roger Randle, Tony Marsh, Tony Brown, Rhys Duggan, Jim Coe and Dallas Seymour; 7 conversions and a penalty goal by Cashmore.

The New Zealand Maori team was: Adrian Cashmore, Roger Randle, Norman Berryman, Tony Marsh, Daryl Gibson (replaced by James Kerr), Tony Brown, Rhys Duggan, Errol Brain (captain, replaced by Deon Muir), Dallas Seymour, Adam Parker (replaced by Dion Waller), Jim Coe, Troy Flavell, Kees Meeuws, Slade McFarland (replaced by Jason Hammond), Kevin Nepia (replaced by Lee Lidgard).

New Zealand Maori 69, Edinburgh Reivers 3
At Hawick, November 11

For New Zealand Maori: Tries by Norman Berryman (2), Greg Feek (2), Bruce Reihana, Troy Flavell, Glen Osborne, Kees Meeuws, Daryl Gibson, Rhys Duggan and Adrian Cashmore; 7 conversions by Cashmore.

The New Zealand Maori team was: Adrian Cashmore, Glen Osborne, Norman Berryman (replaced by Caleb Ralph), Daryl Gibson (replaced by Leon MacDonald), Bruce Reihana, Tony Brown, Aaron Flynn (replaced by Rhys Duggan), Deon Muir (captain), Glenn Marsh (replaced by Robbie Ford), Troy Flavell, Jim Coe (replaced by Ron Cribb), Norm Maxwell, Kees Meeuws, Slade McFarland (replaced by John Akurangi), Greg Feek.

New Zealand Maori 24, Scotland 8
At Edinburgh, November 14

For New Zealand Maori: Tries by Glenn Marsh and Adrian Cashmore; conversion and 4 penalty goals by Cashmore.

The New Zealand Maori team was: Adrian Cashmore, Bruce Reihana, Caleb Ralph, Daryl Gibson (replaced by Leon MacDonald), Norm Berryman (replaced by Glen Osborne), Tony Brown, Rhys Duggan, Deon Muir (captain), Glenn Marsh, Troy Flavell, Jim Coe (replaced by Ron Cribb), Norm Maxwell, Kees Meeuws, Slade McFarland (replaced by John Akurangi), Lee Lidgard (replaced by Greg Feek).

New Zealand Maori 53, Glasgow Caledonians 15
At Perthshire, November 18

For New Zealand Maori: Tries by Glen Osborne (2), Deon Muir, Caleb Ralph, Kees Meeuws and Slade McFarland; 4 conversions and 5 penalty goals by Cashmore.

The New Zealand Maori team was: Adrian Cashmore, Glen Osborne, Caleb Ralph, Daryl Gibson (replaced by Norman Berryman), James Kerr, Ray MacDonald (replaced by Bruce Reihana), Rhys Duggan, Deon Muir (captain), Glenn Marsh, Hare Makiri (replaced by Troy Flavell), Dion Waller, Jim Coe (replaced by Robbie Ford), Kees Meeuws, John Akurangi (replaced by Slade McFarland), Greg Feek (replaced by Lee Lidgard).

1999

New Zealand Maori 20, Fiji Warriors 10
At Lautoka, July 30

For New Zealand Maori: Tries by James Kerr, Glenn Marsh and Leon MacDonald; conversion and a penalty goal by MacDonald.

The New Zealand Maori team was: Todd Miller, Karl Te Nana, Norman Berryman, Leon MacDonald, James Kerr (replaced by Glen Osborne), Ray MacDonald (replaced by Glen Jackson), Craig McGrath, Ron Cribb (replaced by Deon Muir), Glenn Marsh, Dallas Seymour, Dion Waller, Jim Coe, Mike Edwards (replaced by John Akurangi), Norm Hewitt (captain, replaced by Slade McFarland), Paul Thomson.

New Zealand Maori 57, Fiji 20
At Suva, August 3

For New Zealand Maori: Tries by Norm Hewitt (3), Glen Osborne (2), Karl Te Nana and Glenn Marsh; 5 conversions and 4 penalty goals by Glen Jackson.

The New Zealand Maori team was: Bruce Reihana, Karl Te Nana (replaced by James Kerr), Caleb Ralph, Norm Berryman, Glen Osborne, Glen Jackson, Rhys Duggan, Deon Muir, Glenn Marsh, Troy Flavell, Dion Waller, Mark Cooksley (replaced by Jim Coe), John Akurangi (replaced by Mike Edwards), Norm Hewitt (captain), Paul Thomson.

2000

New Zealand Maori 18, Scotland 15
At New Plymouth, June 17

For New Zealand Maori: Tries by Deon Muir and Matua Parkinson; conversion and 2 penalty goals by Adrian Cashmore.

The New Zealand Maori team was: Adrian Cashmore, Norm Berryman (replaced by Roger Randle), Daryl Gibson, Mark Mayerhofler, Caleb Ralph, Glen Jackson (replaced by Bruce Reihana), Rhys Duggan, Deon Muir (replaced by Hare Makiri), Matua Parkinson, Glenn Marsh, Paul Tito (replaced by Mark Cooksley), Dion Waller, Greg Feek (replaced by Mike Edwards), Norm Hewitt (captain), Joe McDonnell.

2001

Australia 41, New Zealand Maori 29
At Sydney, June 9

For New Zealand Maori: 2 tries by Carlos Spencer; conversion and 4 penalty goals by Glen Jackson. Conversion and a penalty goal by David Hill.

The New Zealand Maori team was: Carlos Spencer, Roger Randle, Caleb Ralph, Daryl Gibson, Bruce Reihana, Glen Jackson (replaced by David Hill), Rhys Duggan, Deon Muir (captain), Taine Randell, Troy Flavell (replaced by Matua Parkinson), Norm Maxwell, Mark Cooksley (replaced by Dion Waller), Deacon Manu, Norm Hewitt (replaced by Slade McFarland), Greg Feek (replaced by Paul Thomson).

New Zealand Maori 43, Argentina 24
At Rotorua, June 26

For New Zealand Maori: Tries by Roger Randle (2), Bruce Reihana (2), Norm Hewitt and Rhys Duggan; 5 conversions and a penalty goal by Carlos Spencer.

The New Zealand Maori team was: Carlos Spencer, Roger Randle, Caleb Ralph, Daryl Gibson, Bruce Reihana, Glen Jackson, Rhys Duggan (replaced by Brendan Haami), Deon Muir (captain), Matua Parkinson, Hare Makiri, Paul Tito, Reece Robinson (replaced by Kristian Ormsby), Deacon Manu, Norm Hewitt (replaced by Slade McFarland), Greg Feek.

2002

Queensland 28, New Zealand Maori 25
At Brisbane, June 4

For New Zealand Maori: Tries by Rhys Duggan, Kristian Ormsby and Reece Robinson; 2 conversions and 2 penalty goals by Glen Jackson.

The New Zealand Maori team was: Carlos Spencer, Bruce Reihana, Ryan Nicholas (replaced by Rico Gear), Mark Mayerhofler, Joe Maddock, Glen Jackson, Rhys Duggan (replaced by Brendan Haami), Deon Muir (captain), Matua Parkinson, Jono Gibbes, Bryce Williams (replaced by Reece Robinson), Kristian Ormsby, Carl Hayman (replaced by Deacon Manu), Slade McFarland (replaced by Corey Flynn), Greg Feek.

New Zealand Maori 43, New South Wales 18
At Sydney, June 8

For New Zealand Maori: Tries by Joe Maddock (2), Willie Walker (2), Blair Urlich, Brendan Haami and Corey Flynn; 4 conversions by Spencer.

The New Zealand Maori team was: Willie Walker, Bruce Reihana, Rico Gear, Mark Mayerhofler, Joe Maddock (replaced by Roger Randle), Carlos Spencer, Brendan Haami, Deon Muir (captain), Blair Urlich, Jono Gibbes, Bryce Williams, Reece Robinson (replaced by Steve Jackson), Carl Hayman, Slade McFarland (replaced by Corey Flynn), Greg Feek (replaced by Tony Penn).

Australia 27, New Zealand Maori 23
At Perth, June 15

For New Zealand Maori: Tries by Bruce Reihana (2) and Rico Gear; conversion and 2 penalty goals by Carlos Spencer.

The New Zealand Maori team was: Willie Walker, Bruce Reihana, Ryan Nicholas, Mark Mayerhofler, Rico Gear, Carlos Spencer, Rhys Duggan, Deon Muir (captain), Matua Parkinson (replaced by Blair Urlich), Jono Gibbes, Bryce Williams (replaced by Kristian Ormsby), Reece Robinson, Carl Hayman (replaced by Deacon Manu), Slade McFarland (replaced by Corey Flynn), Greg Feek.

New Zealand Barbarians 37, New Zealand Maori 22
At Albany, June 21

For New Zealand Maori: Tries by Bruce Reihana (3) and Joe Maddock; conversion by Carlos Spencer.

The New Zealand Maori team was: Willie Walker (replaced by Roger Randle), Bruce Reihana, Ryan Nicholas, Mark Mayerhofler, Rico Gear (replaced by Joe Maddock), Carlos Spencer (replaced by Riki Flutey), Rhys Duggan, Deon Muir (captain), Matua Parkinson, Blair Urlich, Bryce Williams, Kristian Ormsby (replaced by Reece Robinson), Carl Hayman (replaced by Deacon Manu), Slade McFarland, Greg Feek.

2003

New Zealand Maori 47, Tonga 12
At Albany, June 2

For New Zealand Maori: Tries by Brad Fleming (2), Joe Maddock, Rico Gear, Christian Cullen, Ryan Nicholas and Glen Jackson; 6 conversions by Jackson.

The New Zealand Maori team was: Christian Cullen, Joe Maddock, Rico Gear, Ryan Nicholas, Brad Fleming, Glen Jackson (replaced by Willie Walker), David Gibson (replaced by Brendan Haami), Taine Randell, Matua Parkinson, Jono Gibbes (captain, replaced by Troy Flavell), Paul Tito, Kristian Ormsby (replaced by Wayne Ormond), Carl Hayman (replaced by Deacon Manu), Slade McFarland (replaced by Scott Linklater), Greg Feek.

England 23, New Zealand Maori 9
At New Plymouth, June 9

For New Zealand Maori: 3 penalty goals by Glen Jackson.

The New Zealand Maori team was: Christian Cullen, Joe Maddock, Rico Gear, Ryan Nicholas (replaced by Bryce Robins), Brad Fleming, Glen Jackson (replaced by Willie Walker), David Gibson, Taine Randell (captain), Matua Parkinson, Troy Flavell, Paul Tito, Kristian Ormsby (replaced by Reece Robinson), Carl Hayman (replaced by Deacon Manu), Slade McFarland, Greg Feek.

New Zealand Maori 65, Canada 27
At Calgary, July 26

For New Zealand Maori: Tries by Brendan Haami (2), Joe Maddock (2), Shayne Austin (2), Troy Flavell, Ron Cribb, Rico Gear and Glen Jackson; 4 conversions and a penalty goal by Willie Walker, 2 conversions by Jackson.

Statistics

The New Zealand Maori team was: Christian Cullen, Joe Maddock, Rico Gear, Norman Berryman (replaced by Bryce Robins), Shayne Austin, Willie Walker (replaced by Glen Jackson), David Gibson (replaced by Brendan Haami), Ron Cribb, Germaine Anaha (replaced by Wayne McEntee), Troy Flavell, Paul Tito (captain), Kristian Ormsby (replaced by Warren Smith), Carl Hayman (replaced by Deacon Manu), Slade McFarland, Joe McDonnell.

New Zealand Maori 52, Canada All Stars 11
At Ottawa, July 30

For New Zealand Maori: Tries by Justin Wilson, Scott Linklater, Bryce Robins, Warren Smith, Ron Cribb, Rico Gear, Joe Maddock and Christian Cullen; 6 conversions by Glen Jackson.

The New Zealand Maori team was: James Arlidge (replaced by Christian Cullen), Justin Wilson, Rico Gear (replaced by Norman Berryman), Bryce Robins, Shayne Austin (replaced by Joe Maddock), Glen Jackson, Brendan Haami, Ron Cribb, Wayne McEntee, Wayne Ormond (replaced by Troy Flavell), Paul Tito (captain), Warren Smith (replaced by Kristian Ormsby), Deacon Manu, Scott Linklater, Greg Feek (replaced by Joe McDonnell).

New Zealand Maori 30, Canada 9
At Toronto, August 2

For New Zealand Maori: Tries by Troy Flavell (2), Christian Cullen, Joe Maddock and Slade McFarland; conversion and a penalty goal by Willie Walker.

The New Zealand Maori team was: Christian Cullen, Joe Maddock, Rico Gear, Norman Berryman, Shayne Austin, Willie Walker (replaced by Glen Jackson), Brendan Haami, Ron Cribb, Wayne McEntee (replaced by Germaine Anaha), Troy Flavell, Paul Tito (captain), Kristian Ormsby (replaced by Warren Smith), Carl Hayman (replaced by Deacon Manu), Slade McFarland (replaced by Scott Linklater), Joe McDonnell.

2004

New Zealand Maori 69, United States 31
At Calgary, June 12

For New Zealand Maori: Tries by Warren Smith (3), Justin Wilson (2), Ryan Nicholas (2), Adrian Cashmore, Caleb Ralph, Hoani MacDonald and Jake Paringatai; 7 conversions by Glen Jackson.

The New Zealand Maori team was: Adrian Cashmore (replaced by Jared Going), Hosea Gear, Justin Wilson, Ryan Nicholas, Caleb Ralph, Glen Jackson (replaced by David Hill), Andrew Fulton (replaced by Craig McGrath), Wayne Ormond (replaced by Jake Paringatai), Wayne McEntee, Warren Smith, Bryce Williams (replaced by Angus MacDonald), Sean Hohneck, Greg Feek, Corey Flynn (captain), Joe McDonnell (replaced by Tony Penn).

New Zealand Maori 26, England A 19 (after extra time)
At Edmonton, June 19

For New Zealand Maori: Tries by Caleb Ralph (2), Glen Jackson and Ryan Nicholas; 3 conversions by Jackson.

The New Zealand Maori team was: Adrian Cashmore, Hosea Gear, Justin Wilson, Ryan Nicholas, Caleb Ralph, Glen Jackson (replaced by David Hill), Andrew Fulton, Wayne Ormond, Wayne McEntee (replaced by Scott Waldrom), Warren Smith, Bryce Williams (replaced by Angus MacDonald), Sean Hohneck, Greg Feek, Corey Flynn (captain, replaced by Scott Linklater), Joe McDonnell.

2005

New Zealand Maori 29, Fiji 27
At Suva, June 3

For New Zealand Maori: Tries by Angus MacDonald, Hayden Pedersen, Shannon Paku and Scott Linklater; 3 conversions and a penalty goal by David Hill.

The New Zealand Maori team was: Shannon Paku, Neil Brew, Rua Tipoki, Luke McAlister, Hayden Pedersen, David Hill (replaced by Riki Flutey), Piri Weepu (replaced by Craig McGrath), Angus MacDonald (replaced by Thomas Waldrom), Marty Holah (replaced by Daniel Braid), Jono Gibbes (captain), Paul Tito, Ross Filipo, Carl Hayman, Scott Linklater, Deacon Manu (replaced by Greg Feek).

New Zealand Maori 19, British & Irish Lions 13
At Hamilton, June 11

For New Zealand Maori: Try by Leon MacDonald; conversion and 2 penalty goals by Luke McAlister, 2 penalty goals by David Hill.

The New Zealand Maori team was: Leon MacDonald, Rico Gear, Rua Tipoki, Luke McAlister, Caleb Ralph, David Hill (replaced by Carlos Spencer), Piri Weepu, Angus MacDonald, Marty Holah, Jono Gibbes (captain), Sean Hohneck, Ross Filipo (replaced by Daniel Braid), Carl Hayman, Corey Flynn, Deacon Manu (replaced by Greg Feek).

New Zealand Maori players and first-class appearances 1995–2005

(Years covered in statistics do not include seasons where players were squad members but failed to appear in a first-class match.)

John Akurangi (Counties) 1998–99: Edinburgh 1998, Scotland 1998, Glasgow 1998, Fiji XV 1999, Fiji 1999. Total: 5.

Germaine Anaha (Wairarapa-Bush) 2003: – Canada (1) 2003, Canada (2) 2003. Total: 2.

James Arlidge (Northland) 2003: Canada All Stars 2003. Total: 1.

Shayne Austin (Taranaki) 2003–04: Canada (1) 2003, Canada All Stars 2003, Canada (2) 2003. Total: 3.

Norman Berryman (Northland) 1995–2004: King Country 1995, Waikato 1995, Bay of Plenty 1996, Western Samoa 1996, Ireland A 1997, Argentina 1997, Western Samoan XV 1997, Western Samoa 1997, Tonga 1998, England 1998, Edinburgh 1998, Scotland 1998, Glasgow 1998, Fiji XV 1999, Fiji 1999, Scotland 2000, Canada (1) 2003, Canada All Stars 2003, Canada (2) 2003. Total: 19.

Daniel Braid (Auckland) 2005: Fiji 2005, British & Irish Lions 2005. Total: 2.

Errol Brain (Counties) 1995–98: King Country 1995, Waikato 1995, Bay of Plenty 1996, Western Samoa 1996, Fiji 1996, Tonga Barbarians 1996, Tonga 1996, Ireland A 1997, Argentina 1997, Western Samoan XV 1997, Western Samoa 1997, Tonga 1998, England 1998. Total: 13.

Neil Brew (Otago) 2005: Fiji 2005. Total: 1.

Robin Brooke (Auckland) 1995: Waikato 1995. Total: 1.

Norm Broughton (Wellington) 1995: King Country 1995, Waikato 1995. Total: 2.

Tony Brown (Otago) 1996–98: Western Samoa 1996, Fiji 1996, Tonga Barbarians 1996, Tonga 1996, Tonga 1998, England 1998, Edinburgh 1998, Scotland 1998. Total: 8.

Adrian Cashmore (Auckland) 1996–2004: Bay of Plenty 1996, Fiji 1996, Argentina 1997, Western Samoa 1997, England 1998, Edinburgh 1998, Scotland 1998, Glasgow 1998, Scotland 2000, United States 2004, England A 2004. Total: 11.

Jim Coe (Counties) 1995–99: King Country 1995, Waikato 1995, Bay of Plenty 1996, Western Samoa 1996, Fiji 1996, Tonga 1996, Ireland A 1997, Argentina 1997, Tonga 1998, England 1998, Edinburgh 1998, Scotland 1998, Glasgow 1998, Fiji XV 1999, Fiji 1999. Total: 15.

Phil Coffin (King Country) 1994–97: King Country 1995, Waikato 1995, Bay of Plenty 1996, Western Samoa 1996, Fiji 1996, Tonga Barbarians 1996, Tonga 1996, Argentina 1997. Total: 8.

Paul Cooke (Otago) 1995: King Country 1995, Waikato 1995. Total: 2.

Mark Cooksley (Counties/Waikato) 1995–2001: King Country 1995, Fiji 1996, Tonga Barbarians 1996, Tonga 1996, Argentina 1997, Western Samoan XV 1997, Western Samoa 1997, Fiji 1999, Scotland 2000, Australia 2001. Total: 10.

Orcades Crawford (Hawke's Bay) 1998: Tonga 1998. Total: 1.

Ron Cribb (North Harbour) 1998–2003: Edinburgh 1998, Scotland 1998, Fiji XV 1999, Canada (1) 2003, Canada All Stars 2003, Canada (2) 2003. Total: 6.

Christian Cullen (Wellington) 2003: Tonga 2003, England 2003, Canada (1) 2003, Canada All Stars 2003, Canada (2) 2003. Total: 5.

Jarrod Cunningham (Hawke's Bay) 1995–97: King Country 1995, Tonga Barbarians 1996, Tonga 1996, Ireland A 1997, Western Samoan XV 1997. Total: 5.

Rhys Duggan (Waikato) 1996–2002: Bay of Plenty 1996, Western Samoa 1996, Tonga Barbarians 1996, Argentina 1997, Western Samoan XV 1997, Western Samoa 1997, England 1998, Edinburgh 1998, Scotland 1998, Glasgow 1998, Fiji 1999, Scotland 2000, Australia 2001, Argentina 2001, Queensland 2002, Australia 2002. Total: 16.

Joe Edwards (Bay of Plenty) 1996: Tonga Barbarians 1996. Total: 1.

Mike Edwards (Wellington) 1999–2000: Fiji XV 1999, Fiji 1999, Scotland 2000. Total: 3.

Greg Feek (Canterbury) 1998–2005: Edinburgh 1998, Scotland 1998, Glasgow 1998, Scotland 2000, Australia 2001, Argentina 2001, Queensland 2002, New South Wales 2002, Australia 2002, New Zealand Barbarians 2002, Tonga 2003, England 2003, Canada All Stars 2003, United States 2004, England A 2004, Fiji 2005, British & Irish Lions 2005. Total: 17.

Ross Filipo (Wellington) 2005: Fiji 2005, British & Irish Lions 2005. Total: 2.

Troy Flavell (North Harbour) 1998–2003: Tonga 1998, England 1998, Edinburgh 1998, Scotland 1998, Glasgow 1998, Fiji 1999, Australia 2001, Tonga 2003, England 2003, Canada (1) 2003, Canada All Stars 2003, Canada (2) 2003. Total: 12.

Brad Fleming (Otago) 2003: Tonga 2003, England 2003. Total: 2.

Riki Flutey (Wellington) 2002–05: New Zealand Barbarians 2002, Fiji 2005. Total: 2.

Aaron Flynn (Canterbury) 1998: Edinburgh 1998. Total: 1.

Corey Flynn (Canterbury) 2002–05: Queensland 2002, New South Wales 2002, Australia 2002, United States 2004, England A 2004, British & Irish Lions 2005. Total: 6.

Robbie Ford (Canterbury) 1998: Edinburgh 1998, Glasgow 1998. Total: 2.

Stu Forster (Otago) 1995–96: Waikato 1995, Fiji 1996, Tonga 1996. Total: 3.

Andrew Fulton (North Harbour) 2004: United States 2004, England A 2004. Total: 2.

Hosea Gear (North Harbour) 2004: United States 2004, England A 2004. Total: 2.

Rico Gear (North Harbour/Nelson Bays) 2002–05: Queensland 2002, New South Wales 2002, Australia 2002, New Zealand Barbarians 2002, Tonga 2003, England 2003, Canada (1) 2003, Canada All Stars 2003, Canada (2) 2003, British & Irish Lions 2005. Total: 10.

Jono Gibbes (Waikato) 2002–05: Queensland 2002, New South Wales 2002, Australia 2002, Tonga 2003, Fiji 2005, British & Irish Lions 2005. Total: 6.

David Gibson (Auckland) 2003: Tonga 2003, England 2003, Canada (1) 2003. Total: 3.

Daryl Gibson (Canterbury) 1996–2001: Western Samoa 1996, Ireland A 1997, Argentina 1997, Western Samoa 1997, Tonga 1998, England 1998, Edinburgh 1998, Scotland 1998, Glasgow 1998, Scotland 2000, Australia 2001, Argentina 2001. Total: 12.

Craig Glendinning (Counties) 1997: Ireland A 1997, Argentina 1997, Western Samoa 1997. Total: 3.

Milton Going (Northland) 1996–97: Bay of Plenty 1996, Western Samoa 1996, Fiji 1996, Ireland A 1997, Argentina 1997, Western Samoa 1997. Total: 6.

Brendan Haami (Taranaki) 2001–03: Argentina 2001, Queensland 2002, New South Wales 2002, Tonga 2003, Canada (1) 2003, Canada All Stars 2003, Canada (2) 2003. Total: 7.

Jason Hammond (Northland) 1998: Tonga 1998, England 1998. Total: 2.

Carl Hayman (Otago) 2002–05: Queensland 2002, New South Wales 2002, Australia 2002, New Zealand Barbarians 2002, Tonga 2003, England 2003, Canada (1) 2003, Canada (2) 2003, Fiji 2005, British & Irish Lions 2005. Total: 10.

Tiwini Hemi (Waikato) 1996: Bay of Plenty 1996. Total: 1.

Norm Hewitt (Wellington/Southland) 1997–2001: Ireland A 1997, Argentina 1997, Western Samoa 1997, Fiji XV 1999, Fiji 1999, Scotland 2000, Australia 2001, Argentina 2001. Total: 8.

David Hill (Waikato) 2001–05: Australia 2001, United States 2004, England A 2004, Fiji 2005, British & Irish Lions 2005. Total: 5.

Steve Hirini (Wellington) 1997: Ireland A 1997, Western Samoan XV 1997. Total: 2.

Sean Hohneck (Waikato) 2004–05: United States 2004, England A 2004, British & Irish Lions 2005. Total: 3.

Marty Holah (Waikato) 2005: Fiji 2005, British & Irish Lions 2005. Total: 2.

Graham Hurunui (Horowhenua-Kapiti) 1995: King Country 1995. Total: 1.

Glen Jackson (Waikato/Bay of Plenty) 1999–2004: Fiji XV 1999, Fiji 1999, Scotland 2000, Australia 2001, Argentina 2001, Queensland 2002, Tonga 2003, England 2003, Canada (1) 2003, Canada All Stars 2003, Canada (2) 2003, United States 2004, England A 2004. Total: 13.

Steve Jackson (Southland) 2002: New South Wales 2002. Total: 1.

Martin Jones (Bay of Plenty) 1997: Western Samoan XV 1997. Total: 1.

Grant Kelly (Canterbury) 1995–96: Waikato 1995, Bay of Plenty 1996, Western Samoa 1996. Total: 3.

James Kerr (Canterbury) 1998–99: Tonga 1998, England 1998, Glasgow 1998, Fiji XV 1999, Fiji 1999. Total: 5.

George Konia (Manawatu) 1995: King Country 1995, Waikato 1995. Total: 2.

Lee Lidgard (Counties) 1996–98: Tonga Barbarians 1996, Ireland A 1997, Argentina 1997, Western Samoan XV 1997, Western Samoa 1997, Tonga 1998, England 1998, Scotland 1998, Glasgow 1998. Total: 9.

Scott Linklater (Waikato) 2003–05: Tonga 2003, Canada All Stars 2003, Canada (2) 2003, England A 2004, Fiji 2005. Total: 5.

Danny Love (Counties) 1995: King Country 1995, Waikato 1995. Total: 2.

Joe Maddock (Canterbury) 2002–03: Queensland 2002, New South Wales 2002, New Zealand Barbarians 2002, Tonga 2003, England 2003, Canada (1) 2003, Canada All Stars 2003, Canada (2) 2003. Total: 8.

Luke McAlister (North Harbour) 2005: Fiji 2005, British & Irish Lions 2005. Total: 2.

Angus MacDonald (Auckland) 2005: Fiji 2005, British & Irish Lions 2005. Total: 2.

Hoani MacDonald (Southland) 2004: United States 2004, England A 2004. Total: 2.

Leon MacDonald (Canterbury) 1998–2005: Edinburgh 1998, Scotland 1998, Fiji XV 1999, British & Irish Lions 2005. Total: 4.

Ray MacDonald (Southland) 1998–99: Tonga 1998, Glasgow 1998, Fiji XV 1999. Total: 3.

Joe McDonnell (Otago/Wellington) 2000–04: Scotland 2000, Canada (1) 2003, Canada All Stars 2003, Canada (2) 2003, United States 2004, England A 2004. Total: 6.

Wayne McEntee (Waikato) 2003–04: Canada (1) 2003, Canada All Stars 2003, Canada (2) 2003, United States 2004, England A 2004. Total: 5.

Slade McFarland (North Harbour) 1995–2003: King Country 1995, Waikato 1995, Bay of Plenty 1996, Western Samoa 1996, Fiji 1996, Tonga 1996, Western Samoan XV 1997, Tonga 1998, England 1998, Edinburgh 1998, Scotland 1998, Glasgow 1998, Fiji XV

1999, Fiji 1999, Australia 2001, Argentina 2001, Queensland 2002, New South Wales 2002, Australia 2002, New Zealand Barbarians 2002, Tonga 2003, England 2003, Canada (1) 2003, Canada (2) 2003. Total: 24.

Craig McGrath (Auckland/Northland/North Harbour) 1997-2005: Samoa 1997, Tonga 1998, Fiji XV 1999, United States 2004, Fiji 2005. Total: 5.

Hare Makiri (Counties) 1998-2001: Glasgow 1998, Scotland 2000, Argentina 2001. Total: 3.

Deacon Manu (Waikato) 2001-05: Australia 2001, Argentina 2001, Queensland 2002, Australia 2002, New Zealand Barbarians 2002, Tonga 2003, England 2003, Canada (1) 2003, Canada All Stars 2003, Canada (2) 2003, Fiji 2005, British & Irish Lions 2005. Total: 12.

Glenn Marsh (Counties) 1998-2000: Edinburgh 1998, Scotland 1998, Glasgow 1998, Fiji XV 1999, Fiji 1999, Scotland 2000. Total: 6.

Tony Marsh (Counties) 1998: Tonga 1998, England 1998. Total: 2.

Eugene Martin (Waikato) 1997: Argentina 1997, Western Samoa 1997. Total: 2.

Dion Matthews (King Country) 1996: Fiji 1996. Total: 1.

Norm Maxwell (Northland/Canterbury) 1997-2001: Ireland A 1997, Western Samoan XV 1997, Western Samoa 1997, Edinburgh 1998, Scotland 1998, Australia 2001. Total: 6.

Chris Mayerhofler (North Harbour) 1995-97: King Country 1995, Waikato 1995, Ireland A 1997, Western Samoan XV 1997. Total: 4.

Mark Mayerhofler (Canterbury) 1996-2002: Bay of Plenty 1996, Western Samoa 1996, Fiji 1996, Tonga Barbarians 1996, Tonga 1996, Argentina 1997, Western Samoan XV 1997, Western Samoa 1997, Scotland 2000, Queensland 2002, New South Wales 2002, Australia 2002, New Zealand Barbarians 2002. Total: 13.

Kees Meeuws (Otago) 1998: England 1998, Edinburgh 1998, Scotland 1998, Glasgow 1998. Total: 4.

Todd Miller (Waikato) 1999: Fiji XV 1999. Total: 1.

Deon Muir (Waikato) 1996-2002: Fiji 1996, Tonga 1996, Tonga 1998, England 1998, Edinburgh 1998, Scotland 1998, Glasgow 1998, Fiji XV 1999, Fiji 1999, Scotland 2000, Australia 2001, Argentina 2001, Queensland 2002, New South Wales 2002, Australia 2002, New Zealand Barbarians 2002. Total: 16.

Kevin Nepia (Auckland/Canterbury) 1995-98: King Country 1995, Waikato 1995, Bay of Plenty 1996, Western Samoa 1996, Fiji 1996, Tonga 1996, Ireland A 1997, Western Samoan XV 1997, Western Samoa 1997, Tonga 1998, England 1998. Total: 11.

Mutu Ngarimu (Poverty Bay/Hawke's Bay) 1995-97: King Country 1995, Tonga Barbarians 1996, Ireland A 1997, Argentina 1997, Western Samoan XV 1997. Total: 5.

Ryan Nicholas (Otago) 2002–04: Queensland 2002, Australia 2002, New Zealand Barbarians 2002, Tonga 2003, England 2003, United States 2004, England A 2004. Total: 7.

Wayne Ormond (Bay of Plenty) 2003–05: Tonga 2003, Canada All Stars 2003, United States 2004, England A 2004. Total: 4.

Kristian Ormsby (Counties) 2001–03: Argentina 2001, Queensland 2002, Australia 2002, New Zealand Barbarians 2002, Tonga 2003, England 2003, Canada (1) 2003, Canada All Stars 2003, Canada (2) 2003. Total: 9.

Glen Osborne (North Harbour) 1995–99: Bay of Plenty 1996, Western Samoa 1996, Edinburgh 1998, Scotland 1998, Glasgow 1998, Fiji XV 1999, Fiji 1999. Total: 7.

Murdoch Paewai (Hawke's Bay) 1996: Tonga Barbarians 1996. Total: 1.

Shannon Paku (Wellington) 2005: Fiji 2005. Total: 1 .

Jake Paringatai (Northland) 2004: United States 2004. Total: 1.

Adam Parker (Canterbury) 1998: Tonga 1998, England 1998. Total: 2.

Matua Parkinson (North Harbour) 2000–03: Scotland 2000, Australia 2001, Argentina 2001, Queensland 2002, Australia 2002, New Zealand Barbarians 2002, Tonga 2003, England 2003. Total: 8.

Hayden Pedersen (Otago) 2005: Fiji 2005. Total: 1.

Tony Penn (Taranaki) 2002–04: New South Wales 2002, United States 2004. Total: 2.

Caleb Ralph (Bay of Plenty/Auckland/Canterbury) 1996–2005: Tonga Barbarians 1996, Tonga 1996, Ireland A 1997, Western Samoan XV 1997, Edinburgh 1998, Scotland 1998, Glasgow 1998, Fiji 1999, Scotland 2000, Australia 2001, Argentina 2001, United States 2004, England A 2004, British & Irish Lions 2005. Total: 14.

Taine Randell (Otago) 1996–2003: Bay of Plenty 1996, Western Samoa 1996, Australia 2001, Tonga 2003, England 2003. Total: 5.

Roger Randle (Hawke's Bay/Waikato) 1996–2002: Tonga Barbarians 1996, Tonga 1996, Tonga 1998, England 1998, Scotland 2000, Australia 2001, New South Wales 2002, New Zealand Barbarians 2002. Total: 8.

Bruce Reihana (Waikato) 1998–2002: – Edinburgh 1998, Scotland 1998, Glasgow 1998, Fiji 1999, Scotland 2000, Australia 2001, Argentina 2001, Queensland 2002, New South Wales 2002, Australia 2002, New Zealand Barbarians 2002. Total: 11.

Bryce Robins (Taranaki) 2003: England 2003, Canada (1) 2003, Canada All Stars 2003. Total: 3.

Reece Robinson (Hawke's Bay/Taranaki) 2001–03: Argentina 2001, Queensland 2002, New South Wales 2002, Australia 2002, New Zealand Barbarians 2002, England 2003. Total: 6.

Eric Rush (North Harbour) 1996-98: Fiji 1996, Tonga Barbarians 1996, Tonga 1996, Western Samoan XV 1997, Western Samoa 1997, Tonga 1998. Total: 6.

Michael Scott (Counties) 1997: Ireland A 1997, Western Samoan XV 1997. Total: 2.

Dallas Seymour (Canterbury/Hawke's Bay/Wellington) 1996-99: Bay of Plenty 1996, Western Samoa 1996, Fiji 1996, Tonga Barbarians 1996, Tonga 1996, Tonga 1998, England 1998, Fiji XV 1999. Total: 8.

Warren Smith (Otago) 2003-04: Canada (1) 2003, Canada All Stars 2003, Canada (2) 2003, United States 2004, England A 2004. Total: 5.

Carlos Spencer (Auckland) 1996-2005: Bay of Plenty 1996, Australia 2001, Argentina 2001, Queensland 2002, New South Wales 2002, Australia 2002, New Zealand Barbarians 2002, British & Irish Lions 2005. Total: 8.

Shane Stone (Bay of Plenty) 1995: King Country 1995. Total: 1.

Karl Te Nana (North Harbour) 1999: Fiji XV 1999, Fiji 1999. Total: 2.

Matthew Te Pou (Thames Valley) 1996: Tonga Barbarians 1996. Total: 1.

Paul Thomson (Auckland) 1996-2001: Tonga Barbarians 1996, Argentina 1997, Western Samoa 1997, Fiji XV 1999, Fiji 1999, Australia 2001. Total: 6.

Rua Tipoki (Bay of Plenty) 2005: Fiji 2005, British & Irish Lions 2005. Total: 2.

Paul Tito (Taranaki) 2000-05: Scotland 2000, Argentina 2001, Tonga 2003, England 2003, Canada (1) 2003, Canada All Stars 2003, Canada (2) 2003, Fiji 2005. Total: 8.

Blair Urlich (North Harbour) 2002: New South Wales 2002, Australia 2002, New Zealand Barbarians 2002. Total: 3.

Scott Waldrom (Wellington) 2004: England A 2004. Total: 1.

Thomas Waldrom (Wellington) 2005: Fiji 2005. Total: 1.

Willie Walker (Otago) 2002-03: New South Wales 2002, Australia 2002, New Zealand Barbarians 2002, Tonga 2003, England 2003, Canada (1) 2003, Canada (2) 2003. Total: 7.

Dion Waller (King Country/Manawatu/Wellington) 1996-2001: Fiji 1996, Tonga Barbarians 1996, Ireland A 1997, Argentina 1997, Western Samoan XV 1997, Western Samoa 1997, Tonga 1998, England 1998, Edinburgh 1998, Glasgow 1998, Fiji XV 1999, Scotland 2000, Australia 2001. Total: 13.

Piri Weepu (Wellington) 2005: Fiji 2005, British & Irish Lions 2005. Total: 2.

Bryce Williams (Auckland) 2002-04: Queensland 2002, New South Wales 2002, Australia 2002, New Zealand Barbarians 2002, United States 2004, England A 2004. Total: 6.

Justin Wilson (Wellington) 2003-04: Canada All Stars 2003, United States 2004, England A 2004. Total: 3.

Players who were selected by the All Blacks after appearing for New Zealand Maori:

Norman Berryman
Tony Brown
Adrian Cashmore
Phil Coffin
Ron Cribb
Rhys Duggan
Greg Feek
Troy Flavell
Corey Flynn
Rico Gear
Jono Gibbes
Daryl Gibson
David Hill
Leon MacDonald
Joe McDonnell
Norm Maxwell
Mark Mayerhofler
Caleb Ralph
Bruce Reihana
Carlos Spencer
Dion Waller

Players who went on to appear for other nations after they appeared for New Zealand Maori, and the teams they played for:

Craig Glendinning (Samoa)
Tony Marsh (France)
Adam Parker (Japan)
Matthew Te Pou (Tonga)

Acknowledgements

The authors wish to take this opportunity to thank all of the players, coaches and administrators, both past and present, who gave up their valuable time and, even more importantly, were prepared to share their memories.

Thanks go also to Brent Drabble for his statistical support, to Heather Gibbon and Ida Te Pou for their dutiful research and patience, and to Mike Stewart, Peter Bush and the teams at Photosport and Pro Sport Photos (Simon Baker) for their images, which have combined to capture the essence of the New Zealand Maori team.

We must also acknowledge the efforts of the teams at Te Puni Kokiri and Huia, without whom this would not have been possible.

Matt Te Pou

Matt Te Pou served in the New Zealand Army for 23 years from 1967 to 1990, a period which included a 12-month tour of Vietnam as part of the allied military forces in 1970 and 1971. He later rose through the rugby coaching ranks, firstly with the Whakatane Marist club and then the Bay of Plenty representative team, prior to coaching the New Zealand Maori team for 10 years between 1995 and 2005. During his time at the helm, the New Zealand Maori team lost just four matches while beating a number of major international touring teams. The New Zealand Maori side was the first team to defeat the 2005 British & Irish Lions. Matt's service to the military, and later to New Zealand rugby, was recognised through award of the following honours: MNZN (Member of the New Zealand Order of Merit); MBE (Member of the British Empire) and BEM (British Empire Medal). He lives in Whakatane, with his wife Ida, where he operates as a business consultant and coach. This is his first book.

Matt McIlraith

Matt McIlraith acted as the New Zealand Maori team's Communications Officer in 2001 while he held the position of Media Manager at the New Zealand Rugby Union. In 2002 and 2003, he was the All Blacks Communications Officer, prior to departing the NZRU midway through 2004 in order to concentrate on writing. A former editor of the national weekly publication *Rugby News*, this is Matt's second book following on from *Ten Years of Super 12*, which was released last year.